Applications of International Trade Theory

Applications of International Trade Theory

THE CARIBBEAN PERSPECTIVE

Roger Hosein

UNIVERSITY OF THE WEST INDIES PRESS
Jamaica • Barbados • Trinidad and Tobago

University of the West Indies Press
7A Gibraltar Hall Road, Mona
Kingston 7, Jamaica
www.uwipress.com

A catalogue record of this book is available from the National Library of Jamaica.

ISBN: 978-976-640-347-8

Cover design by Richard Rawlins.

Printed in the United States of America.

Contents

Figures

Tables

Acknowledgements

I would like to acknowledge my wife, Denise Hosein, and my children, Ava, Desiree, Amartya, Daniel and Jayelle. Many thanks to my students since 2001, who endured versions of the text. However, this book would not have been completed without the assistance of Rebecca Gookool, Jeetendra Khadan, Justin Joseph and Ranita Seecharan, all diligent research assistants. Most significantly, though, I would like to acknowledge the research assistance of Rishi Singh, a truly dedicated researcher and a definite friend.

1.

International Trade

Theory and Application

Learning Objectives

a. Define international trade.
b. Identify the main economic trends in the global marketplace.
c. Examine China's emergence as one of the forerunners of global economic activity.
d. Identify the main implications of China's continued sovereignty for the CARICOM region.

1.0 An Overview of the Global Economy

Since the early seventeenth century, trade patterns between and among countries have emerged. More so, through any trading arrangement, whether bilateral or multilateral, the general corollary has been the dominance of one or a few economies. Over the past few decades, there have been many events that have spurred the direction and composition of trade throughout the world. The effect of this trade dynamism has manifested itself in the national accounts as well as the developmental efforts of various countries.

Table 1.1 shows the trends in world output growth in the period 1990–2008. The world economy as a whole appears to be carrying an improved growth performance after the dampening influence of the events of 11 September 2001. In particular, world output, which averaged 2.7 per cent per annum in the period 1990–2000 with a growth rate of 4 per cent in 2000, experienced a sharp decline in 2001 on account of the events of 9/11.

Since 2001, however, world economic activity has displayed renewed signs of economic buoyancy with a world output growth of 3.4 per cent in 2005 (the average growth rate for the period 2001–5 was 2.6 per cent). In the developed world, the persistently strong growth player since 1990 has been the United States, with the Japanese economy displaying a commendable recovery effort since its negative growth performance in 2002.

The growth performance of developing countries has been much stronger than the overall average, with a growth performance of 6.3 per cent in 2005 as compared to 2.5 per cent among developed economies in the same year. In this regard, the growth of the Chinese economy has to be emphasized and is illustrated in table 1.2.

Table 1.1: World output growth, 1990–2008 (percentage change over previous year)

Region/country	Annual average, 1990–2000	1999	2000	2001	2002	2003	2004	2005	2006	2007	2008
World	2.7	2.9	4.0	1.3	1.8	2.5	3.8	3.4	4.0	3.8	2.1
Developed countries	2.4	2.7	3.5	1.1	1.3	1.7	3.0	2.5	2.8	2.5	0.7
Japan	1.4	0.1	2.8	0.4	–0.3	1.4	2.6	2.6	2.4	2.1	–0.6
United States	3.4	4.1	3.8	0.3	2.4	3.0	4.4	3.2	2.9	2.2	1.1
European Union											
Euro area	2.0	2.8	3.5	1.6	0.9	0.5	1.8	1.6	2.9	2.8	0.8
France	1.7	3.2	3.8	2.1	1.2	0.5	2.1	1.2	2.2	2.1	0.7
Germany	1.6	2.0	2.9	0.9	0.2	–0.1	1.0	0.9	2.9	2.5	1.3
Italy	1.6	1.7	3.0	1.8	0.4	0.3	1.0	0.0	1.7	1.5	–1.0
United Kingdom	2.7	2.8	3.8	2.1	1.7	2.2	3.1	1.8	2.8	3.0	0.7
Southeast Europe and CIS	–4.3	3.4	8.1	5.6	4.9	6.9	7.5	6.2	7.2	8.2	5.4
Developing countries	4.8	3.5	5.4	2.4	3.5	4.7	6.4	6.3	7.1	7.3	5.5
Developing countries, excluding China	4.0	3.2	5.1	1.5	2.7	3.9	5.7	5.3	6.0	6.2	4.4

Source: UNTCAD Handbook of Statistics (various years).

Table 1.2: Growth performance of Chinese economy, 1990–2009

Year	1990–2000	1999	2000	2001	2002	2003	2004	**2005**	2006	2007	2008	2009
China	9.85	7.6	8.4	8.3	9.1	10.0	10.1	**11.3**	12.7	14.2	9.6	9.1

Source: World Development Indicators (various years).

1.1 World Trade by Region

Table 1.3 shows the world merchandise trade by major regions for the year 2008. The world as a whole had an export level in 2008 tallying $15.8 trillion (all currency in US dollars unless otherwise noted). This represented a 16 per cent growth over 2007 export values. With the exception of North America, all major regions listed in table 1.3 exceeded the world average for the period 2000–8. In fact, since 2006 there has been a persistent improvement in the trade performance of all players, with 2008 representing peak performances for all regions with the exception of the North American and European regions.

Table 1.3: World merchandise trade by major regions, 2008 (US$bn and annual percentage change)

	Exports					Imports				
	Value	Annual percentage change				Value	Annual percentage change			
	2008	2000–2008	2006	2007	2008	2008	2000–2008	2006	2007	2008
World	15,775	12	16	16	15	16,120	12	15	15	15
North America	2,049	7	13	11	10	2,909	7	11	6	7
South and Central America[1]	602	15	21	14	21	595	14	22	25	30
Europe	6,456	12	13	16	12	6,833	12	15	16	12
CIS	703	22	25	20	35	493	25	30	35	31
Africa	561	18	19	18	29	466	17	16	24	27
Middle East	1,047	19	22	16	36	575	17	12	25	23
Asia	4,355	13	17	16	15	4,247	14	16	15	20

[1]Includes Caribbean
Source: World Trade Report (2009).

World imports followed suit as all major regions experienced an expansion of their imports in 2006. This trend continued into 2008, with a general trade growth being exhibited by all regions.

Foreign Direct Investment (FDI) Flows Internationally

As table 1.4 illustrates, world foreign direct investment (FDI) inflows increased from $207.9 billion in 1990 to $1,114.2 billion in 2009 with a peak value of $1,833.3 billion in 2007. Similarly, world FDI outflows increased from $238.7 billion in 1990 to $1,100.9 billion in 2009. World FDI outflows also peaked in 2007 at $1,996.5 billion. FDI inflows to developed economies fluctuated but increased from $172.1 billion in

Table 1.4: World FDI inflows to developed and developing economies, 1990–2009 (US$mn)

Year	World		Developed economies		Developing economies	
	FDI inflows	FDI outflows	FDI inflows	FDI outflows	FDI inflows	FDI outflows
1990	207,878.4	238,681.4	172,067.2	225,965.1	35,736.3	147,313.5
1991	161,212.7	200,196.6	117,027.4	186,508.9	43,950.8	161,602.8
1992	169,238.1	202,904.7	112,583.2	178,102.6	54,872.3	186,103.1
1993	227,694.0	244,788.0	144,004.3	204,013.7	80,420.4	225,478.2
1994	259,468.8	288,508.0	151,827.9	239,817.1	105,141.2	279,827.7
1995	341,085.9	358,176.8	218,738.4	304,559.1	117,544.1	334,720.2
1996	392,921.9	397,706.7	234,867.8	333,074.2	151,746.4	386,811.3
1997	487,877.8	484,896.2	284,013.0	400,474.7	191,763.7	553,632.0
1998	701,123.8	693,094.7	503,851.0	637,850.3	186,626.3	574,355.4
1999	1,092,052	1,104,937.0	849,051.9	1,014,086.0	232,507.3	736,516.3
2000	1,396,539	1,239,149.0	1,134,293.0	1,092,747.0	253,178.8	868,919.9
2001	825,924.6	743,464.6	596,304.9	662,198.8	217,844.9	856,229.7
2002	716,127.5	652,181.2	547,777.8	599,895.2	155,528.4	861,568.5
2003	632,598.8	616,922.9	442,156.5	577,323.3	166,336.6	927,442.0
2004	648,146.1	730,256.6	380,021.7	637,360.0	233,227.2	1,035,676.0
2005	916,277.0	778,725.0	542,312.0	646,206.0	334,285.0	117,463.0
2006	1,305,852.0	1,215,789.0	857,499.0	1,022,711.0	379,070.0	174,389.0
2007	1,833,324.0	1,996,514.0	1,247,635.0	1,692,141.0	499,747.0	253,145.0
2008	1,697,353.0	1,857,734.0	962,259.0	1,506,528.0	620,733.0	292,710.0
2009	1,114,189.0	1,100,993.0	565,892.0	820,665.0	478,349.0	229,159.0

Source: IMF International Financial Statistics (various years).

1990 to $565.9 billion in 2009. FDI inflows to developed economies peaked in 2007 at $1,247.6 billion. FDI outflows from developed economies also fluctuated, increasing from $226.0 billion in 1990 to $820.1 billion in 2009. There was a significant increase in FDI inflows to developing economies from $35.7 billion in 1990 to $478.3 billion in 2009. Similarly, over the same time interval, developing economies' FDI outflows increased significantly from $147.3 billion to $229.2 billion. Developing economies' FDI inflows were the highest in 2008 at $620.7 billion, while their FDI outflows were the highest in 2004 at $1035.7 billion.

World Exports of Merchandise and Commercial Services

Table 1.5 shows the level of commercial services exports and imports in 2008. In particular, world commercial services exports increased by 13, 19 and 11 per cent annually in the time interval from 2006 to 2008. Over the same period, world commercial services imports increased by 12, 18 and 11 per cent annually. It can also be seen that merchandise services trade followed a similar suit, increasing by 12, 18 and 11 per cent.

1.2 What Is Globalization?

Globalization refers to the development of an extensive worldwide pattern of economic relationships among nations. The process of globalization promotes economic integration as well as a merging of cultural, political and social systems across geographic boundaries. Globalization gained special attention in the late 1990s, a time of increasing worldwide integration of markets for goods, services and capital. One of the changes that occurred at that time was the increased role of multinational corporations (MNCs) in the world economy. Another change was the increased intervention by the International Monetary Fund (IMF), World Trade Organization (WTO) and World Bank (WB)

Table 1.5: World exports and imports in services in US$bn and as a percentage of total exports and imports

	Value	Annual percentage change			
	2008	2000–2008	2006	2007	2008
Commercial services exports	3,730	12	13	19	11
Merchandise services trade	15,775	12	16	16	15
Commercial services imports	3,470	12	12	18	11

Source: World Trade Report (2009).

in the domestic policies and affairs of many economies. With globalization, the spread of free market capitalism has been extended to almost every country of the world (Friedman 2000, 7–8).

Globalization can be measured by a variety of ratios, such as the share of world exports

Table 1.6: World exports and imports and net inflows and outflows of FDI as a percentage of GDP, 1980–2009

	World exports	World imports	World FDI net inflows	World FDI net outflows
1980	18.69253	19.71289	0.55981	0.56287
1981	19.05936	19.73195	0.678557	0.495938
1982	18.449	18.91473	0.548124	0.270356
1983	18.22748	18.49648	0.46962	0.360884
1984	19.09806	19.33941	0.517471	0.458746
1985	18.83203	19.00408	0.487274	0.519822
1986	17.35933	17.49171	0.618105	0.712877
1987	17.63307	17.80236	0.84013	0.907026
1988	18.04357	18.37876	0.921814	0.997924
1989	18.61788	19.08517	1.088472	1.203419
1990	18.86908	19.14777	1.015762	1.139384
1991	18.82168	18.96858	0.755364	0.882203
1992	19.37685	19.35027	0.726234	0.805063
1993	19.23599	19.22225	0.945797	0.937761
1994	19.88587	19.76723	0.978897	1.021855
1995	20.97348	20.80194	1.163052	1.142776
1996	21.29206	21.06451	1.302817	1.24068
1997	22.23606	21.84948	1.611504	1.491358
1998	22.33405	22.04089	2.427302	2.258072
1999	22.38919	22.26637	3.925549	3.168235
2000	24.35872	24.47072	5.044298	3.601449
2001	24.18002	24.26161	2.799178	2.047733
2002	24.05603	23.73586	2.258357	2.028157
2003	24.26038	24.0802	1.73588	1.81503
2004	25.76751	25.7105	1.821873	2.436229
2005	26.77658	26.90104	2.533366	2.378928
2006	28.17214	28.29583	3.102052	3.081601
2007	28.67881	28.60233	4.247429	4.522216
2008	29.25659	29.7639	3.056585	3.465812
2009	24.19956	24.29118	2.028594	2.236068

Source: World Development Indicators (various years).

or imports as a percentage of the world's gross domestic product (GDP). Other good measures of globalization include the share of world FDI inflows as a percentage of GDP and world FDI net outflows as a percentage of GDP.

As table 1.6 illustrates, over the period from 1980 to 2009 the share of world exports in world GDP increased gradually from 18.8 per cent to 24 per cent. Similarly, there was a gradual increase in the share of world imports in world GDP from 19.8 per cent to

Table 1.7: Relative importance of China in the global economy with reference to several key macroeconomic variables, 1975, 1980, 1985 and 1990–2009

	China GDP (% of world GDP)	China exports (% of world exports)	China imports (% of world imports)	China FDI inflows (% of world FDI inflows)
1975	0.9	n.a.	n.a.	n.a.
1980	1.0	2.0	n.a.	n.a.
1985	1.5	1.9	2.1	2.9
1986	1.6	1.7	1.8	2.2
1987	1.7	1.8	1.5	1.7
1988	1.8	1.7	1.7	2.0
1989	1.8	1.6	1.5	1.7
1990	1.8	1.6	1.2	1.6
1991	2.0	1.7	1.3	2.6
1992	2.2	1.8	1.7	6.4
1993	2.5	1.9	2.2	11.8
1994	2.7	2.3	2.2	13.1
1995	2.9	2.3	2.3	10.5
1996	3.1	2.4	2.5	10.3
1997	3.3	2.7	2.5	9.2
1998	3.4	2.8	2.6	6.1
1999	3.6	3.0	2.8	3.2
2000	3.7	3.5	3.1	2.4
2001	4.0	3.8	3.5	5.0
2002	4.2	4.7	3.9	6.6
2003	4.5	5.7	4.9	7.3
2004	4.8	6.6	5.7	7.2
2005	5.2	7.5	6.0	6.9
2006	5.6	8.5	6.3	5.1
2007	6.2	9.4	6.7	5.9
2008	6.6	9.9	6.8	8.0
2009	7.4	10.0	8.0	6.7

Source: World Development Indicators (various years).

24.3 per cent. The share of world FDI net inflows in world GDP increased from 0.6 per cent to 2.0 per cent, and the share of world FDI net outflows increased from 0.6 per cent to 2.2 per cent.

The Chinese economy has experienced rapid growth in recent times; as such, the rest of this chapter provides an overview of the Chinese economy over the last few decades.

Table 1.8: China's current account balance, exports of goods and services, foreign direct investment and total population, 1990–2009

	Current account balance (current US$bn)	Exports of goods and services (constant 2000 US$bn)	Imports of goods and services (constant 2000 US$bn)	Foreign direct investment, net (BOP, current US$bn)	Population (millions)
1990	12.0	63.6	48.8	2.7	1,135.19
1991	13.3	70.4	56.0	3.5	1,150.78
1992	6.4	79.2	74.8	7.2	1,164.97
1993	−11.6	89.3	99.8	23.1	1,178.44
1994	6.9	115.1	109.9	31.8	1,191.84
1995	1.6	125.3	124.1	33.8	1,204.86
1996	7.2	141.1	142.0	38.1	1,217.55
1997	37.0	173.5	157.8	41.7	1,230.08
1998	31.5	185.9	172.9	41.1	1,241.94
1999	21.1	211.7	200.8	37.0	1,252.74
2000	20.5	279.6	250.7	37.5	1,262.65
2001	17.4	307.7	282.6	37.4	1,271.85
2002	35.4	394.1	326.7	46.8	1,280.4
2003	45.9	502.9	428.6	47.2	1,288.4
2004	68.7	640.4	556.9	53.1	1,296.08
2005	160.8	791.8	631.6	67.8	1,303.72
2006	253.3	981.0	733.0	56.9	1,311.02
2007	371.8	1,175.5	835.1	121.4	1,317.89
2008	436.1	1,274.4	866.7	94.3	1,324.66
2009	297.1	1,142.8	902.7	34.3	1,331.46

Source: World Development Indicators (various years).

1.3 China's Increasing Trade Openness and the Implications for World Trade

China currently has a population of 1.3 billion people, which accounts for 20 per cent of the world's population. As the macroeconomic variables indicate, the Chinese economy has been doing phenomenally well, to the extent that any discussion of the global economy should provide a brief introductory discussion on this economy.

As shown in table 1.7, China's share in world GDP increased consistently from 0.9 per cent in 1975 to 7.4 per cent in 2009. There was also a significant increase in China's exports as a percentage of world exports from 2.0 per cent in 1980 to 10.0 per cent in 2009. China's imports as a percentage of world imports also increased from 2.1 per cent in 1985 to 8.0 per cent in 2009. China's FDI inflows as a percentage of world FDI inflows also increased considerably in the time interval, from 2.9 per cent in 1980 to 6.7 per cent in 2009.

China's export of goods and services to the rest of the world expanded by 1,697 per cent over the period from 1990 to 2009, moving from $63.6 billion in 1990 to $1,142.8 billion in 2009, as seen in table 1.8. Imports of goods and services by the Chinese economy increased from $48.8 billion in 1990 to $902.7 billion in 2009: a 1,749 per cent change. Foreign direct investment inflows into the Chinese economy also increased considerably from $2.7 billion in 1990 to $34.3 billion in 2009: an increase of 1,170.4 per cent. Although the population of China only increased by 17.3 per cent between 1990 and 2009, China's 1.33 billion people were still approximately one-fifth of the global population.

Table 1.9, drawn from Dale Jorgenson and Khuong Vu (2005), provides an illustration of the relative size and growth of the Chinese economy.[1] The clear indication is that the Chinese economy is growing at a rapid pace and in the process is having a very favourable impact on the growth of global GDP.

Given that the price levels of a significant amount of goods and services from China are much lower than in Organisation for Economic Co-operation and Development (OECD) economies, using purchasing power parity (PPP) estimates actually leads to an increase in the representative economic size of the Chinese economy, as illustrated in table 1.10.[2] In particular, in nominal terms the GDP of China was 18.1 per cent of that of the United States in 2005 but in PPP terms was 67 per cent for the same year. Similarly, while Chinese nominal per capita income was 4 per cent of that of the United States, its PPP income per capita was 15.1 per cent.

Table 1.9: China's contribution to global GDP growth

	Share in global GDP		Growth of GDP (%)		Share in world GDP growth (%)	
	1989–95	2004	1989–95	1995–2003	1989–95	1995–2003
China	7.64	10.91	9.94	7.13	30.3	22.6

Source: Jorgenson and Vu (2005).

Table 1.10: Comparison of US, Japanese and Chinese GDP and per capita GDP in nominal US dollars and PPP, 2005

Country	Nominal GDP (US$1bn)	GDP in PPP $ billion	Nominal GDP per capita	Per capita GDP in PPP
United States	12,458	12,458	42,130	42,130
Japan	4,571	3,914	35,880	30,720
China	2,262	8,359	1,700	6,386

Source: EIU (various years).

China's 2001 accession into the World Trade Organization (WTO) has had tremendous implications for world trade. China now has the ability to use the WTO's dispute-settlement mechanism when defending itself against antidumping charges and other trade-related disputes.

Countries having factor endowments and export products similar to those of China are facing a much higher degree of economic rivalry today as compared to the last fifty years. Additionally, China's emergence has impacted negatively on Southeast Asia since FDI has been redirected from there into China.

The rapid growth of the Chinese economy has positively impacted on Chinese citizens, many of whom were able to move above the poverty line. At the same time, however, Chinese growth spells bad news for many other economies.

Implications of a Rapidly Growing Chinese Economy for CARICOM Economies[3]

The rapid growth of China is likely to have several direct effects on Caribbean economies. These direct effects may be classified into four broad groups.

The first effect on the Caribbean economies is a *complementary* effect. This effect realizes that as China grows it will need a greater amount of goods and services to help meet the requirements of its expanding population. In terms of its sheer size and increasing income, this will open new markets for economies external to China. The critical question here is whether or not China is becoming a new engine for economic growth and a conduit for economic growth in the Caribbean. The economic literature provides, in a much broader context, evidence that there has been a shifting in cross-country growth linkages over time. Haltmaier (2007) found that in recent years China's growth has had a much more pronounced impact on the economic growth performance of other economies, and this will therefore benefit the Caribbean.

Additionally, many Caribbean economies are heavily dependent on tourism, and the Chinese economy will become a very important source economy for tourism flows in the future. Table 1.11 shows that for the Trinidad and Tobago economy alone, tourism inflows increased sixfold between 2002 and 2009. In this regard, the Caribbean tourism industry will need to do its homework and establish the relevant chain of plans and policies to benefit from potential future tourist inflows from China.

Table 1.11: Stopover arrivals from China to Trinidad and Tobago, 2002–2009

	2002	2003	2004	2005	2006	2007	2008	2009
January	16	70	13	129	27	124	152	179
February	16	14	27	29	53	27	36	313
March	11	33	19	78	28	208	225	169
April	18	31	43	22	54	197	209	191
May	19	9	34	37	91	241	301	192
June	31	5	26	45	45	126	100	278
July	42	16	63	42	27	121	288	120
August	18	45	53	35	67	192	167	173
September	29	47	54	42	65	131	97	132
October	26	35	24	20	134	134	195	–
November	23	45	46	58	62	192	116	–
December	29	27	29	58	195	131	152	–
Total	278	377	431	595	848	1,824	2,038	1,747

Source: Central Statistical Office of Trinidad and Tobago.

The second effect of the growing Chinese economy is that it is now one of the world's largest net savings economies; in the future there will be greater outflows of FDI from China. FDI outflows from China play an important role in China's international economic positioning. China now has some 95,000 approved outward FDI projects covering a wide range of areas including trade, transportation, resource exploration, tourism and manufacturing in more than one hundred various economies. China's outward investment thrust has been motivated more by the need to access natural resources, markets and strategic assets. In 1990, China had an FDI outflow of $0.8 billion with an aggregate

Table 1.12: Outward FDI from China's basic indicators, 1990, 2000, 2005 and 2008

	1990	2000	2005	2008
FDI outflows (US$bn)	0.8	0.9	12.3	52.2
Outward stock (US$bn)	4.5	27.8	57.2	147.9
Ratio of outward stock to GDP (%)	1.2	2.3	2.6	3.4
Ratio of outward stock to world (%)	0.3	0.1	1.4	2.8

Source: World Investment Report (2009).

stock of $4.5 billion; by 2008, FDI outflows had increased to $52.2 billion and outward stock had increased to $147.9 billion. China's ratio of outward stock of FDI to GDP was 1.2 per cent in 1990 and increased to 3.4 per cent in 2008, while China's share in global FDI outflows increased from 0.3 per cent in 1990 to 2.8 per cent in 2008 (see table 1.12). In 2005, China had a presence in 163 host economies.

Chinese firms have already started to plough their way into the Caribbean sphere in a number of areas, including the construction sector. Table 1.13 provides a brief description of some of the work two Chinese companies are currently undertaking in one CARICOM member state, Trinidad and Tobago.

In this regard, and given the expected growth of the Chinese economy and its greater participation in the global economy, CARICOM governments may find it pragmatic to woo and fawn over FDI from the Chinese economy in a greater way.

Third, China will also likely have a pronounced impact on the demand for some basic commodities – for example, crude oil. In particular, in the medium-term period, China's demand for oil and gas is expected to increase. China is abundant in coal, and this will help meet some of its industrial energy demand in the future, but this will not be so for oil and gas. Specifically, China has become a very prolific consumer of crude oil and as it stands is the second-largest consumer of oil on a daily basis, after the United States (the United States currently consumes approximately 21 million barrels of crude oil per day, while China consumes 6.5 million barrels).[4] This would certainly provide some opportunities for the Trinidad and Tobago economy in particular, which produces both crude

Table 1.13: FDI from China in Trinidad and Tobago

Foreign construction company	Origin	Contract	Contract period	Value (TT$mn)
Shanghai construction company	Shanghai, China	Social Development Towers, St Vincent, POS	3 months commencing February/March 2006	368.0
China Jiangan	China	34 housing units, El Dorado Road, Tunapuna	March 2004– March 2006	6.6
China Jiangan	China	30 housing units, Green Street, Tunapuna	April 2004– February 2005	4.8
China Jiangan	China	296 apartments, Lady Young Road, Morvant	November 2004– March 2007	664.0

Source: Trinidad and Tobago Business Guardian, 6 February 2006, http://legacy.guardian.co.tt /archives/2006-02-02/bussguardian1.html

oil and natural gas and of late has started to produce liquefied natural gas (LNG). China's consumption of natural gas has grown by as much as 13 per cent between 2000 and 2005, with consumption in 2005 standing at forty-six billion cubic metres, some 39 per cent higher than the previous year.[5]

Another direct impact of a larger Chinese economy on CARICOM states is the effect of Chinese exports on third markets (competitive effects). This will lead to increased competition and can potentially squeeze CARICOM economies out of important third markets. Table 1.14 shows that while the significance of the US market for Barbados improved from 14.9 per cent to 21.0 per cent between 1991 and 2008 and for Jamaica from 29.9 per cent to 40.3 per cent in the same interval of time, for China it improved from 8.6 per cent to 17.7 per cent.

There will also be increased competition from China in the home markets of CARICOM economies. This is another competitive effect. The maquilas of Mexico lost 254,000 jobs between 2002 and 2005 on account of cheap Chinese imports. From another perspective, foreign direct investment flows to the Brazilian economy fell from US$26.6 billion

Table 1.14: Relative shares of exports of selected CARICOM countries and China to the United States, 1991–2008

	Barbados	Jamaica	China
1991	14.9	29.9	8.6
1992	16.9	37.3	10.1
1993	18.6	39.4	18.5
1994	19.1	36.4	17.7
1995	16.0	36.9	16.6
1996	14.1	37.1	17.7
1997	14.7	33.4	17.9
1998	16.1	39.8	20.7
1999	17.5	37.3	21.5
2000	15.8	39.2	20.9
2001	15.0	33.0	20.4
2002	16.5	28.4	21.5
2003	14.5	28.6	21.1
2004	20.0	21.5	21.1
2005	13.4	25.6	21.42
2006	20.1	30.4	21.0
2007	14.2	37.2	19.1
2008	21.0	40.3	17.7

Source: Compiled from UN Comtrade Database.

in 2001 to US$11 billion in 2003, partly on account of a redirection of FDI flows to the Chinese economy.

1.4 Conclusion

This chapter provided a brief data sketch of the global economy, providing an indication of the growth performance of various regions. The chapter also provided a preliminary outline of the growing importance of the Chinese economy in the international trading arena.

Summary of Key Points

- The world economy as a whole appears to be carrying an improved growth performance after the dampening influence of the events of 9/11.
- The growth performance of developing countries has been much stronger than the overall average.
- *Globalization* refers to the development of an extensive worldwide pattern of economic relationships among nations.
- The Chinese economy is growing at a rapid pace and in the process is having a very favourable impact on the growth of global GDP.
- The rapid growth of China is likely to have several effects on Caribbean economies: more demand for tourism and domestic commodities as well as greater outflows of FDI from China but increased competition from Chinese exports to third markets.

Multiple Choice

1. What is globalization?
    a) the total inflow and outflow of capital by countries around the world
    b) the integration of markets, nation-states and technologies that allows nation-states to communicate further, faster, deeper and cheaper
    c) the extensive worldwide pattern of economic relationships between nations
    d) the unification of global prices
    e) b and c

2. The average growth rate of the Chinese economy over the period 2000 to 2009 was
    a) 9 per cent
    b) 9.5 per cent
    c) 8 per cent
    d) 10.3 per cent
    e) 7.6 per cent

3. The average growth rate of all developing countries over the period 2000 to 2008 was
    a) 4.6 per cent
    b) 4 per cent
    c) 5.4 per cent
    d) 3.5 per cent
    e) 3 per cent

4. What is/are the consequence(s) of China's increasing trade openness for Caribbean economies?
    a) a greater inflow of tourists
    b) a reduction in FDI inflows
    c) greater competition for third markets
    d) a and c
    e) b and c

5. *As China grows, it will need a greater amount of goods to help meet the requirements of its expanding population in terms of its sheer size and growing income.*
    What implication does the above statement have for the Caribbean economies?
    a) China is becoming a new engine for economic growth and a conduit for economic growth in the Caribbean.
    b) China's residents will migrate to the Caribbean.
    c) The Caribbean is becoming a new engine for economic growth and a conduit for economic growth in China.
    d) The Caribbean's residents will migrate to China.

Short Essay

1. What are the benefits of global economic growth for Caribbean economies?
2. What are the main drivers of international demand and supply?
3. What has been the growth performance of China over the period 1995–2009?
4. Briefly describe China's international trading status for the period 1995–2009.
5. Discuss in detail the projected impact of the growth of the Chinese economy on (a) CARICOM economies and (b) the rest of the world.

Key Trade Terms

- International trade
- Merchandise trade
- Commercial services
- Globalization
- Exports/imports
- Trade openness
- Current account balance
- Complementary effect
- Caribbean Community (CARICOM)

The Pure Theory of International Trade
Supply

Learning Objectives
a. Define Mercantilism.
b. Compare absolute and comparative advantage.
c. Define revealed comparative advantage (RCA) and how it is measured.
d. Identify the problems in quantifying RCA measures.

2.0 Introduction

The question of how international trade should operate has been the subject of much debate for several centuries. Starting with the mercantilist era (approximately the sixteenth to eighteenth century), the main thrust of the mercantilist school was that exports should be encouraged and imports discouraged. Towards the end of the eighteenth century the mercantilist views began to lose their sway and laissez-faire trade policy became more common. However, the question of how trade should be conducted remains as important today as it was several centuries ago – should government intervene and if so by how much?

At a superficial level, one can argue that people would trade in those goods and services that would make the most money for them as private economic agents. What is not so clear though is who ends up making the money from trade and whether the gains made by some people are greater than the losses made by others. Furthermore, if two nations are engaged in trade, does that mean that if one gains the other has to lose, and if so, is this a sufficient basis to disallow trade?

2.1 The Mercantilist View

The mercantilist view (popular from the sixteenth to the middle of the eighteenth century in such countries as Britain, Spain, France and the Netherlands) held that the most important way for a nation to become rich and powerful was to export more than it imported. The difference would be settled by an inflow of precious metals – mostly gold.

In the mercantilist system, the notion of economic wealth was conditioned by the amount of precious metals that the country carried. The mercantilist reasoned that with a higher stock of wealth, the economy could produce a higher quantity of goods and services to meet the needs of the population and in so doing increase the standard of living of the entire population.

In the mercantilist system, an increase in the amount of gold bullion was interpreted as representing an increase in real wealth. The rationale for this line of reasoning in England can be found in the fact that more wealth meant that the economy could finance the royal navy, which was critical in maintaining the economy's imperial position. In addition, a greater volume of gold in circulation meant that higher volumes of economic activity could be facilitated.

Given that the resources that represented wealth, in particular gold, were deemed as being fixed in supply, trade was beneficial only to those countries that carried a surplus on their trade account:

> The ordinary means . . . to increase our wealth treasure is by Foreign Trade, wherein we must ever observe this rule; to sell more to strangers yearly than we consume of theirs in value. For suppose that when this Kingdom is plentifully served with the Cloth, Lead, Tin, Iron, Fish and other native commodities, we do yearly export the overplus to foreign countries to the value of twenty two hundred thousand pounds; by which means we are enabled beyond the Seas to buy and bring in foreign wares for our use and consumptions, to the value of twenty hundred thousand pounds. By this order duly kept in our trading, we may rest assured that the Kingdom shall be enriched yearly two hundred thousand pounds, which must be brought to us in so much Treasure; because that part of our stock which is not returned to us in wares must necessarily be brought home in treasure. (Thomas Mun 1664)

The mercantilist system of trade, which preceded the rise of free trade, was characterized by the following:

- A bias in trade policy towards exports: This was evidenced by the imposition of strict bans and quotas on imported goods. Specifically, the British Navigation Acts of 1651 and 1660 attempted to reduce the amount of trade its colonies engaged with non-English traders. In some cases, the export of certain raw materials was also prohibited. For example, in the case of textiles England sought to limit the amount of wool traded in order to maintain its monopoly on the textile market.
- The existence of trade monopolies: The governments of the day permitted single merchants or groups of merchants to act in a manner and form that tended to be monopolistic in nature. They were allowed to set price levels. These practices existed in the English, Spanish, Belgian and Dutch markets.
- The existence of a lucrative informal sector: Given the amount of bans and quotas in existence, traders from England, Holland, Belgium and Spain found it profitable to trade with Caribbean colonies. From these colonies the traders obtained cheap raw materials. The colonies also provided a ready market for manufactured goods. Additionally, a very lucrative trade emerged with the smuggling of bullion.

Mercantilism today, although somewhat disguised and diluted, is still practised in some countries. Modern policies that encourage exports and discourage imports are influenced by the same factors that motivated mercantilism during the seventeenth and eighteenth centuries. Today, however, the focus in not so much on building wealth but more so on either generating or maintaining the level of employment. Modern trade policies therefore favour exports, given the link between the expansion in exports and generation of employment.

There are many weaknesses in the mercantilist argument. In particular, an expansion in the amount of money a country has encourages an increase in its domestic price level, and this in turn can reduce the international competitiveness of that economy with the possibility that import expenditures exceed export revenues.

2.2 Absolute Advantage

One of the first economists to challenge the mercantilist orthodoxy was Adam Smith, who as early as 1776 noted that nations parallel households and that free trade among specialized nations would improve the welfare of all nations. In the *Wealth of Nations*, Smith argued that the mercantilist position on trade was incorrect and free trade offered the best portfolio of opportunities for all countries. His main suggestion was that with free trade, the nations of the world could specialize in the production of those commodities in which they had an absolute advantage and import those commodities in which they had a disadvantage. International specialization would therefore lead to an increase in world output, and all nations would benefit.

The theory of absolute advantage set out in this section is based on the following list of assumptions:

1. There are two countries, two commodities and two factors of production.
2. Factors are easily substitutable between productive options.
3. The analysis is for a particular period of time with a given level of technology.
4. Constant cost economies of scale are assumed so that changes in production have no effect on the costs of production.
5. There are no barriers to trade in existence between trade partners.

To portray Smith's thinking on absolute advantage, we shall proceed with an example. In table 2.1 we illustrate the output per man-hour for the Jamaican and Trinidad and Tobago economies as concerns the production of methanol and sugar.

Observe that Trinidad and Tobago can produce methanol six times as efficiently as Jamaica, while Jamaica can produce sugar three times as efficiently as Trinidad and Tobago. Suppose that Trinidad and Tobago exchanged twelve barrels of methanol (the man-hour equivalent of two tons of sugar) with Jamaica to obtain six tons of sugar. These four extra tons of sugar represent a gain of two man-hours of Trinidad and Tobago time. Jamaica will also benefit, for the twelve barrels of methanol it received would have taken it six

Table 2.1: Output per man-hour: Absolute advantage

	Trinidad and Tobago	Jamaica
Methanol (barrels)	12	2
Sugar (tons)	2	6

hours to produce. These six hours can now be used by the Jamaicans to produce thirty-six tons of sugar. Thus Jamaica by exchanging six tons of sugar for twelve barrels of methanol can gain five man-hours.

Smith therefore argued for greater specialization on an international basis to improve global resource allocation and by extension global output. Note, though, that world output is only increased in Smith's argument if each nation holds an absolute advantage in the production of at least one commodity.

David Ricardo (1951, 133–49) was able to expand on some of Smith's ideas by explaining the conditions under which an economy with no absolute advantage could trade and gain.

2.3 Comparative Advantage

Smith's definition of mutually beneficial trade was an effective rebuttal to mercantilism. However, Smith's analysis left an unanswered question. Why would trade occur between two countries if one had an absolute advantage in the production of both goods? In the late eighteenth and nineteenth centuries, the United Kingdom was the most advanced country in the world with an absolute advantage in the production of most goods. Given this situation, why would the United Kingdom trade with less productive areas such as those in the Americas? David Ricardo, a British economist, developed the answer. Expanding on Adam Smith's work on absolute advantage, Ricardo formulated the theory of comparative advantage.[1]

Ricardo illustrated the principle of comparative advantage by drawing reference to the following example: "Two men can make both shoes and hats, and one is superior to the other in both employments, but in making hats he can only exceed his competitor by one fifth or 20 percent, and in making shoes he can excel him by one third or 33 percent; will it not be for the interest of both that the superior man should employ himself exclusively in making shoes and the inferior man in making hats?" (Ricardo 1817).

The theory of comparative advantage states that it is beneficial for two countries to trade, although one country may be able to produce all of the items traded cheaper than the other. Emphasis is placed on the ratio between how easily two countries can produce different kinds of goods. In this case the absolute cost of production is not emphasized.

To illustrate the main ideas associated with the theory of comparative advantage we can proceed as follows. Let us assume we had a situation such as that shown in table 2.2.

Trinidad and Tobago can produce more of both methanol (M) and sugar (S) than Jamaica per man-hour. (This is not an unusual position, as many developed economies have factor endowment attributes that enable them to produce more of all commodities at lower per unit costs than developing economies.)

Table 2.2: Output per man-hour: Comparative advantage

	Trinidad and Tobago	Jamaica
Methanol (barrels)	12	2
Sugar (tons)	6	4

Observe that if Trinidad and Tobago were to exchange twelve barrels of methanol for twelve tons of sugar with Jamaica, then it would be giving up one hour's worth of effort but receiving two hours' worth of its productive capability in sugar, so that it benefits by six tons of sugar. In turn, if Jamaica were to produce twelve barrels of methanol, it would need to deploy six hours of labour. Jamaica saves three man-hours when it exchanges twelve tons of sugar for twelve barrels of methanol with Trinidad and Tobago, as the Jamaicans utilize only three hours of labour to produce twelve tons of sugar.

Thus, with an exchange of twelve barrels of methanol for twelve tons of sugar, Trinidad and Tobago gains six tons of sugar and Jamaica twelve barrels of methanol: 12M = 12S is called the international terms of trade, but it is not the only terms of trade at which both nations benefit. Let us investigate this point a bit further.

Recall that in Trinidad and Tobago one man-hour can produce either 12M or 6S; this means that it will not be in Trinidad and Tobago's best interest to give up 12M for less than 6S. If this were the case, Trinidad and Tobago could simply take one man-hour and produce 6S. In a parallel vein of reasoning, Jamaica can utilize one man-hour to produce 2M or 4S. In this scenario, it will not be practical for Jamaica to give up more than 24S to obtain 12M. If such were the case, it would be best for Jamaica to produce methanol itself, as it would be too costly to import.

Thus we have established some boundaries within which trade will be beneficial for both economies, and these boundaries are as follows:

• Trinidad and Tobago must get more than 6S for 12M.
• Jamaica must not be required to give up more than 24S for 12M.

The international terms of trade must therefore be such that 12M trade for at least 6S for Trinidad and Tobago and less than 24S for Jamaica: 6S < 12M < 24S.

Observe that 18s (24s − 6s) represents the total gain from trade. The distribution of the gains from trade depends on the actual value at which the terms of trade settles. The closer the terms of trade settles to 6S, the more Jamaica gains from trade. Similarly, if they settle closer to 24S, then Trinidad and Tobago reaps the lion's share of trade.

Adam Smith and David Ricardo based their theories on the assumption that output is a function of a single homogeneous factor of production: labour. Using this argument, we can express the cost of producing methanol in terms of the cost of producing sugar.

Let initial conditions be such that in Trinidad and Tobago, one man-hour can be used to produce 12M or 6S; alternatively, 1M requires $\frac{1}{12}$ of a man-hour and 1S requires $\frac{1}{6}$ of a man-hour. In Jamaica, 1M requires $\frac{1}{2}$ of a man-hour, while 1S requires $\frac{1}{4}$ of a man-hour. This information is summarized in table 2.3.

Table 2.3: Man-hours to produce methanol and sugar

	Trinidad and Tobago	Jamaica
Man-hours to produce 1M	$\frac{1}{12}$	$\frac{1}{2}$
Man-hours to produce 1S	$\frac{1}{6}$	$\frac{1}{4}$

Let $(P_S/P_M)_T$ and $(P_S/P_M)_J$ represent the price/cost relation in Trinidad and Tobago and Jamaica, respectively:

$$(P_S/P_M)_T = ((\tfrac{1}{6})/(\tfrac{1}{12})) = 2$$

$$(P_S/P_M)_J = ((\tfrac{1}{4})/(\tfrac{1}{2})) = \tfrac{1}{2}$$

Since $(P_S/P_M)_J < (P_S/P_M)_T$, then in Jamaica sugar is relatively cheaper to produce. Trade needs to take place somewhere between Jamaica's price and Trinidad and Tobago's price: $\tfrac{1}{2} < P_S/P_M < 2$. As long as a terms of trade holds within this range of values, Trinidad and Tobago can buy sugar from Jamaica, and trade will be initiated.

2.4 Comparative Advantage and the Developing Countries

Comparative advantage is an important concept to both policymakers and practitioners. The nature of an economy's comparative advantage has utility, as it can help identify the implications of a shift in a policy regime and determine the influence on economic welfare. An understanding of comparative advantage can help provide clearer directives regarding the direction that an economy's trade and investment regime should adhere to in order to benefit from explicit differences in international factor endowments and relative demand.

The classical theory of international trade suggests that if an economy has an absolute advantage in the production of all commodities, specialization and trade can transpire if each trading nation has a comparative advantage in the production of at least one commodity.

The classical economists noted a wide array of benefits that free international trade offers to participating nations, including a greater utilization of formerly idle resources as improved levels of output are brought on stream through enhanced export levels.

Greater resource utilization promotes a higher level of income, which in turn facilitates a greater degree of consumption of foreign goods and services. Higher income levels working through the accelerator principle can also help to promote a greater degree of investment. Researchers have also argued that international trade offers the opportunity to not only realize the full employment of scarce resources but also promote the optimal allocation of scarce resources.

Participation in free trade also allows some dynamic benefits such as access to foreign capital and technology, stimulation of entrepreneurial capability and an encouragement of innovation.

At the same time, some developmental economists such as Raul Prebisch (1959) and Hans Singer (1950) argued that the production of goods along comparative advantage lines will cause developing countries to continue to produce mainly primary goods for exports. Primary goods generally have low prices and income elasticity of demand, which in turn translates into low levels of relative income compared to economies producing manufacturing goods.

2.5 An Enquiry into the Revealed Comparative Advantage of Trinidad and Tobago

Quantifying comparative advantage is a detailed involvement. Several difficulties easily arise when such a calculation is being undertaken. One of the difficulties is that comparative advantage in its theoretical nakedness occurs in a world with perfectly functioning markets.

Another problem in quantifying revealed comparative advantage occurs when we consider aggregation. It is well understood that economic welfare and allocative efficiency in the use of resources occurs when nations engage in international trade in those commodities in which they carry a comparative advantage. However, this relationship becomes blurred as we try to discern the comparative advantage for a commodity that is itself comprised of several commodities. In particular, what this means is that while an economy may have a comparative advantage in some parts of a commodity, it may have a comparative disadvantage in other parts.

A third problem arises because an economy's comparative advantage may appear to be what an economy's post-trade data reflects, while with actual data this may not be the case. As Vollrath (1991) notes, "Both applied economists and policy makers need to be sensitive about the gap between inferred and the true comparative advantage. Ferreting out the trade impacts or real economic determinants, government intervention and imperfect information represents a challenging area needing additional research".

Bela Balassa (1965) in an evaluation of the factors that determine the comparative advantage of an economy noted that "comparative advantage appears to be the outcome of a number of factors, some measurable, others not, some easily pinned down, others less so. One wonders, therefore, whether more could not be gained if instead of enunciating general principles and trying to apply these to explain actual trade flows, one took the observed pattern of trade as a point of departure".

On this basis, Balassa promoted the line of enquiry focusing on post-trade equilibrium rather than pre-trade equilibrium.[2] Concerning post-trade equilibrium, Balassa highlights that it "reflects relative costs as well as differences in non price factors" (cited in Volrath 1991).

Economic conditions have the ultimate influence on the economy's comparative advantage. In turn, the pattern of international comparative advantage influences trade, production and consumption patterns of any particular good. Using data on trade, production and costs (which are "post trade" data), one can estimate an economy's comparative advantage (the word *estimate* here is indicative of "revealed").

Theoretically, the construction of a comparative advantage index requires a focus on pre-trade relative price levels in an undistorted world where factor and product markets operate in equilibrium. In practice, however, economic analysts are constrained to use data generated by a post-trade equilibrium process. One crude measure that can be used to indicate a country's comparative advantage is calculated as

$$C_{ij} = X_i / WX_i \qquad (2.1)$$

where

X_i = quantity of the commodity i exported by country j,
WX_i = quantity of the commodity i exported by the world as a whole.

Table 2.4: Index of Trinidad and Tobago's share (volume) of world exports in selected energy sector products, 1975–1998

Year	LPG	Aviation gasoline	Motor gasoline	Kerosene	Jet fuel	Gas-diesel oil	Residual fuel oil
1975	100.0	100.0	100.0	100.0	100.0	100.0	100.0
1976	119.0	214.9	62.0	139.9	139.4	123.5	137.4
1977	120.3	209.7	101.7	104.2	69.9	87.6	109.8
1978	169.0	197.1	52.3	59.4	63.2	72.5	93.4
1979	223.6	156.9	53.3	64.1	69.6	81.8	85.1
1980	284.9	238.8	52.2	48.4	73.8	101.9	94.6
1981	227.6	310.3	41.0	27.2	23.5	76.4	64.4
1982	157.3	481.8	27.8	23.6	20.8	60.2	52.6
1983	148.4	366.1	4.3	0.0	34.5	21.4	19.6
1984	84.7	63.5	17.0	17.9	36.5	35.2	30.3
1985	132.0	43.1	14.7	7.1	47.1	28.4	35.2
1986	94.3	51.5	12.9	0.0	45.4	25.6	36.9
1987	78.5	60.6	15.5	0.0	49.2	25.7	37.2
1988	63.7	25.1	12.9	0.0	49.3	25.9	35.4
1989	42.7	31.0	8.4	0.0	31.8	31.7	28.9
1990	75.1	69.6	11.3	0.0	12.8	24.8	31.6
1991	377.8	79.8	14.2	0.0	14.2	24.8	38.7
1992	493.8	64.0	12.7	0.0	13.9	30.0	30.0
1993	820.0	85.5	14.9	0.0	11.6	36.4	32.6
1994	734.5	67.2	12.0	0.0	33.7	25.6	29.1
1995	805.6	72.1	19.4	0.0	28.5	26.9	25.9
1996	878.1	70.5	17.4	0.0	29.2	27.3	25.2
1997	577.3	70.3	10.9	0.0	38.4	27.6	22.9
1998	608.1	34.1	41.4	0.0	30.5	32.4	24.7

Source: Derived from data in the *United Nations Trade Statistics Yearbook* (various years).

This measure indicates the share of total world output of commodity i attributable to country j. For convenience, the trend in the variable C_{ij} is presented in index format. As $C_{ij} \to 1$, the comparative advantage of country j in the export of commodity i increases.

The *United Nations Trade Statistics Yearbook* provides detailed trade data that can be used to calculate indices such as expression 2.1 (the discussion focuses on energy statistics as they are easily available). Not all trade data lend themselves to analysis in this (quantity) format, however.

As shown in table 2.4, Trinidad and Tobago's export share in 1998 as compared to 1975 of all the listed energy products decreased substantially, except liquid propane gas (LPG), which increased some sixfold. Since 1993, however, Trinidad and Tobago's share of world output of motor gasoline and jet fuel have also shown some signs of improvement, increasing from 14.9 and 11.6 in 1993 to 41.4 and 30.5 in 1998, respectively.

While the indexed version of the export share of a country in world exports is partly reflective of the comparative advantage of that country, more robust measures are available in the literature. One widely used measure was introduced by Balassa (1965) and is called the "revealed comparative advantage" index. The revealed comparative advantage (RCA) of a country is indicated by the country's trade performance with respect to individual industries. The RCA index is calculated based on the actual export performance of a country:

$$\text{RCA}_i = \frac{T_{xi}}{T_{xt}} \bigg/ \frac{W_{xi}}{W_{xt}} \qquad (2.2)$$

where

T_{xi} = a country's exports of good i,
T_{xt} = a country's total exports,
W_{xi} = world exports of good i,
W_{xt} = total world exports.

The theoretical range of the RCA for commodity i (RCA_i) is $0 < \text{RCA}_i < \infty$. A country is said to have a revealed comparative advantage in exporting a commodity, i, if

$$1 < \text{RCA}_i < \infty$$

Structural shifts in the comparative advantage position of Trinidad and Tobago for ten different products that Trinidad and Tobago exports and for which data are available are shown in table 2.5.

In 1970, the only commodities of those listed in table 2.5 in which Trinidad and Tobago did not have a comparative advantage were non-alcoholic beverages (111) and methanol (51,211). After 1990, we can observe a changing pattern in the structure of trade for energy sector products. Particularly, ammonia (52,261), urea (56,216) and methanol (51,211) have been experiencing upward movements in their respective RCA scores, while scores for crude petroleum (333) and refined petroleum products (334) have been persistently on the decline throughout the data period. By the end of the data period, Trinidad and Tobago had RCA indices greater than unity for cocoa (72), non-alcoholic beverages (111), crude petroleum (333), refined petroleum products (334), urea (56,216), natural

Table 2.5: Revealed comparative advantage indices for various export commodities of Trinidad and Tobago, 1970–2009

Codes	Sugar	Cocoa	Non-alcoholic beverages	Crude petroleum	Petroleum products, refined	Iron and steel products	Gas, natural and manufactured	Urea	Ammonia	Methanol
	61	72	111	333	334	673	34	56,216	52,261	51,211
1970	8.792	2.616	0.318	2.027	27.720	n.a.	n.a.	n.a.	18.355	0.131
1975	2.937	1.222	0.085	3.083	13.279	0.006	n.a.	n.a.	37.225	0.063
1980	0.854	0.929	0.151	4.364	17.376	0.002	0.308	2.412	67.303	n.a.
1985	4.149	0.608	0.000	8.240	0.000	1.667	0.204	59.033	341.199	1,219.298
1990	5.123	3.431	6.563	8.239	13.409	9.158	0.432	69.957	126.981	101.543
1995	6.608	1.650	15.708	5.906	18.429	0.009	4.713	82.482	405.752	n.a.
1996	3.945	0.953	15.273	4.698	15.797	0.012	2.233	67.489	318.952	176.587
1997	6.695	1.044	17.866	6.212	14.211	0.036	2.321	75.682	319.109	257.230
1998	6.088	1.016	24.840	4.568	20.250	0.022	3.201	58.163	395.624	295.519
1999	6.134	0.935	15.556	3.644	18.148	0.043	9.268	52.051	459.721	277.245
2000	5.553	0.964	12.013	2.394	15.529	0.009	10.157	34.944	287.725	211.651
2001	2.596	2.095	10.410	1.896	12.290	0.009	7.358	31.475	280.243	141.115
2002	3.454	1.186	13.030	3.246	13.179	0.009	12.031	42.921	362.078	154.150
2003	1.438	2.182	7.189	1.723	13.027	0.005	14.855	31.882	267.691	158.173
2004	2.875	2.616	6.261	2.419	4.827	0.008	24.347	31.635	349.293	213.429
2005	1.638	3.319	6.023	2.456	8.621	0.008	14.662	26.412	236.326	195.338
2006	1.408	3.512	4.501	2.061	7.026	0.002	24.160	21.401	178.161	156.250
2007	0.950	3.102	4.183	2.080	4.179	0.009	22.897	26.234	275.153	189.821
2008	0.177	5.775	2.987	1.387	5.650	0.001	15.749	25.301	196.559	158.464
2009	0.119	5.469	5.532	2.019	5.348	0.004	24.375	22.803	159.913	137.493

Source: Computed using data from UNCOMTRADE (Sitc Rev 1).

and manufactured gas (34), methanol (51,211) and ammonia (52,261). Even at this level of aggregation, the analysis shows that the revealed comparative advantage position of the Trinidad and Tobago economy has graduated away from a narrow focus on petroleum products towards petrochemical products such as ammonia, urea and methanol.

2.6 Conclusion

This chapter focused on some of the early trade theories from mercantilism to comparative advantage theory. The mercantilists focused on trade as a basis to acquire wealth and emphasized the benefits of export revenues outstripping import expenditures. The theory of absolute advantage emphasized the gains that nations and the world economy could realize from trade if each nation hosted an absolute advantage in at least one commodity. David Ricardo, however, showed that even if nations held no absolute advantage, trade would still be beneficial if each nation had a comparative advantage in at least one commodity.

Appendix 2.1: Measuring Revealed Comparative Advantage (RCA)

The idea of measuring RCA was developed by Liesner (1958) and later refined by Balassa (1965). RCA indices have been used by a vast number of researchers trying to shed light on the RCA of various nation-states. Porter (1990) used the concept of RCA to help identify strong sectoral clusters, while Ferto and Hubbard (2003) used RCA indices to analyse the competitiveness of the Hungarian food sectors.

The predominant measure of revealed comparative advantage used in the literature is that formulated by Balassa (1965) and can be expressed as follows:[3]

$$B = (X_{ij}/X_{it}) / (X_{nj}/X_{nt})$$ 2.3

where

X = exports,
i = a country,
j = a commodity,
t = a set of commodities,
n = a set of countries.

The index has a theoretical range from zero to infinity and is based on post-trade and not on pre-trade data. This range can be divided into two substantive groups:

$$0 < B < 1$$

$$1 < B < \text{infinity}$$

That is, the Balassa index is asymmetrically distributed.

Because of this asymmetry, the following concerns emerge. If the Balassa index (B) has a higher mean than the median score, then the distribution will be skewed to the right. The implication of this asymmetry is that those sectors with a weight in excess of unity will be overestimated in relation to those with an RCA score less then unity.

From a methodical point of view, the RCA index is devised to compare relative specialization in different products nation-wise – that is, to allow comparison of the dominance of different products of a given nation with a pattern seen among a larger group of countries.

The Hillman Condition

Hillman (1980) examined the relationship between the Balassa index and pre-trade relative prices. He focused on cross-country comparisons for a specific sector, using homothetic preferences and treating all other goods as a Hicksian composite good.

Hillman considered the post-trade-equilibrium-based Balassa index as a measure of comparative advantage and what pre-trade indices suggest. Hillman illustrated that it was inappropriate to use the B index in making cross-country comparisons. Specifically, Hillman noted that when making cross-country comparisons, the B index is independent of Ricardian-premised comparative advantage.

He provided a theoretical basis for the Balassa index and a diagrammatic illustration of the necessary and sufficient conditions that will facilitate correspondence between the post-trade Balassa index and pre-trade relative prices. The condition is verifiable empirically.

Significantly, he outlined the following condition for the B index to reflect the comparative advantage status of an economy that pre-trade relative prices would suggest. Hillman illustrated that in pre-trade equilibrium, comparative advantage meant the following condition held:

$$\text{Hillman condition:} \quad [1 - (X_{ij}/W_i)] > [(X_{ij}/X_j)(1 - X_j/W)] \quad (2.4)$$

In this formulation,

X_{ij} = exports of commodity i by country j,
X_j = aggregate exports (all commodities),
W_i = world export of commodity i,
W = aggregate world exports.

As outlined, the Hillman condition has three parts:

$X_{ji,t}/X_{jt}$: the share of a country's exports in a particular commodity as a proportion of total exports of a group of reference economies in that sector (this is a market share term),
$X_{ji,t}/X_{i,t}$: the share of exports in sector relative to the economy's aggregate exports (this is an export penetration term), and
(X_{it}/X_t): the size of the economy to total exports, relative to the world (this provides an indication of the relative size of the economy).

Violation of the Hillman condition occurs in two regards. First, if the country exports only one commodity ($X_{ji,t} = X_{i,t}$), or second, if the economy is the sole supplier of the commodity ($X_{ji,t} = X_{jt}$). Hinloopen and Marrewijk (2006) noted that the Hillman condition is violated in the general environment where the economy has a highly concentrated market and export specialization.

To convert the Hillman condition into an operationally testable format, Marchese and Nadal de Simone (1989) utilized the following version of the Hillman index:

Hillman condition modified: $(1 - X_{ij}/W_i) / (X_{ij}/X_j) (1 - X_j/W)$ (2.5)

Using expression 2.5, for a score greater than unity, the B index represents a good indicator of comparative advantage. Marchese and Nadal de Simone (1989) argued that researchers should investigate whether the Hillman condition holds before proceeding to use the Balassa index to examine the comparative advantage stance of an economy.

Summary of Key Points

- According to the mercantilists, the most important way for a nation to become rich and powerful is to export more than it imports. The difference would be settled by an inflow of precious metals – mostly gold.
- A country is said to have an absolute advantage over another country in the production of a good if an equal quantity of resources can produce more in the former country than the latter. The theory of absolute advantage is grounded in Adam Smith's rebuttal of the mercantilist view.
- David Ricardo formulated the theory of comparative advantage, which states that it can be beneficial for two countries to trade even though one country can produce all of the items traded cheaper than the other. Emphasis is placed on the respective opportunity cost ratios of both countries in the production of goods.
- The revealed comparative advantage (RCA) of a country is indicated by the country's trade performance with respect to individual industries. The RCA index is calculated based on the actual export performance of a country.

Multiple Choice

1. According to the theory of comparative advantage, all of the reasons listed below are reasons countries trade except
   a) Exporting countries have a political advantage over the other countries.
   b) Domestic prices in one country are higher than in other countries.
   c) Raw material prices in one country are higher than in other countries.
   d) Labour is more productive in one country than in other countries.

2. The mercantilist school of thought would advocate all of the following except
   a) Imports should be encouraged.
   b) Monopolies should be encouraged.
   c) Exports should be encouraged.
   d) A balance of payments surplus should be encouraged.

3. The source of a country's comparative advantage in a particular good can be attributed to all of the following except

    a) economies of scale
    b) superior technology
    c) low demand
    d) relative abundance of the factor of production needed to produce the good

4. The mercantilist school of thought were subscribers to which of the following conventions?

    a) restriction of exports
    b) free international trade
    c) trade policies which promoted the accumulation of bullion
    d) all of the above

5. Adam Smith showed that

    a) With trade, one nation gains and the other loses.
    b) Mercantilism is beneficial to all countries.
    c) Trade can be beneficial to all participating nations.
    d) Government intervention is necessary in implementing trade policy.

Short Essay

1. Describe the trends in world trade over the period 1999–2008.
2. Explain in detail the concepts of absolute and comparative advantage.
3. Explain and illustrate equilibrium conditions under autarky; use diagrams where appropriate.

Key Trade Terms

- Mercantilism
- Absolute advantage
- Comparative advantage
- Classical theory
- Revealed comparative advantage
- Economic welfare
- Allocative efficiency
- Hillman condition

3.

Terms of Trade

Learning Objectives

- a. Define net barter terms of trade and income terms of trade and how each is measured.
- b. Identify trends in the terms of trade for CARICOM economies.
- c. Distinguish between single factoral terms of trade (SFTOT) and double factoral terms of trade (DFTOT).

3.0 Introduction

In this chapter, we review a variety of terms of trade indices. As illustrated in the previous chapter, the number of goods produced by the home country (HC) and the foreign country (FC) is conditioned by their various opportunity costs for producing the two goods. The actual international exchange ratio will therefore fall between the limits set by the opportunity costs for producing these goods in each country, dependent also on the relative strength of demand in each of these economies. This international exchange ratio influences the level of each economy's export revenues and import expenditures.

3.1 Net Barter Terms of Trade

The first terms of trade index presented in this chapter, and the one most often encountered in the trade literature, is the net barter terms of trade (NBTT), which can be represented as

$$NBTT = (E^P_i/M^P_i) \times 100$$

where

E^P_i = export price index,
M^P_i = import price index.

A value above 100 indicates an improvement in the NBTT and a fall below 100 indicates a worsening of the NBTT.

A change in the terms of trade affects the command of one unit of export on imports.

Let us assume that initially one barrel of methanol produced for export in the HC purchased one ton of sugar produced in the FC. A favourable change in the HC's net barter terms of trade, however, implies that an increase in the price of methanol may result in this same barrel of methanol fetching more than one ton of sugar.

3.2 Trends in the Terms of Trade of Trinidad and Tobago

In table 3.1, which shows the NBTT of the Trinidad and Tobago economy, three distinct patterns are recognizable:

- 1973–80, when the NBTT improved considerably;
- 1981–93, when the falloff in the price of crude oil led to a rapid deterioration in the country's terms of trade; and
- 1994–98, when the NBTT realized a general improvement on account of improvements in the price of crude oil and petrochemicals (these are two key sets of goods exported by the Trinidad and Tobago economy).

Specifically, the price of crude oil, a very important traded item in the export basket of Trinidad and Tobago, increased in 1974 on account of the Yom Kippur War and again in 1979 on account of the Persian War. These two events led to a rapid improvement in the NBTT of Trinidad and Tobago until 1980. Thereafter, the falloff in the price of crude oil led to a collapse in Trinidad and Tobago's terms of trade until around 1993. Beyond 1993, with the resurgence in the price of crude oil and the buoyancy in the price of other major export commodities from Trinidad and Tobago (such as methanol, ammonia and urea), there was an improvement in the economy's NBTT.

3.3 Income Terms of Trade

The income terms of trade may be represented as follows:

$$YTT = P_x Q_x / P_m = NBTT \times Q_x$$

where

YTT = income terms of trade,
P_x = price of exports,
Q_x = quantity of exports,
$P_x Q_x$ = volume of exports,
P_m = price of imports.

Observe that the YTT differs from the NBTT by the inclusion of the quantity of exports sold. The YTT should be calculated in those economies where a change in the relative price of exports encourages a change in the amount of exports supplied, or vice versa.

For Trinidad and Tobago, the time has probably come or is close to arriving when policymakers need to look at the income terms of trade as compared to the commodity net

Table 3.1: Net barter terms of trade, 1968–1998

Year	NBTT (all sections)
1968	153.1
1969	147.2
1970	144.2
1971	146.8
1972	137.0
1973	153.7
1974	180.3
1975	181.5
1976	181.6
1977	192.1
1978	183.9
1979	214.6
1980	228.2
1981	222.7
1982	188.5
1983	185.6
1984	184.2
1985	177.7
1986	127.4
1987	116.7
1988	100.0
1989	104.5
1990	115.5
1991	105.7
1992	98.3
1993	93.0
1994	101.5
1995	108.7
1996	111.4
1997	120.2
1998	110.4

Source: Coker (1998).

Table 3.2: Income terms of trade, 1968–1998

Year	YTT (all sections)
1968	162.5
1969	159.5
1970	156.8
1971	154.5
1972	147.4
1973	164.2
1974	207.1
1975	183.2
1976	210.2
1977	208.3
1978	181.0
1979	205.6
1980	210.7
1981	183.5
1982	159.0
1983	153.2
1984	174.5
1985	177.7
1986	125.7
1987	113.1
1988	100.0
1989	108.8
1990	133.6
1991	123.8
1992	120.1
1993	107.9
1994	128.6
1995	168.6
1996	150.2
1997	159.7
1998	163.1

Source: Coker (1998).

barter terms of trade. The income terms of trade caters for feedback from changes in the output levels of the exporting country on the export prices of its main export commodities. At present, Trinidad and Tobago is the world's number one exporter of ammonia, methanol and urea. As the data in table 3.2 reflects, Trinidad and Tobago's YTT improved from 1988 to 1998 (Coker 1998).

3.4 Comparing the Income Terms of Trade (YTT) and the Net Barter Terms of Trade (NBTT)

It is not necessary for the income terms of trade and the commodity terms of trade to move in the same direction. In particular, a country's NBTT may fall if the export prices of its main exports fall. However, if the quantity of goods an economy exports increases as a consequence, then the YTT may actually increase.

Example 3.1: Consider the following scenario, where the superscript 99 and 00 represent the years 1999 and 2000, respectively. The base year is 1999.

$$P_x^{99} = 100$$

$$P_x^{00} = 95$$

$$P_m^{99} = 100$$

$$P_m^{00} = 110$$

$$Q_x^{99} = 100$$

$$Q_x^{00} = 120$$

$$\text{NBTT}^{99} = \frac{P_x^{99}}{P_m^{99}} = \frac{100}{100} = 100 \text{ (expressed as a percentage)}$$

$$\text{NBTT}^{00} = \frac{P_x^{00}}{P_m^{00}} = \frac{95}{110} = 86$$

That is, a 14 per cent decline.

$$\text{YTT}_y^{99} = \frac{P_x^{99}}{P_m^{99}} Q_x^{99} = \frac{100}{100} \frac{100}{100} = 100$$

$$\text{YTT}_y^{00} = (0.8636)(120)$$

$$= 103.6$$

This illustrates that although the net barter terms of trade declined, the income terms of trade increased by some 3.6 per cent. This signals that for less-developed countries (LDCs), which account for a major export share of a particular export market, the YTT must be calculated, as it carries important extra information.

Table 3.3: Terms of trade in developed and developing economies, 1990–2009

		Terms of trade	
	Year	Developed countries	Developing countries
	1990	103	101
	1991	104	101
	1992	104	100
	1993	104	101
	1994	105	102
	1995	105	102
	1996	103	102
	1997	104	103
	1998	105	100
	1999	105	99
	2000	100	100
	2001	102	98
	2002	102	97
	2003	103	98
	2004	103	98
	2005	101	101
	2006	100	103
	2007	101	104
	2008	98	104
	2009	102	101

Source: UNCTAD Statistical Handbook (various years).

Table 3.3 illustrates the terms of trade of both developed and developing economies for the time interval between 1990 and 2009. Observe that while the terms of trade for developed economies remained relatively consistent from 1990 to 2009, for developing economies it fluctuated but eventually settled at 101 in 2009, thus representing a decline from its 2008 peak value.

3.5 Comparing the Terms of Trade of CARICOM Countries

The data in table 3.4 suggest that the terms of trade of Antigua and Barbuda, Guyana, Jamaica and St Kitts worsened during the period 1991–98. The same can also be said for the terms of trade of Dominica, St Lucia, St Vincent and the Grenadines, and Suriname,

Table 3.4: Terms of trade (1995 = 100) of some CARICOM member states, 1991–1998

	1991	1992	1993	1994	1995	1996	1997	1998
Antigua and Barbuda	105.17	123.58	85.89	72.83	100.00	33.60	37.87	35.63
Bahamas	99.23	97.74	105.26	105.26	100.00	100.10	106.21	105.68
Barbados	89.98	93.40	96.02	87.95	100.00	102.80	103.93	105.39
Belize	89.89	91.60	102.13	104.28	100.00	102.00	102.41	103.12
Dominica	109.26	106.20	101.32	101.42	100.00	100.10	102.60	105.27
Guyana	126.37	109.19	111.37	97.56	100.00	93.20	84.16	83.49
Jamaica	99.75	92.77	90.64	96.62	100.00	92.40	95.54	93.25
St Kitts	98.56	102.80	99.40	99.90	100.00	98.90	98.80	99.89
St Lucia	122.18	116.93	113.31	105.37	100.00	94.50	101.68	104.63
St Vincent and the Grenadines	124.27	113.21	105.29	108.34	100.00	103.10	102.79	100.73
Suriname	112.01	106.85	107.39	103.20	100.00	103.50	102.67	102.06

Source: Itam et al. (2000).

which, although still above 100, deteriorated during the period 1991–98. Part of the reason for the deteriorating terms of trade of these CARICOM economies is shown in table 3.5. For Dominica, St Lucia and St Vincent, bananas accounted for a significant part of their export earnings, and although the price offered by the European Union export market for bananas from these countries remained above the price level in the more competitive US market, overall it was in a state of decline.

Fluctuating export prices have both direct and indirect effects on CARICOM economies. A change in the export prices for any country affects the capacity of the country to import foreign goods, the country's international reserves, the government's fiscal accounts and also the level of income in the industries concerned. Adverse movements in the price of key export commodities could be offset by increases in production. However, there are resource limits on the extent to which this can be done, assuming the demand exists. The reduction in the capacity of a country to import goods can affect its economic development. The indirect effect of price fluctuations occurs through the exchange rate. In floating exchange rate regimes, falling export prices can trigger current account deficits and prompt a worsening of a country's balance of payments (BOP), thus encouraging a depreciation of a country's currency with attendant consequences.

Table 3.5: Prices of bananas and sugar in the EU and US markets, 1999–2001

Commodity	Unit	Jan–Dec 99	Jul–Sept 00	Oct–Dec 00	Jan–Mar 01	Apr–Jun 01	July–Sept 01	Nov 01
Bananas (EU)	$mn/ton	850.4	611.0	628.2	910.2	834.9	686	650.8
Bananas (US)	$mn/ton	373.8	354.1	399.4	587.4	599.2	650.9	496.0
Sugar (EU)	Cents/kg	59.17	54.2	52.89	53.0	53.12	52.6	52.6
Sugar (US)	Cents/kg	46.6	42.1	47.56	47.44	46.9	46.8	47.0

Source: UNECLAC (2001).

3.6 Illustration of the Two Factor Terms of Trade: Single and Double Factoral

Another terms of trade index sometimes encountered in the international trade literature is the single factoral terms of trade (SFTOT), which takes into account the export
productivity of the home country. It is the net barter terms of trade adjusted for changes
in the productivity of exports and may be calculated as follows:

$$SFTOT = NBTT \times Z_x$$

where Z_x is an export productivity index for the HC. Alternatively, the SFTOT is computed as the product of the NBTT and export productivity.

Trade practitioners also calculate a double factoral terms of trade (DFTOT). The
DFTOT may be calculated as follows:

$$DFTOT = NBTT \times (Z_x/Z_m)$$

where Z_m is an index of import productivity. Of all the terms of trade indices listed in
the literature, the double factoral terms of trade is the most difficult and is rarely ever
imputed. Specifically, the DFTOT from the HC's perspective reflects the number of units
of domestic factors embodied in the exports of the HC's exchange per unit of the foreign
factors embodied in the HC's imports.

In practice, although LDCs may find that the SFTOT and YTT are the most useful for
their analytical purposes, it is the net barter terms of trade that is most often calculated.
Even so, the most favourable position for any LDC exists when all of its terms of trade
increase.

Example 3.2:

Let P_x^{1999}, P_m^{1999}, P_x^{2000}, P_m^{2000} be as in the previous example (example 3.1).

$$Z_x^{1999} = 100, Z_x^{2000} = 125$$

$$\text{SFTOT} = (0.8636)\,(125) = 108\%$$

$$\text{Let } Z_m^{2000} = 110$$

$$\text{This means that } \left. Z_x^{00} \middle/ Z_m^{00} \right. = \frac{125}{110} \times 100 = 113.6\%$$

$$\text{So that, DFTOT} = (0.8636)\,(113.6\%) = 98\%$$

Overall, the terms of trade that an analyst calculates hinges on the purpose for which it is required, although all of them build on the relative price change between the import and export sector. In general, though, when the terms of trade is referred to in this text, it is in reference to the net barter terms of trade.

3.7 The Transfer Problem and the Terms of Trade

When countries are linked by trade, changes in world prices lead to benefits for some only. Changes in the terms of trade result in a transfer of income (real) between trading partners. To illustrate this, let us commence by assuming the HC makes a transfer of value $T to the FC. To make this transfer, let us assume that the HC reduces its expenditure outlay by $T and as a consequence the FC increases its expenditure outlay by $T more than its current aggregate production level. Let us assume a two-good world with the HC specializing in cloth and the FC specializing in food.

A pertinent question at this point is does a transfer of this nature influence the terms of trade? A change in purchasing power would only impact on the world demand curve while leaving world supply intact (world demand would change on account of a change in the distribution of income). Because the HC makes the transfer, the HC's demand for food from the world market decreases while the FC's demand for food on the world market rises. The net effect on the demand for food depends on the relative size of the demand for food by the HC and FC – that is, the demand curve for food can shift inwards or outwards.

If we define the international terms of trade as P_f/P_c, then the change in demand can lead to either an improvement or a worsening of the terms of trade. Let m and m* be the marginal propensity to import of the HC and FC, respectively. In this regard we have

$$mT = \text{loss in demand for food by the HC}$$

Let the FC import clothing. m*T represents import expenditure on clothing from the transfer, and so, $T - m^*T = (1 - m^*)T$ is the amount spent by the FC from the transfer on food.

$$\text{Change in food demand} = T\,(1 - m^*) - mT$$

Thus the change in food demand is positive only if $T(1 - m^*) > mT$. The terms of trade of the HC worsens with the transfer if $T(1 - m^*) > mT$ as this would increase P_f/P_c.

Alternatively, note that

$$T(1 - m^*) - mT$$

$$= T - m^*T - mT$$

$$= T[1 - (m^* + m)]$$

So that the change in demand for food is negative and hence the P_f/P_c ratio falls only if the sum of the marginal propensity to import of the HC and FC exceeds unity. If the sum of the marginal propensities to import does fall short of unity, economists speak of the secondary burdens of the transfer to acknowledge the fact that price changes create an international redistribution of income additional to the initial loan or grant.

3.8 Conclusion

This chapter outlined the various terms of trade indices and how they are calculated. The net barter terms of trade was outlined simply as the ratio of the export price index to the import price index. The income terms of trade was also presented as the net barter terms of trade adjusted for the quantity of exports. The NBTT and the YTT were identified as the most commonly used measures of a country's terms of trade, but for completeness the SFTOT and the DFTOT were also detailed.

The SFTOT was presented as the NBTT adjusted by an export productivity index. The DFTOT is presented as the NBTT adjusted by the ratio of the export and import productivity indices.

Summary of Key Points

- The net barter terms of trade (NBTT) is a ratio of the export price index to the import price index.
- The income terms of trade (YTT) differs from the NBTT by the inclusion of the quantity of exports sold. NBTT and YTT may not necessarily move in the same direction.
- The single factoral terms of trade (SFTOT) takes into account the export productivity of the home country. It is the net barter terms of trade adjusted for changes in the productivity of exports.
- The double factoral terms of trade (DFTOT) is calculated as the product of the NBTT and a ratio of export to import productivity.

Multiple Choice

1. Which of the following statements is true?
   a) Under no circumstances can the terms of trade index be calculated.
   b) The terms of trade measures the command of one unit of export on imports.
   c) A positive change in the terms of trade is always beneficial.
   d) A change in the terms of trade is always detrimental to an economy.

2. A change in the terms of trade of a country results in which of the following:
   a) a transfer of real income between countries
   b) no change in the economic environment
   c) a transfer of income between trading partners
   d) a transfer of goods and services between countries

3. An improvement in the NBTT is indicated by which of the following:
   a) any increase in the index
   b) any decrease in the index
   c) an increase above 100
   d) a fall below 100

4. A small country would benefit from trade because
   a) a small nation tends to be more productive than a large nation
   b) a large nation tends to be more productive than a small nation
   c) income levels in small nations tend to be lower than in their trading partners
   d) none of the above

5. Assuming a two-nation world, if the terms of trade in one country is 1.5, what is the terms of trade of its trading partner?
   a) ¾
   b) ⅔
   c) ³⁄₂
   d) ⁴⁄₃

Short Essays

1. Illustrate and discuss the trends in the net barter terms of trade for any named CARICOM economy.
2. How is the net barter terms of trade calculated? Use a numerical example to help illustrate your answer.
3. Plot the NBTT against the trade balance of the CARICOM economy named CARICOM economy in essay 1.
4. Besides the NBTT, what are the other indices used to measure the terms of trade?

Key Trade Terms

- Terms of trade
- Net barter terms of trade
- Income terms of trade
- Single factoral terms of trade
- Double factoral terms of trade
- Distribution of income
- Marginal propensity to import

4.

Gains from Trade in Neoclassical Theory

Learning Objectives

a. Define opportunity cost from an economic perspective.
b. Understand what a production possibility frontier (PPF) illustrates.
c. List the properties of indifference curves.
d. Understand how changes in income and prices affect the combinations of commodities that a consumer can purchase.
e. Define autarky.
f. Define gains from trade and distinguish between gains from exchange and gains from specialization.

This chapter provides a basic overview of some of the relevant neoclassical tools of economics that are used in the theory of international trade.

4.0 The Concept of Opportunity Cost

In economics the concept of cost is quite different from that of accounting. The accountant measures cost in terms of dollars and cents, while the economist measures cost in terms of what is given up or the sacrifice of one option for another. This type of cost is called opportunity cost.

In economics, we use the term *opportunity cost* to refer to the cost of one choice in terms of the benefits of the next best alternative. Thus the opportunity cost of studying international trade theory is the income that the student may have earned in that time period if he or she had opted to get a job instead.

Production Possibility Frontier

The production possibility frontier (PPF) illustrates the combination of goods an economy (or firm) can produce if it utilizes all its available factors of production. If the economy is not producing the quantities indicated along the boundary of the PPF, resources are being managed inefficiently and some factors will remain unemployed. The production possibility frontier shows there are limits to production, so an economy, in order to achieve allocative efficiency, must decide which combination of goods and services should be produced.

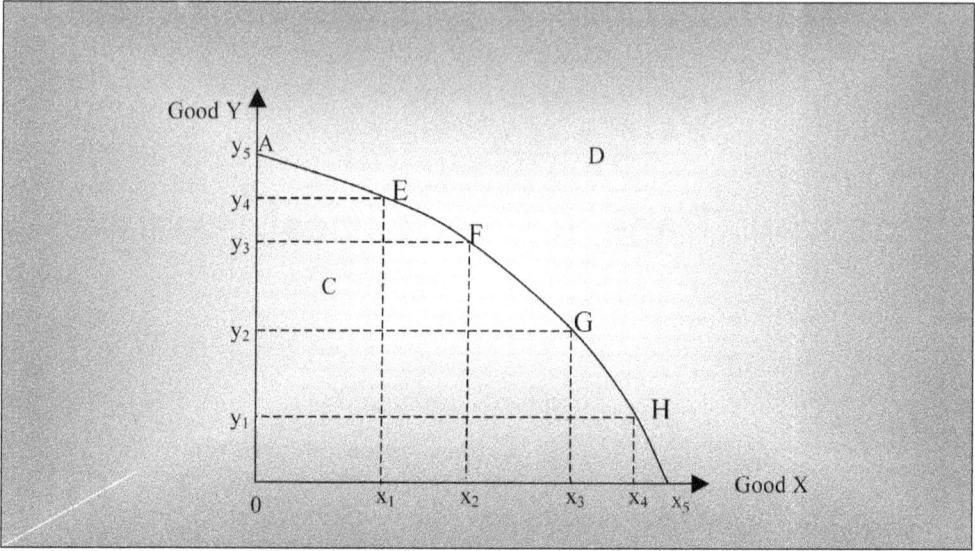

Figure 4.1: A production possibility frontier

Referring to figure 4.1, let us assume that an economy can use its resources to produce two goods: clothing (X) and food (Y). The economy can produce y_5 units of Y and 0 units of X, or x_5 units of X and 0 units of Y, or any combination of X and Y along the curve. Because the economy has a limited amount of scarce resources, it cannot produce at point D. At the same time, while the economy can easily produce at point C, this output combination is very much within the boundaries of the production possibility capabilities of the country. Point C represents an inefficient production point, as some of the economy's resources remain idle or unemployed.

Note that this economy can choose to operate anywhere within or on the production possibility curve. Thus at point E the firm can produce y_4 units of Y and x_1 units of X, while at point F the firm can produce y_3 units of Y and x_2 units of X, and so on. In order to produce the bundle of goods illustrated by point F, the firm has to give up the bundle of goods represented by point E. We say that the opportunity cost of producing F is E. The slope of the PPF shows the marginal rate of transformation of one good into another.

Table 4.1: Alternative bundles of clothing and food conferring equal satisfaction

Bundle	Clothing (C)	Food (F)
A	30	1
B	18	2
C	13	3
D	10	4
E	8	5
F	7	6

4.1 Indifference Curves

Indifference curves are another set of tools used in economics to explain consumer behaviour in different market situations. An indifference curve is the locus of all the possible combinations of two or more goods that yield the same level of satisfaction to a consumer. For illustrative purposes, consider the data in table 4.1, which shows the combinations of clothing and food that yield the same level of satisfaction to a consumer.

The information in table 4.1 can be used to plot the indifference curve for the consumer as shown in figure 4.2.

In the real world, economic agents make trade-offs between the goods they consume; indifference curve analysis can help to make these trade-offs clearer. In the indifference curve in figure 4.2, in moving from market bundle A to B, the consumer gives up twelve units of clothing to obtain a single extra unit of food. Similarly, to move from market bundle B to C, the consumer gives up five units of clothing for a single unit of food. The slope of the indifference curve illustrates that the consumer will be willing to give up less and less units of clothing for food if he or she wishes to remain at the same level of satisfaction – that is, on the same indifference curve. To quantify the amount of clothing a consumer is willing to give up for food, economists calculate the marginal rate of substitution (MRS). The marginal rate of substitution of food for clothes details the number of units of food sacrificed for one unit of clothing. The MRS is therefore the slope of the indifference curve. Observe from figure 4.2 that the indifference curve has a negative slope.

Properties of Indifference Curves

1. Indifference curves do not intersect. This is a mathematical impossibility in that it would imply that one point is characterized by two different levels of satisfaction.

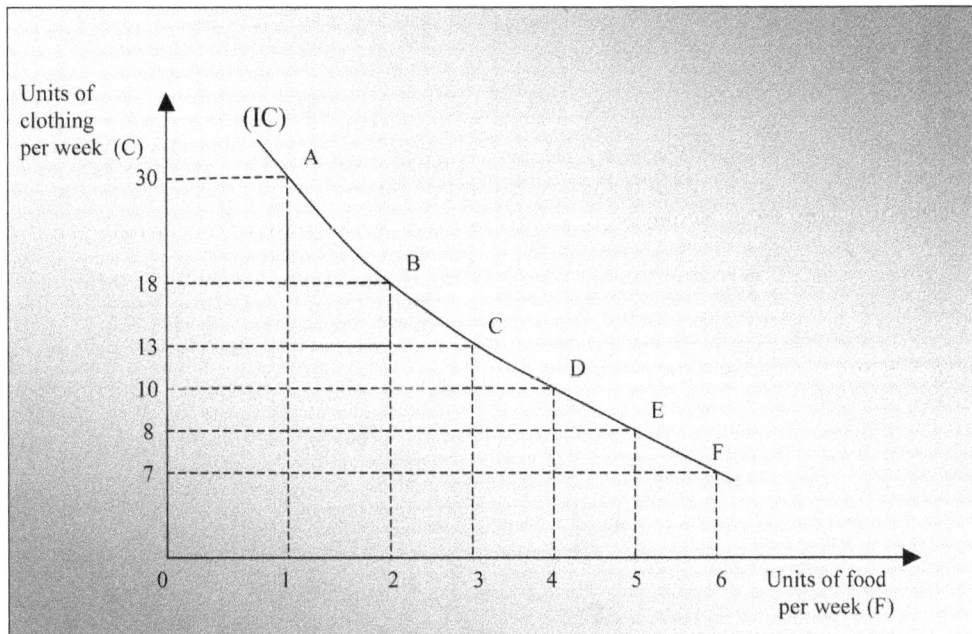

Figure 4.2: An indifference curve

2. Indifference curves slope downwards from left to right. This implies that there is an opportunity cost involved in increasing the consumption of one commodity in relation to the other. The slope is also called the marginal rate of substitution.
3. The curve is convex to the origin. The convexity of the curve reflects the nature of the opportunity cost – that is, it is decreasing over the length of the curve.
4. The further away an indifference curve is from the origin the higher the level of satisfaction.
5. There are an infinite number of indifference curves in welfare space: collectively these are called an indifference map.

Indifference Map

An indifference map represents a set of indifference curves, which illustrates the preferences of a consumer. In the indifference map shown in figure 4.3, IC_5 represents the highest level of welfare and IC_1 the lowest. Observe that

$$IC_5 > IC_4 > IC_3 > IC_2 > IC_1$$

where ">" implies preferred.

4.2 Budget Line

The budget line of a consumer shows all the combinations of clothing (C) and food (F) that a consumer can buy given the prices of clothing (P_c) and food (P_f) and the consumer's money income (Y).

Algebraically,

$$Y = P_c c + P_f f$$

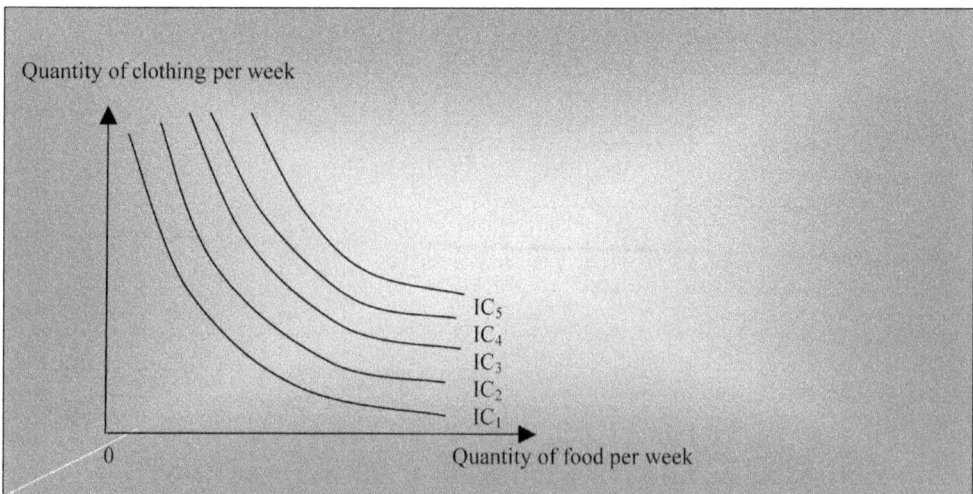

Figure 4.3: An indifference map

where c is the number of units of clothing purchased at the price P_c and f is the number of units of food purchased at the price P_f. The right-hand side of the equation reads that the sum of expenses on clothing ($P_c c$) and food ($P_f f$) is equal to the income of the household, assuming that the consumer does not save any proportion of his or her income. With this budget line, the intercept on the vertical (clothing) axis is Y/P_c and the intercept on the horizontal (food) axis is Y/P_f. The slope of the budget line, therefore, is $-P_f/P_c$. We can plot this budget line as illustrated in figure 4.4.

Changes in Income (Y)

The budget line of a consumer will shift outwards away from the origin if Y increases, ceteris paribus, and inward towards the origin if Y decreases. Thus let the original income level of the consumer be Y and let Y_1 and Y_2 be income levels lower and higher than Y, respectively. Given P_c, then

$$Y_1/P_c < Y/P_c < Y_2/P_c$$

and

$$Y_1/P_f < Y/P_f < Y_2/P_f$$

This is illustrated in figure 4.5.

Other things constant, an increase in income allows the household to buy more of both goods (Y_2/P_f and Y_2/P_c), while a decrease in income means that the household has to buy less of both goods (Y_1/P_f and Y_1/P_c).

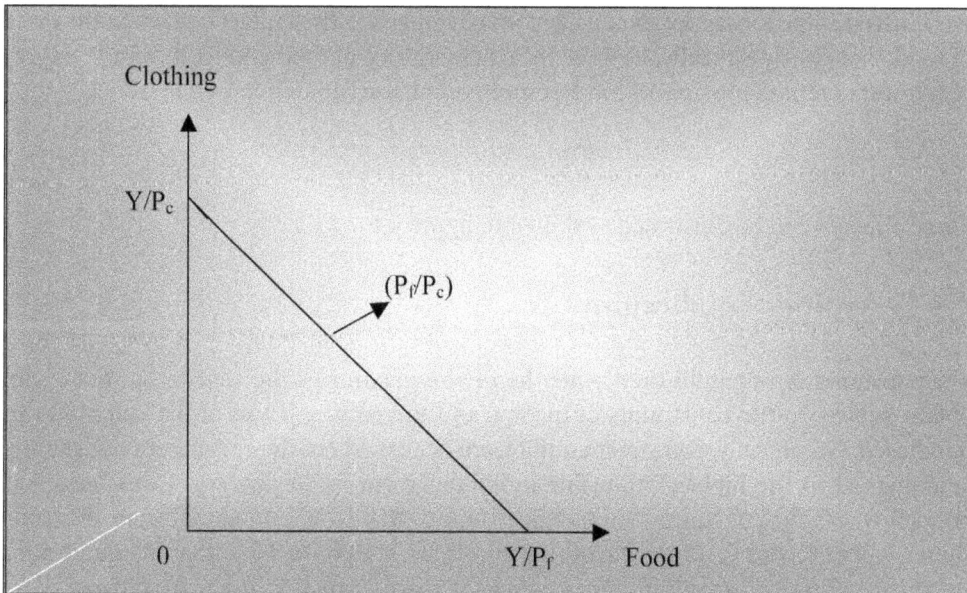

Figure 4.4: The budget line

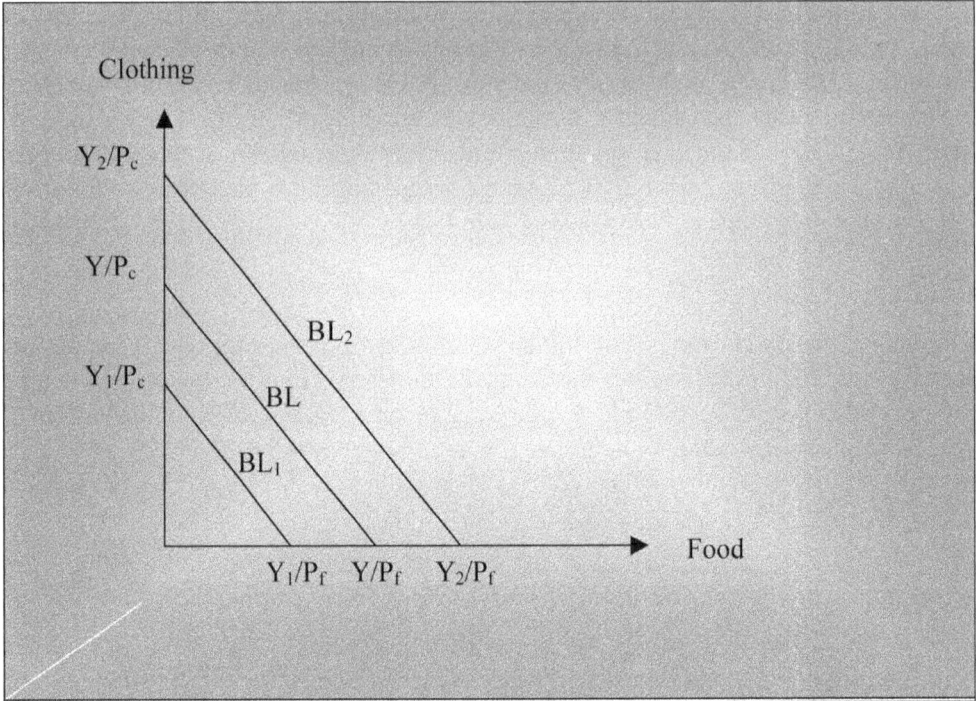

Figure 4.5: A shift in the budget line

Price Changes and the Budget Line

If the price of one of the goods entering a consumer's market bundle changes, then the slope of the consumer's budget line will change – that is, as the price of one good changes it becomes relatively cheaper or more expensive resulting in a pivot of the budget line. For illustrative purposes, let us consider what happens to the budget line when the price of food changes. Specifically, let P_f be the original price of food and let P^1_f and P^2_f represent lower and higher prices of food, respectively. Clearly,

$$Y/P^1_f > Y/P_f > Y_2/P^2_f$$

These changes can be illustrated as shown in figure 4.6.

4.3 Consumer Equilibrium

The consumer is in equilibrium when he or she maximizes the welfare he or she can obtain subject to the constraints of income and the market prices of the commodities purchased. Graphically, consumer equilibrium occurs where the consumer's budget line is tangential to the highest attainable indifference curve. In figure 4.7, this occurs at point B where the consumer's budget line is tangential to IC_2. In equilibrium this consumer will purchase C_2 units of clothing and F_2 units of food. Note that in equilibrium the marginal rate of substitution of clothes for food is equal to the price ratio of these two commodities, or to the slope of the budget line.

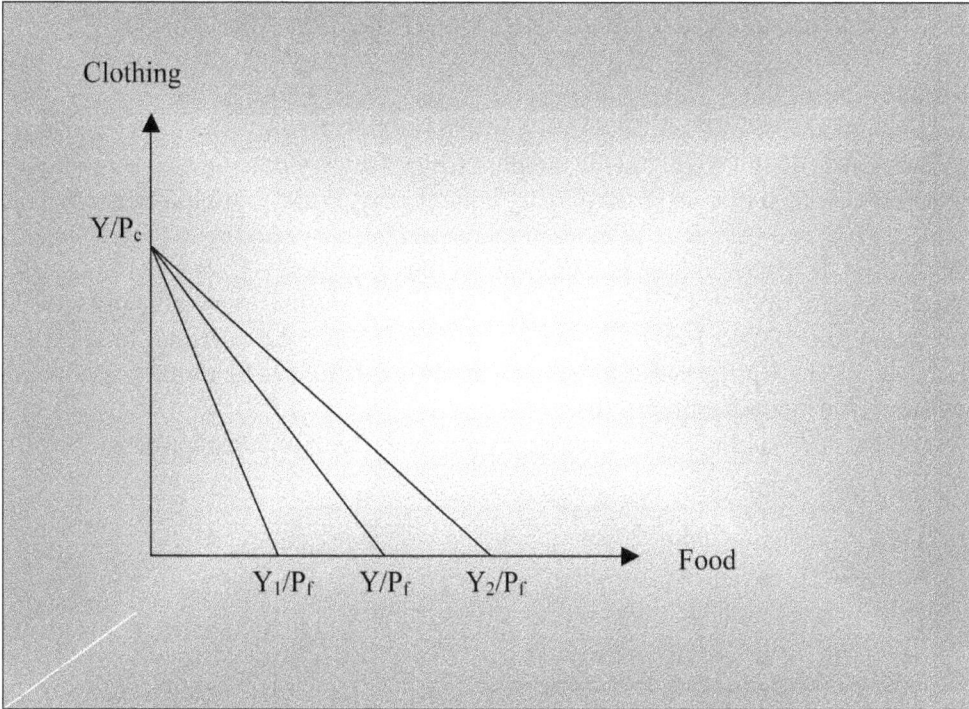

Figure 4.6: The budget line when the price of food changes

Point D is not attainable given the consumer's income and the prices of food and clothing currently existing on the market place, while points A and C are obtainable but are not welfare-maximizing points.

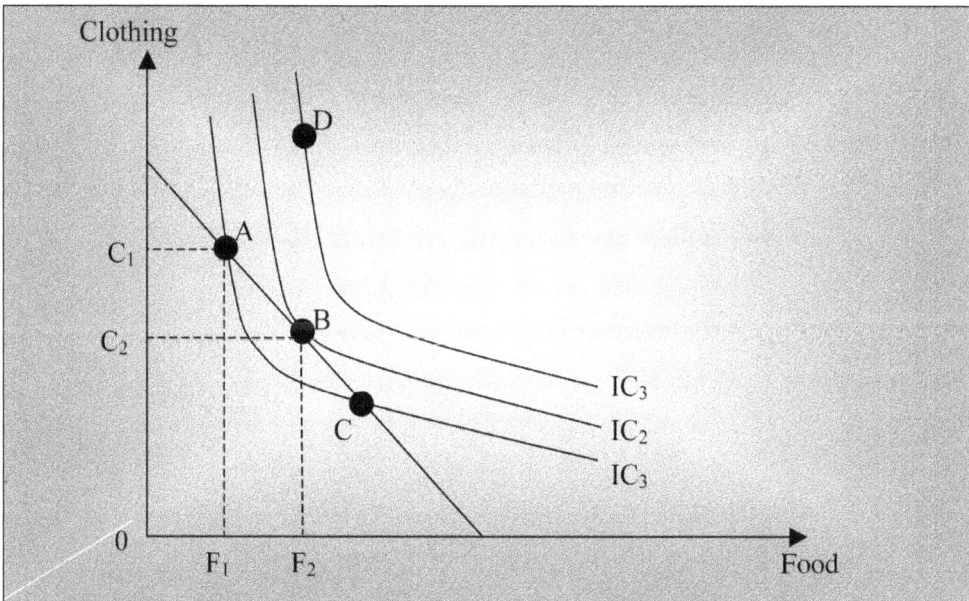

Figure 4.7: Consumer equilibrium using indifference curve analysis

4.4 The Price Consumption Curve and the Demand Curve

In figure 4.8, the upper panel shows the varying slopes of the budget line of a consumer at the alternative price levels for food P_0, P_1 and P_2 where $P_2 < P_1 < P_0$. With these alternative price levels for food, the consumer in his or her various equilibrium conditions purchases Q_0 units of food at price P_0, Q_1 units at price P_1 and Q_2 units at price P_2. The second panel plots the price of food on the vertical axis against the respective quantities of food demanded on the horizontal axis. Thus at price P_0, Q_0 units of food is purchased, while at price P_1, Q_1 units are purchased, and so on. The points a_0, a_1 and a_2 when combined in the lower panel of the diagram trace the demand curve for food by this consumer. Note that the points a_0, a_1 and a_2 in the upper part of figure 4.8 trace out the consumer's price consumption curve.

The rest of this chapter is couched on several fundamental assumptions:

1. Consumers are utility optimizers.
2. Firms are profit maximizes.
3. Workers are income maximizers.
4. Perfect factor mobility exists within national borders.
5. Transportation costs are negligible.
6. Policy-induced barriers to trade are zero.
7. The economy as a whole is perfectly competitive.

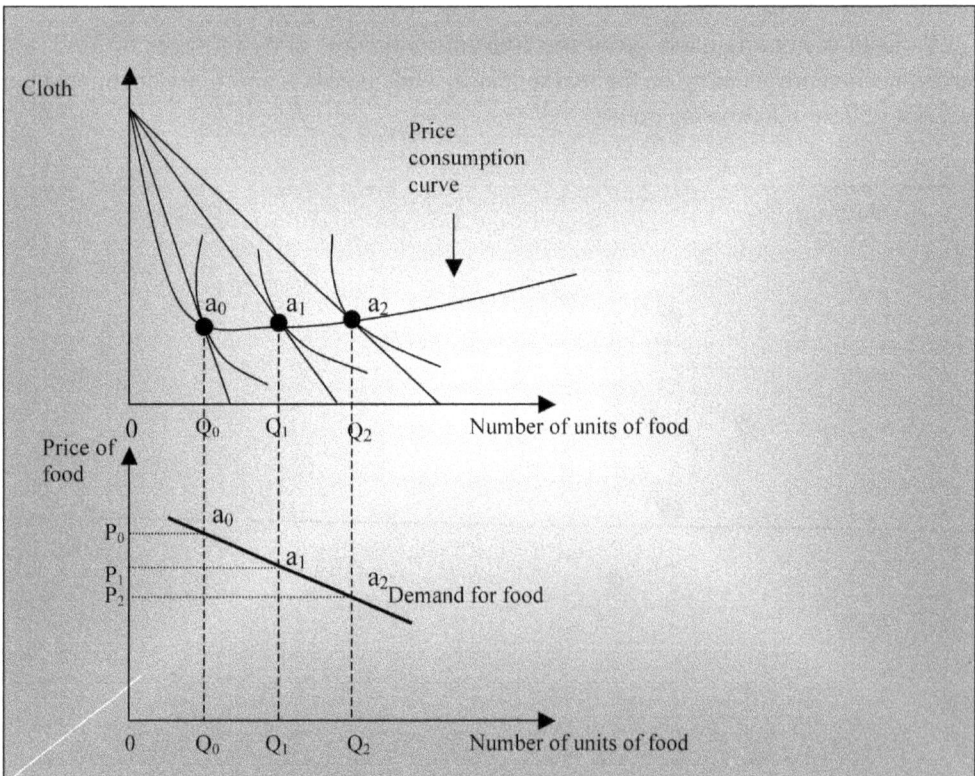

Figure 4.8: The derivation of a consumer's demand curve

4.5 Factor Intensity of a Production Process

The factor intensity of any production process refers to how much of each factor of production it employs. A capital-intensive method of production is one that uses relatively more capital than labour. In a world characterized by two factors of production, labour and capital, factor intensity refers to the ratio of capital to labour employed by a particular method of production. Let us assume that some output level X could be produced using two different methods of production. This is represented by the isoquant, IQ_0, in figure 4.9. We can geometrically illustrate factor intensities by the slope of the ray through the origin representing the particular production process, so that M_1 is the more capital-intensive process as compared to M_2, which is more labour intensive. For any isoquant, its upper part reflects more capital-intensive production and its lower part more labour-intensive production.

4.6 General Equilibrium in a Closed Economy (Autarky)

An autarkic economy is one that does not participate in international trade. In an autarkic system, general equilibrium conditions can be explored by merging the consumer preference mapping, in this case IC_0 and IC_1, with the production possibility frontier (see figure 4.10). Given a preference price relative of P_x/P_y, the autarkic system is in equilibrium producing y_0 units of good Y and x_0 units of good X. General equilibrium in this autarkic system occurs at a point such as E_0 where consumers are in equilibrium and the economy is operating on the frontier of its production possibilities. At E_0 the existing pricing structure is such that neither consumers nor firms can improve their economic position.

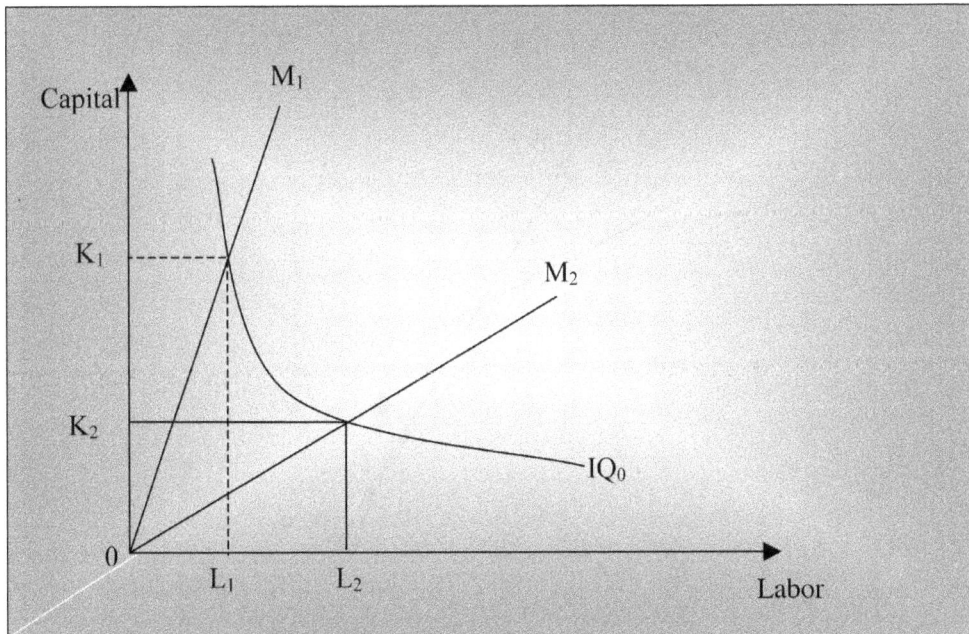

Figure 4.9: Factor intensity reversal

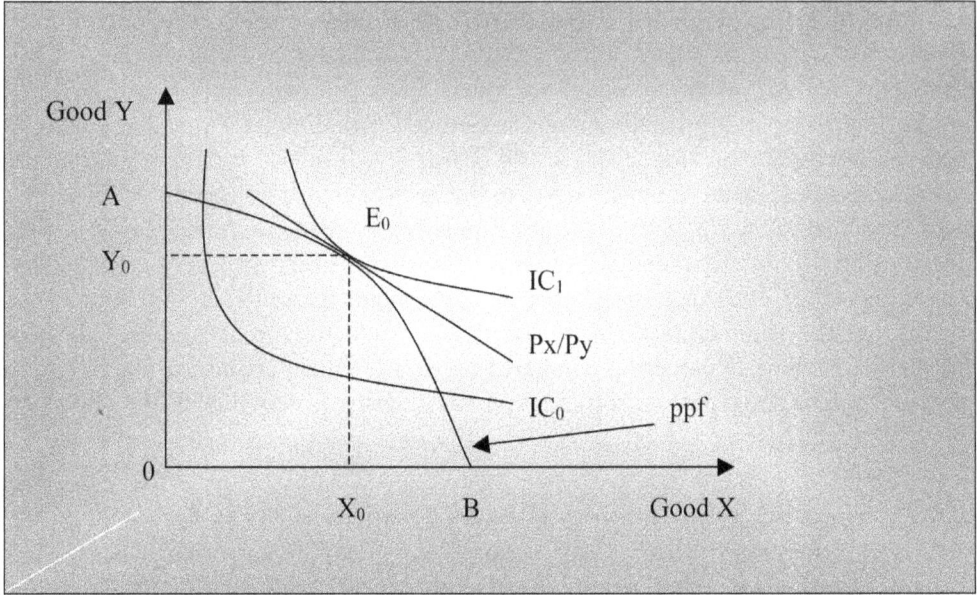

Figure 4.10: Autarky in a closed economy

4.7 Gains from Trade

To illustrate gains from trade, it is best in the first instance to investigate economic outcomes under conditions of autarky. In an autarkic situation, let the home country (HC) produce y_1 units of commodity Y and x_1 units of commodity X (this is illustrated in

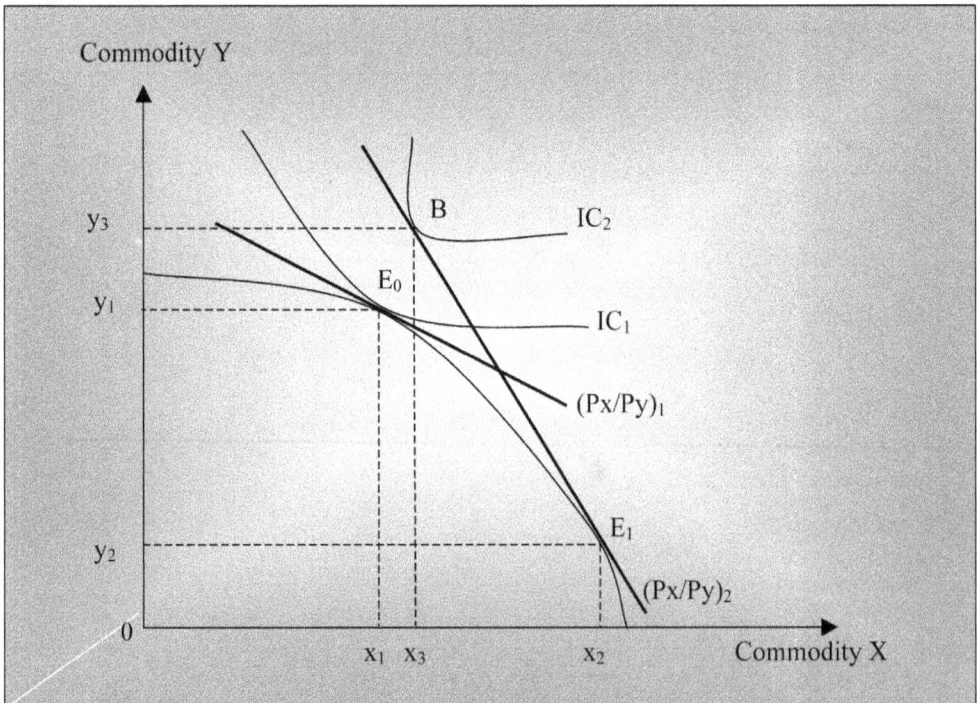

Figure 4.11: Gains from trade for the HC

figure 4.11). In this environment, consumers are forced to consume y_1 and x_1 units of Y and X, respectively. In the autarkic system the exchange of X for Y takes place at the price level $(P_x/P_y)_1$. With free trade, a formerly autarkic economy can now exchange commodities at the international terms of trade. Let us assume that this international terms of trade occurs at the price ratio $(P_x/P_y)_2$. By construct, this international terms of trade offers a higher price of commodity X, and as a consequence the HC would now produce and export more of X. With this new international terms of trade, the HC's production of X increases to x_2 units with production taking place at point E_1. Given the relatively cheaper cost of obtaining commodity Y, HC consumers can move to point B on the higher indifference curve IC_2, consuming y_3 units of Y. At point B the HC consumes x_3 units of X. Since the HC produces x_2 units of X, it means that at point B the consumer is exchanging $x_3 - x_2$ units of X for $y_3 - y_2$ units of Y. Very clearly then, with free trade the welfare of consumers in the HC increases.

4.8 Decomposing the Gains from Trade

It is in fact possible to decompose the gains from trade into two sub-components: gains from exchange and gains from specialization. In this regard, consider figure 4.12. If the economy moves from an autarkic position to free trade, consumers will move from IC_0 at a point e_0 to IC_2 and consume at a new point e_2. If the free trade price relative, $(Px/Py)_2$, is superimposed onto the autarkic equilibrium level of production and consumption, e_0, then we can note the following. The gains from exchange (or consumption gains) are the

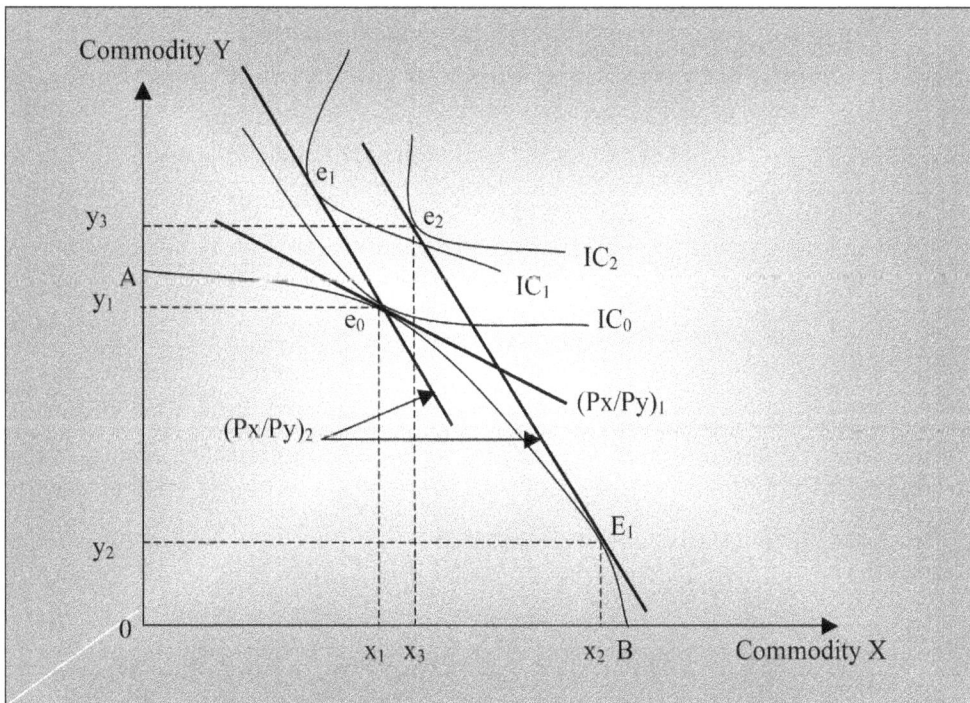

Figure 4.12: Gains from exchange and specialization

benefits from moving from IC_0 to IC_1, and the gains from specialization occur when we move from point IC_1 to IC_2.

More specifically, the consumption gain reflects the fact that the household moves away from the more expensive domestic export good X and towards the less expensive foreign good Y. The gain from consumption is measured as the difference between IC_0 and IC_1. With free trade, each country is allowed to specialize in the production of those commodities in which it has a comparative advantage. Specialization increases the home country's real income. The increase in real income shifts the budget line outwards parallel to itself and facilitates movement by the consumer onto a higher indifference curve from the point e_1 to e_2.

4.9 Specialization and Export Concentration in Trinidad and Tobago

There is a broad amount of trade overlap between trading partners. Many countries produce and export the same commodities, sometimes even to each other (this is the often discussed intra-industry trade issue and will be detailed in chapter 7). For any country, we can obtain an idea of its export "specialization" by using a specialization index (S). Such an index may be calculated as follows:

$$S = \sum_{i=0}^{9} \left(Xsitc_{ij} / X_j \right)^2 \quad i=0,\ldots\ldots,9$$

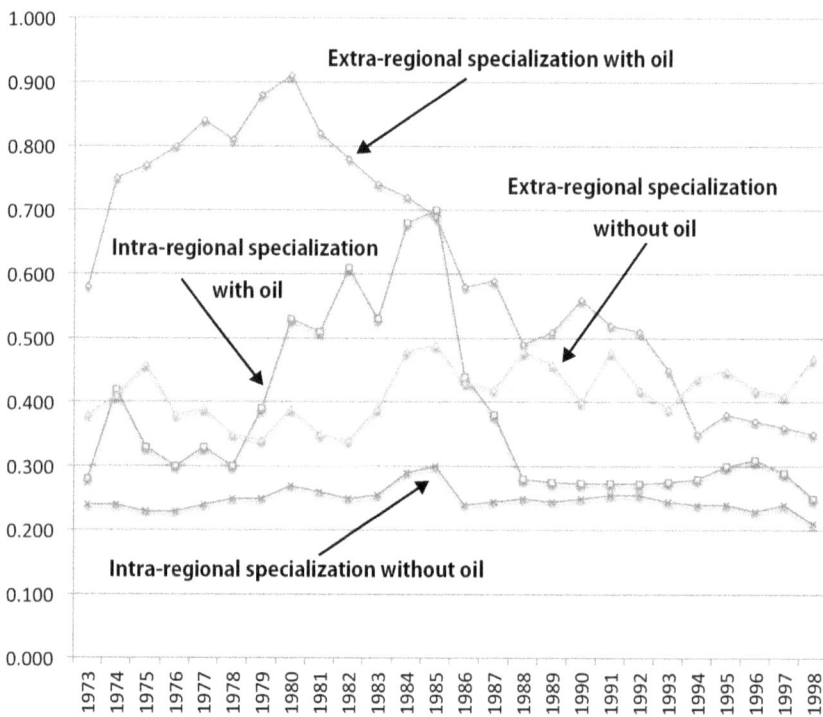

Figure 4.13: Intra- and extra-regional specialization with and without oil, 1973–1998

where

$Xsitc_{ij}$ = the exports of $sitc_i$,
i = the 0–9 single-digit exports sectors,
j = 1 or 2 (1 represents intra-CARICOM exports and 2 represents extra-regional exports).

Figure 4.13 plots four specialization indices for Trinidad and Tobago: exports with and without oil, to both the intra-regional and extra-regional markets.[1] For intra-regional exports including oil, there has been a greater degree of diversification in Trinidad and Tobago's exports to its CARICOM partners after 1985, as characterized by a fall in the index's value from 0.66 in 1985 to 0.21 by 1998. The non-oil version of this index also hints (although less markedly) to increasing diversification, as evidenced in a marginal decline in the value of this index from 0.201 in 1973 to 0.173 in 1998.

As concerns the extra-regional markets, when oil is included, the relevant specialization index escalates between 1973 and 1980 from 0.585 to 0.87. (During this period the export of oil, approximated here as the exports of sitc 3, increased from $189.2 million to $2,293.5 million: almost twelvefold.) With the decline in the exports of oil after 1980, the concentration of Trinidad and Tobago exports in this area dampened and together with increasing competitiveness of the non-oil areas (occasioned by devaluations in 1985 and 1988 and the dismantling of barriers to free trade in the late 1980s) led to a falloff in the value of this index to 0.31 in 1994, improving marginally thereafter to 0.33 in 1998.[2] When oil is excluded, the extra-regional specialization index shows clear signs of increasing specialization. In particular, this version of the specialization index increased from 0.33 in 1973 to 0.42 by 1998, the increase appearing even more pronounced when it is considered that the index stood at 0.30 in 1979.

In general, these specialization indices portray that in the context of Trinidad and Tobago there are signs that the export basket inclusive of oil has broadened to both intra- and extra-regional markets. Perhaps more significant though, these specialization indices reflect that the extent of export commodity diversification is significantly greater within the protected regional market.

4.10 Foreign Countries and Gains from Trade

With free trade, the foreign country (FC) also gains. In figure 4.14, the gains from trade in the FC are displayed. In the FC, the autarkic terms of trade is $(Px/Py)_3$ and the corresponding HC terms of trade is $(Px/Py)_1$. Let us assume that the international terms of trade is $(Px/Py)_2$. Observe that at this international price ratio, the FC benefits from a higher price for its export good, good Y. Consequently, the FC's production of Y expands from y_4 to y_5 and production of X contracts from x_4 to x_5. The new price relative allows the FC to move to a higher indifference curve (from IC^{FC}_0 to IC^{FC}_1) and consumer equilibrium to move from e_1 to e_2.

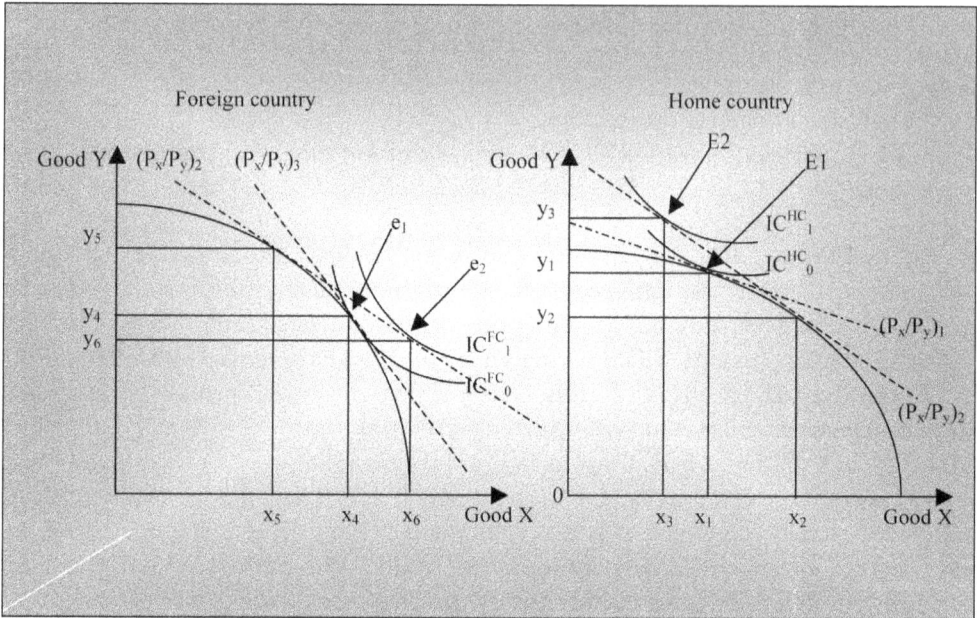

Figure 4.14: Gains from trade in the foreign country

4.11 Conclusion

This chapter introduced and discussed some of the basic neoclassical tools used in international trade theory. The chapter also introduced and discussed gains from trade. These foundational tools are utilized throughout the rest of this book to illustrate the various terms of trade.

Summary of Key Points

- Opportunity cost is measured terms of what is given up, or the sacrifice of one option for another.
- The production possibility frontier (PPF) illustrates the combination of goods an economy (or a firm) can produce if it utilizes all its available factors of production.
- An indifference curve is the locus of all the possible combinations of two or more goods that yield the same level of satisfaction to a consumer.
- The budget line of a consumer shows all the combinations of two commodities that can be purchased given the price of each commodity and the consumer's income level.
- Graphically, consumer equilibrium occurs where the consumer's budget line is tangential to the highest attainable indifference curve.
- Gains from trade can be decomposed into consumption gains (gains from exchange), which reflect the fact that the household moves away from the more expensive domestic export good X and towards the less expensive foreign good Y, and gains from specialization.
- Specialization increases the home country's real income. The increase in real income shifts the budget line outwards parallel to itself and facilitates movement by the consumer onto a higher indifference curve.

Multiple Choice

1. Under conditions of autarky, the domestic price relative of a country can be determined by which of the following tools?

   a) the production possibility curve
   b) the indifference curve
   c) the indifference map
   d) the production possibility curve and the indifference curve

2. Why is a discussion of indifference curves important for an understanding of trade theory?

   a) to show welfare levels
   b) to show resource prices
   c) to indicate tastes and prices
   d) to indicate productivity levels

3. With trade, the economic welfare of a trading economy can be maximized because

   a) trade allows the country to consume at its highest possible indifference curve
   b) the marginal rate of substitution is lowest
   c) more of both goods are produced
   d) the country can tax imports

4. Equilibrium in autarkic conditions occurs under which of the following conditions:

   a) at a point above the PPF
   b) at a point that is tangential to the PPF
   c) at a point that intersects the PPF
   d) at a point that is lower than the PPF

5. Which of the following statements is true?

   a) A consumer is in equilibrium when his or her welfare is maximized under the constraints of his or her own income and market prices.
   b) The economy is in equilibrium where the terms of trade is tangential to the highest possible indifference curve.
   c) none of the above
   d) a and b only

Short Essays

1. Explain the concept of consumer equilibrium using indifference curve analysis.
2. Show the income and substitution effects of a price fall for a normal and inferior good.

Key Trade Terms

- Opportunity cost
- Production possibility frontier
- Indifference curves
- Marginal rate of substitution
- Indifference map
- Budget line
- Consumer equilibrium
- Price consumption curve
- Isoquant
- Autarky
- Gains from trade
- Gains from exchange
- Gains from specialization
- Export concentration
- Specialization index
- Intra-regional
- Extra-regional

5.

Offer Curves

Learning Objectives

a. Define offer curve (OC).
b. Derive the offer curves for the home country (HC) and foreign country (FC).
c. Identify factors influencing a shift of the OC.
d. Understand how a shift of the OC affects the HC's terms of trade.

5.0 Introduction

In many regards, the best way to analyse international trade is to remain focused on supply and demand. One of the simplest ways to present this type of analysis is via the use of offer curves. Offer curves show the quantity of a product that can be exported or offered for every quantity of another type of product or import. This chapter reviews the theoretical literature concerning offer curves and their various uses in international trade.

Figure 5.1 displays production and consumption conditions in the HC with two alternative terms of trade: tot_0 and tot_1. With the first international price relative (tot_0), the

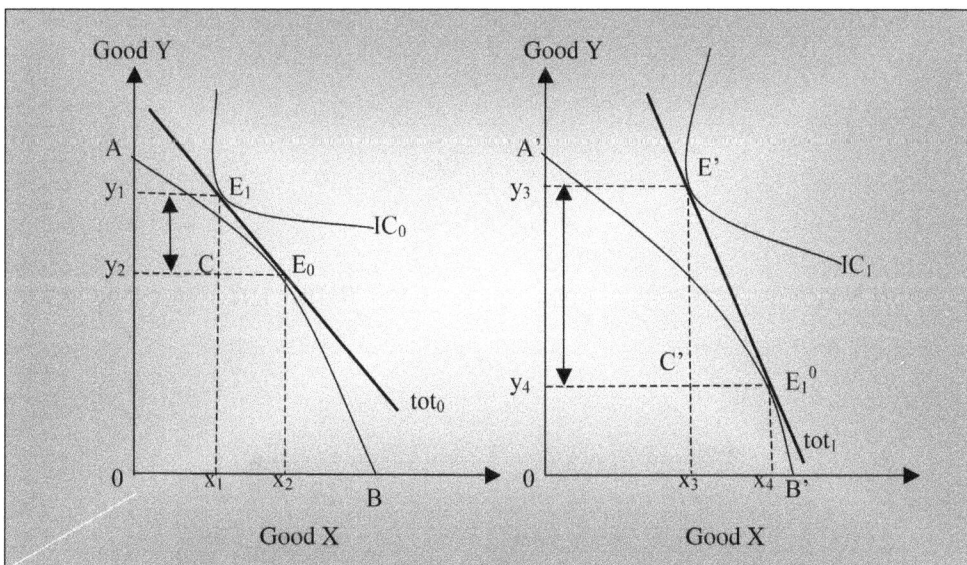

Figure 5.1: Trade triangles at two possible terms of trade

HC imports $y_1 - y_2$ units (b_0 in figure 5.2) of Y and exports $x_2 - x_1$ (a_0 in figure 5.2) units of X. The triangle CE_1E_0 traces out the amount of the good exported (CE_0), the amount imported (CE_1) and the terms at which they are exchanged E_0E_1.

Suppose that the terms of trade were in fact indicated by tot_1. (Note that tot_1 is steeper than tot_0 and hence indicates that the relative price of good X is now higher.) In such a scenario, the HC would produce and export more X, $x_4 - x_3$ (a_1 in figure 5.2), import more Y, $y_3 - y_4$ (b_1), and move onto a higher indifference curve (IC_1). The trade triangle $C`E`E_1^0$ is larger than Ce_1e_0, indicating that, at alternative terms of trade, trading partners will offer alternative amounts of X for Y.

Alternative Relative Prices (Terms of Trade) and Export-Import Combinations on the HC Offer Curve

To explore the idea of offer curves more closely, we can proceed by making reference to the figure 5.2. At a terms of trade such as tot_0, the home country offered a_0 units of commodity X to the foreign market and purchased b_0 units of Y from its trade partners. Let us label the point on tot_0 at which a_0 and b_0 are exported and imported, respectively, as e_0. The corresponding points for tot_1, tot_2 and tot_3 are e_1, e_2 and e_3, so that we can form the HC offer curve of exports for imports by tracing out the curve associated with these e_i points (i = 0, 1, 2, 3). Note that the offer curve starts from the origin, indicating that in autarky there is no trade.[1] A hypothetical offer curve is shown in figure 5.3. Note, for example, the HC is willing to offer 120 units of crude oil to obtain 190 units of bauxite.

The shape of the offer curve of a country can be discussed in terms of the microeconomic concept of elasticity, in a number of varied ways. In this section, we shall focus on one particular definition, in which we identify the offer curve of the country as dealing with the elasticity of demand for imports along the offer curve.

The elasticity of demand for imports varies along the length of the offer curve. The

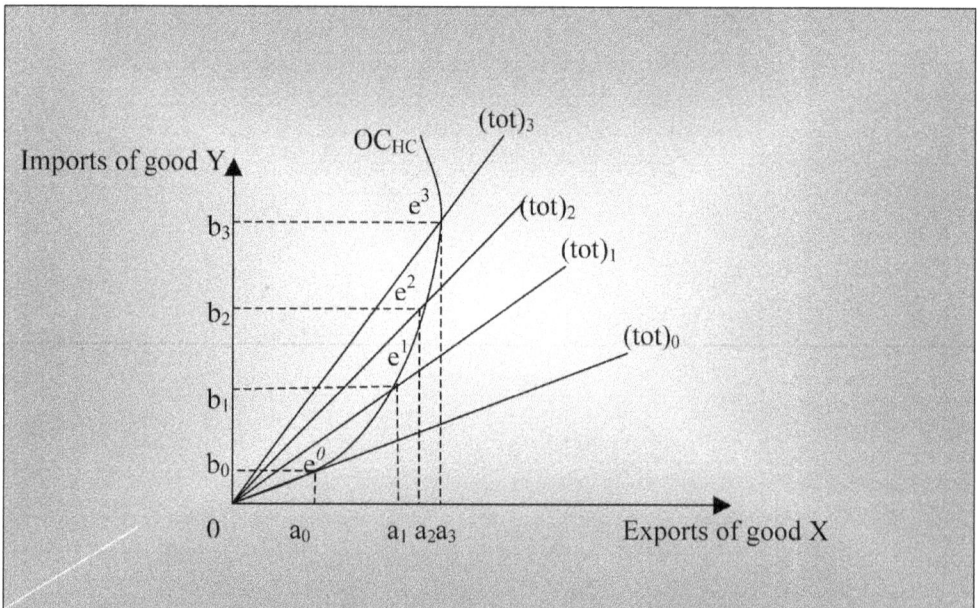

Figure 5.2: Deriving the offer curve for the HC

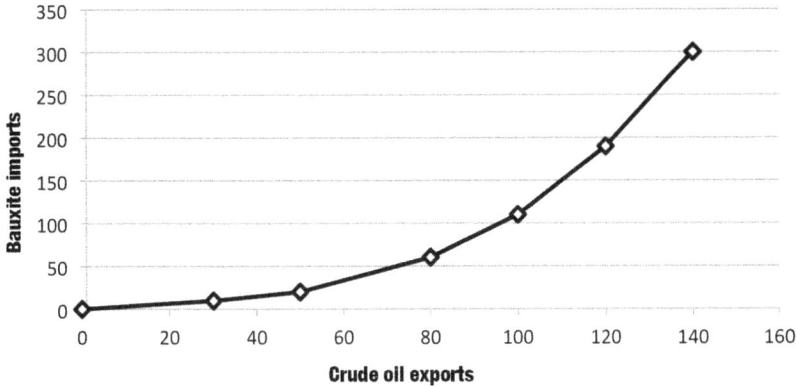

Figure 5.3: Offer curve of the HC

elasticity of imports at any point is given by the slope of the curve at that point. More specifically, the import elasticity of demand can be given by the ratio $^{OB}/_{OA}$. In the first of the three panels in figure 5.4, the import elasticity of demand is elastic, as OB > OA. In the second case, OB < OA, which implies that at point C the offer curve is inelastic, whereas in the third case, OB = OA, so the offer curve at that point exhibits unit elasticity.

In order to further explore the elasticity characteristics of offer curves we can make reference to figure 5.5. Let us assume that the price of the HC's substantive export good increases so that its terms of trade improves from tot_1 to tot_2. This would mean that the trade triangle of the HC expands in size as imports expand from y_1 to y_2 and exports increase from x_1 to x_2. Note that in the elastic segment of the offer curve, as the price of X increases, the amount of imports increases more than proportional. In the inelastic segment of the offer curve, if the price of a substantive export commodity rises so that the terms of trade moves from tot_4 to tot_5 in figure 5.5, then the exports of the HC would fall, although it would still import more (imports increase by $y_5 - y_4$). In the unit elasticity range of the offer curve, a change in the relative price of exports will lead to an

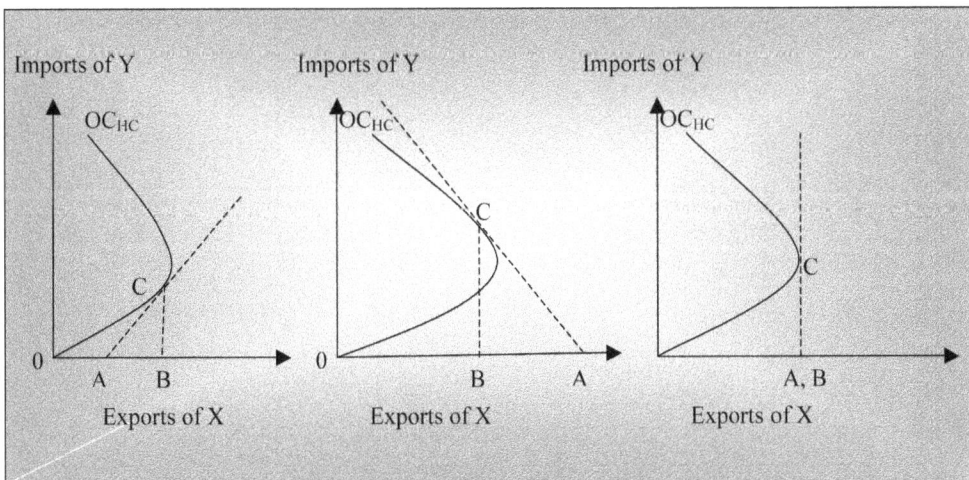

Figure 5.4: The elasticity of demand for imports along an offer curve

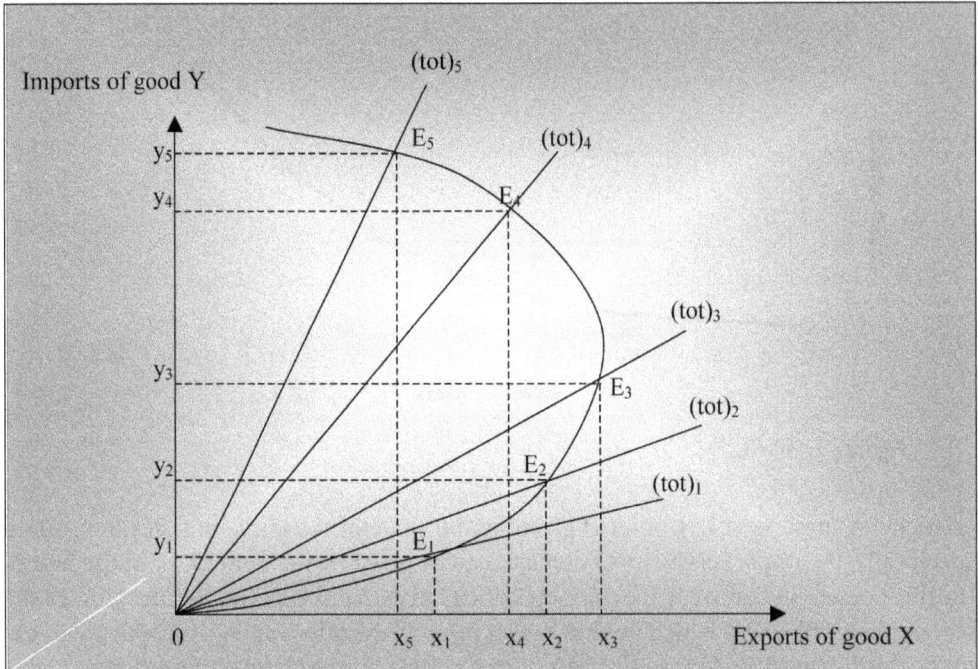

Figure 5.5: Elasticity ranges and export quantities given up to acquire imports

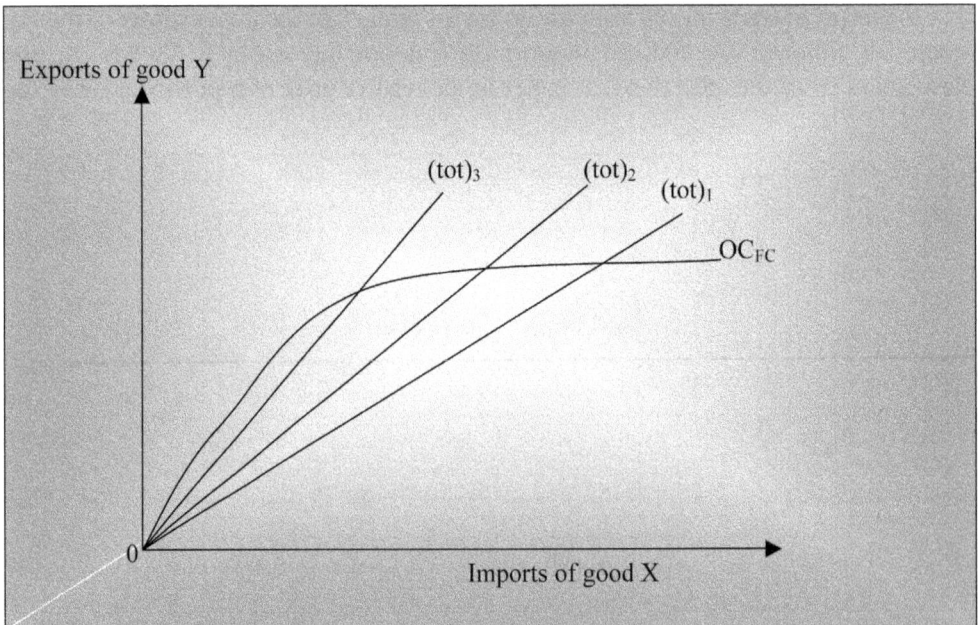

Figure 5.6: The FC's offer curve

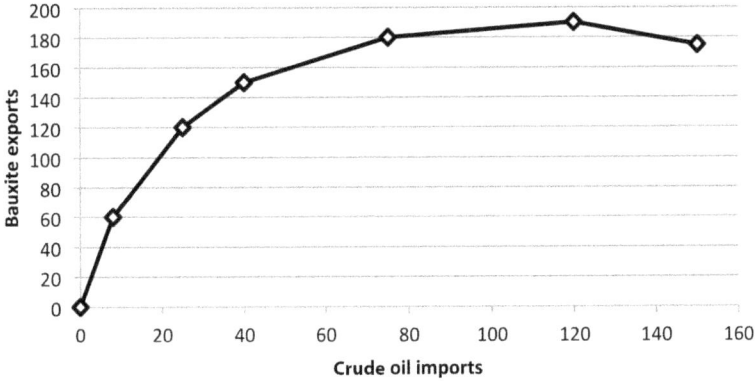

Figure 5.7: Offer curve of the FC

equi-proportional change in the amount of imports. Figure 5.7 uses hypothetical data to provide a simple illustrative outline of the offer curve of the FC.

5.1 Offer Curves and the Equilibrium Terms of Trade

For completeness, figure 5.6 shows the offer curve of the FC. Note the changes in the labelling of the various axes. Figure 5.6 shows how the FC offers its export of good Y on the international market at various terms of trade. As the relative price of Y increases, the FC (which we are assuming has a comparative advantage in the production of good Y) is willing to exchange more of Y on the market for X.

It is possible to use offer curve analysis to arrive at the international terms of trade. In figure 5.8 the international terms of trade will settle where the two offer curves intersect.

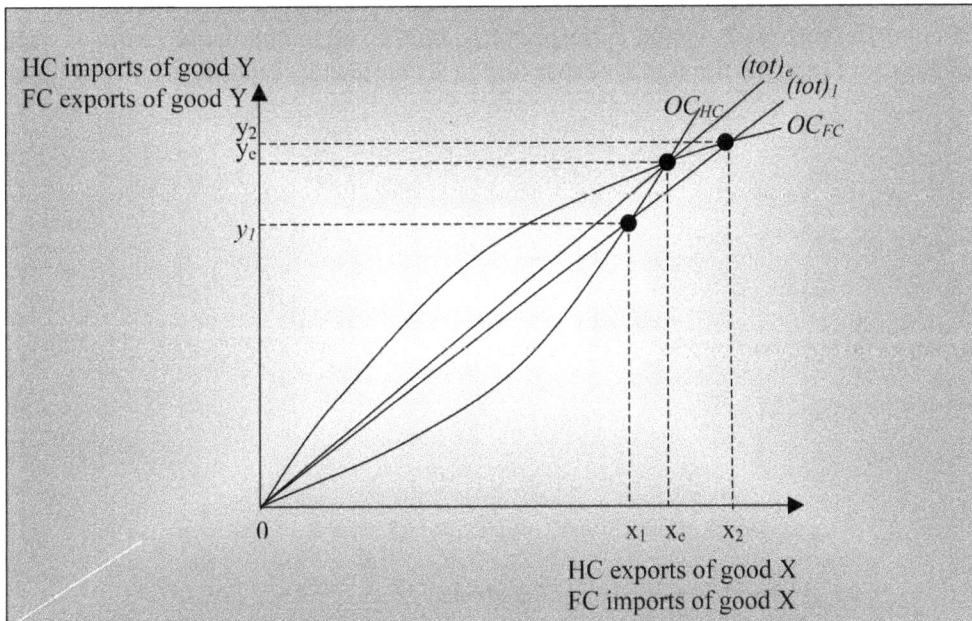

Figure 5.8: Offer curves and the terms of trade

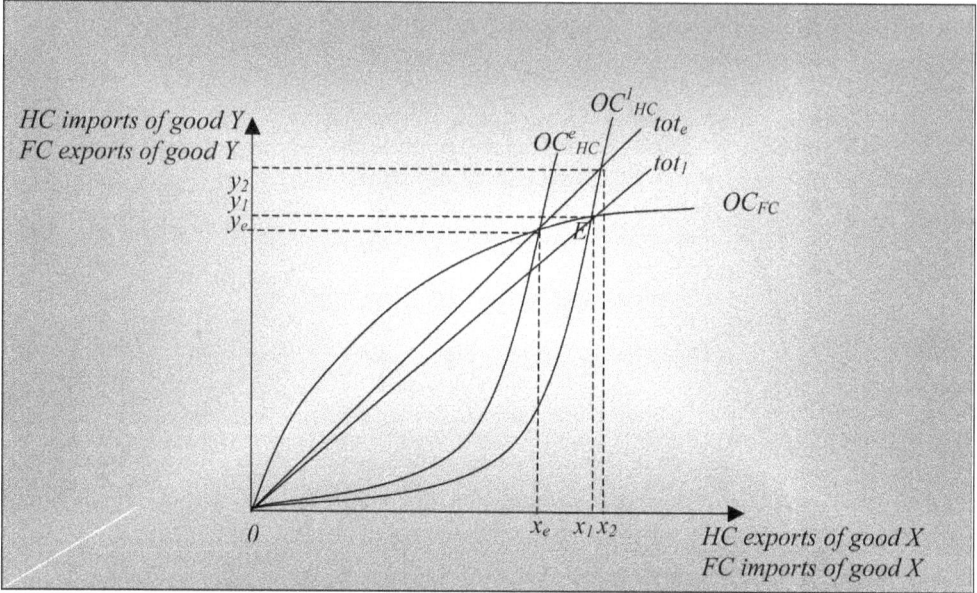

Figure 5.9: Offer curves for HC and FC

Thus with offer curves of OC_{HC} and OC_{FC} for the HC and FC, respectively, the international terms of trade would settle at $(tot)_e$ with the HC exporting x_e units of good X and importing y_e units of good Y. At this same terms of trade, the FC would export y_e units of good Y and import x_e units of good X. Other terms of trade such as $(tot)_1$, for example, would not result in an equilibrium pattern of trade between the HC and FC, for at such a terms of trade, the FC would be prepared to purchase x_2 units of X while the HC would only be prepared to engage x_1 units of its production of X for exports.

Following from the previous diagram, whereas the HC and FC's offer curves intersect at import/export levels y_e and x_e, respectively, on tot_e, at an alternative terms of trade such as tot_1, the HC, through an expansion of its productive capacity, exports x_1 units

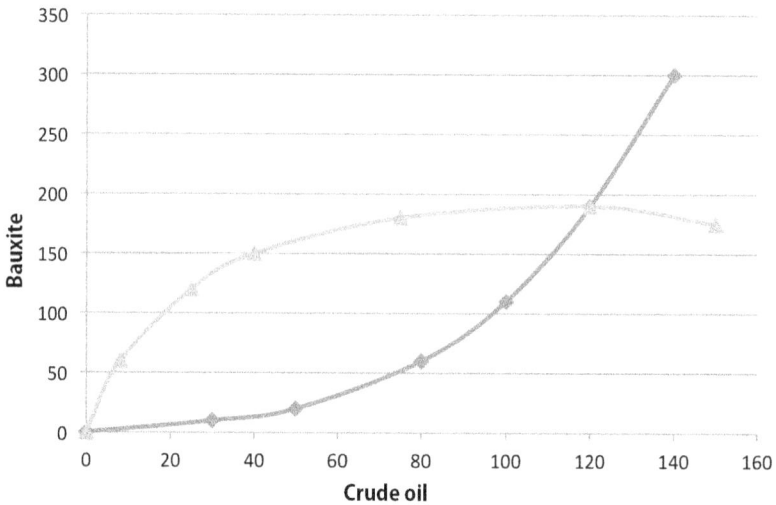

Figure 5.10: Hypothetical offer curves for HC and FC

of good X instead of the previous x_e units. Hence the FC is now able to import a greater quantity of good X from the HC per unit of good Y exported. Point E on the diagram (figure 5.9) shows the equilibrium import/export conditions between the HC and the FC, where x_1 units of good X is exported by the HC (and imported by the FC) while y_1 units of good Y is imported into the HC (and exported from the FC). In figure 5.10, 120 barrels of crude oil exchange for 190 tonnes of bauxite so that the exchange rate is 1 barrel of crude oil = 190/120 tonnes of bauxite.

5.2 Factors Influencing a Shift of the Offer Curve

There are a number of factors (discussed from the HC's perspective) that can cause a country's offer curve to shift:

- If the HC experiences a change in its tastes in favour of the imported good, then at every terms of trade it will give up more exports to obtain more of the imported good.
- An increase in the income of residents of the HC will also shift its offer curve rightwards, as it would imply an increase in the demand for imports, for which a greater amount of exports have to be given up.
- In a similar vein of reasoning, a resource boom or an expansion in production in the domestic economy can also encourage a rightward shift of the HC's offer curve.

Changes in offer curves affect trade volumes; they affect the area of any trade triangle. Suppose, for example, the HC experiences an increase in its willingness to trade. This means that at the existing terms of trade, the country is willing to export and/or import more, such that the net impact is an increase in trade. If, in turn, the country experienced a decreased willingness to trade, then we move to OC^1_{HC} (see figure 5.11).

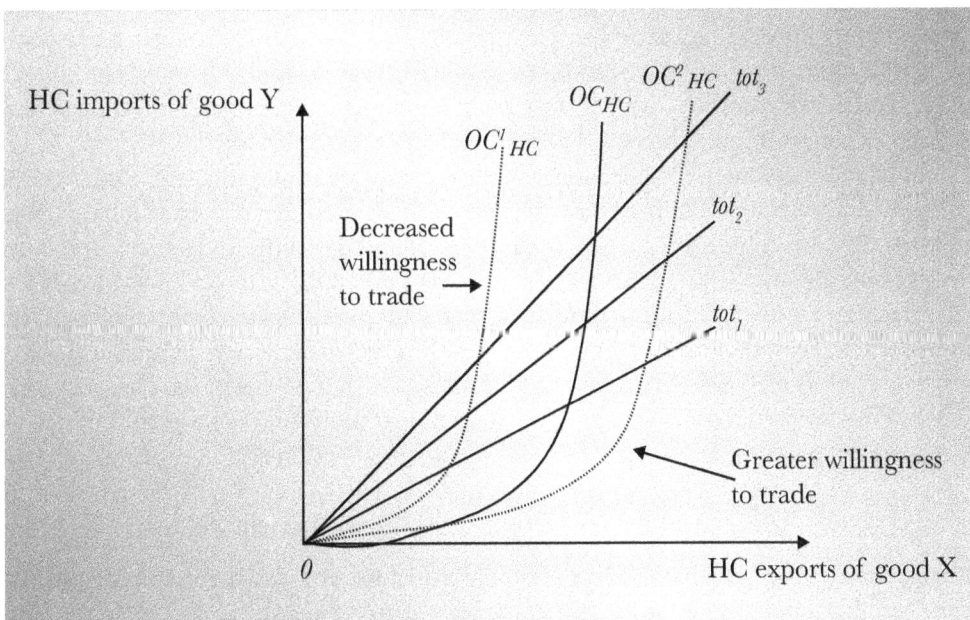

Figure 5.11: Shifts in the HC's offer curve

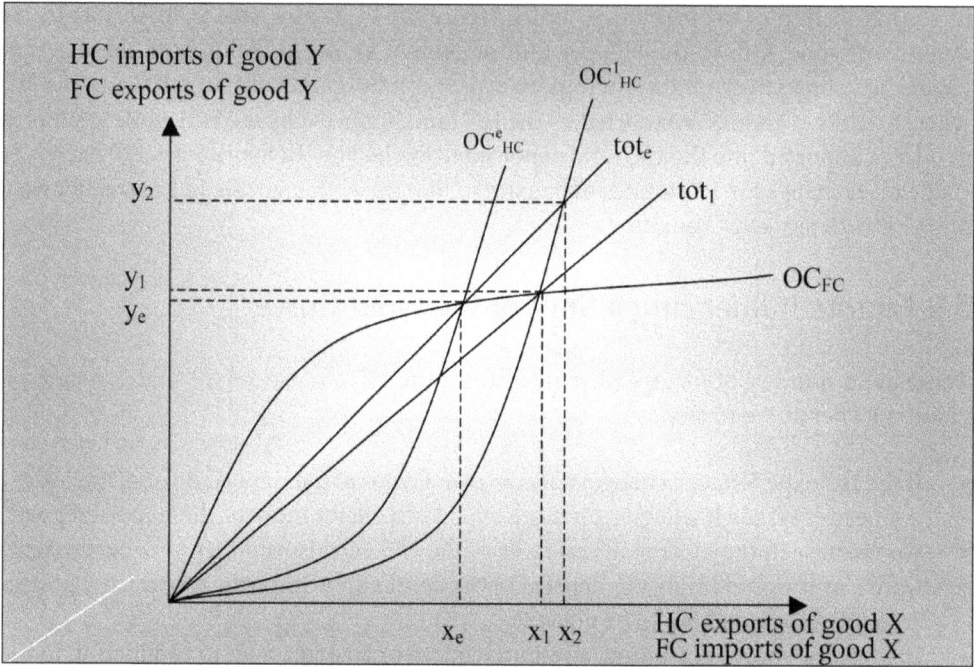

Figure 5.12: The effect of a shift of the OC on the HC's terms of trade

If the HC is a small economy, then it will not be able to impact on the international terms of trade. In such a situation the OC_{FC} and the terms of trade facing the HC would both coincide on the same straight line. As figure 5.11 also clearly reflects, fluctuations in the OC_{HC} have no influence on the international terms of trade. The size of a country, however, is an empirical question. For example, if Suriname or Montserrat were to increase their demand for steel, it is hardly likely that the world price of steel would be affected; if so, it would be affected only marginally. Regardless, some countries, although small in terms of gross domestic product or land area, may be significant world producers of particular commodities – for example, urea, ammonia and methanol in Trinidad and Tobago or coffee in Colombia.

Let us now explore the implications for the terms of trade of a shift in the offer curve of the HC. For example, let us assume that the HC has a sudden and favourable change towards the consumption of the imported good Y. This shifts the HC's offer curve outwards from OC^e_{HC} to OC^1_{HC}. With the initial offer curve OC^e_{HC}, the HC was in equilibrium trading x_e units of X for y_e units of Y at the international terms of trade, tot_e. The new offer curve results in the formation of a new terms of trade, tot_1, at which the HC imports y_1 units of Y in exchange for x_1 units of X, which it now exports. Thus a change in the offer curve of the HC changes the international terms of trade and the volume of goods entering trade.[2]

The Shape of Offer Curves and Price Stability in the Market

It is not always the case that markets clear. Figure 5.13 shows a situation of multiple free trade equilibrium. Point A in figure 5.13 shows the world demand and supply for food in balance. If the price of food, however, were to rise above A, say to P_1, the quantity

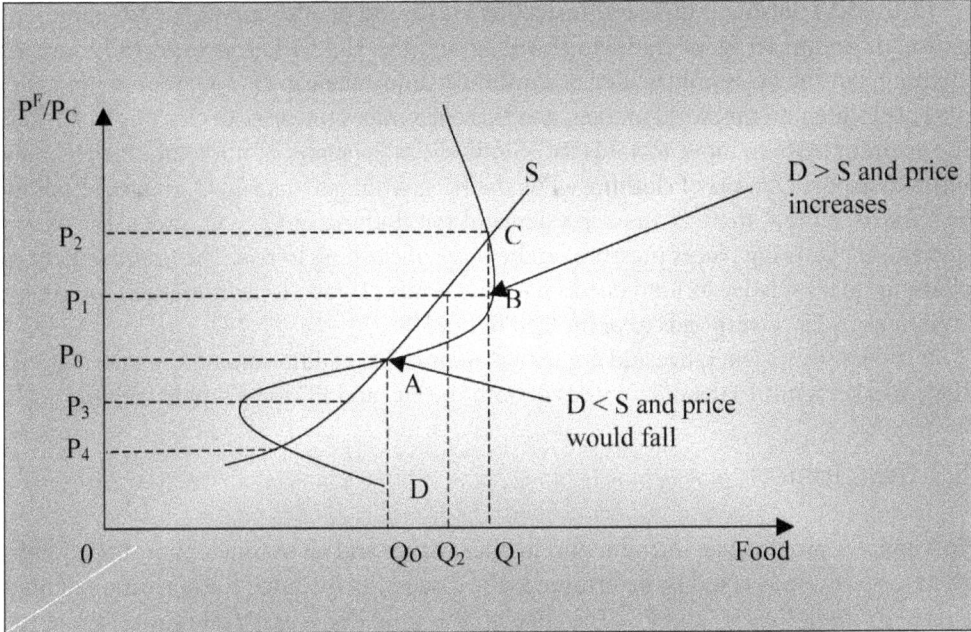

Figure 5.13: Multiple equilibrium using demand and supply

demanded of this commodity in the international market place would rise from Q_0 to Q_1 but the quantity supplied would only be Q_2. $Q_1 - Q_2$ represents excess demand for this commodity in the international market place. Excess demand in the market place would result in the price level being competed upwards until an equilibrium price such as P_2 is attained.

In a similar vein of reasoning, if the world price of food were to fall below P_0, say to P_3, then this would lead to an excess world supply of food, and this in turn would motivate world food prices downwards, to P_4.

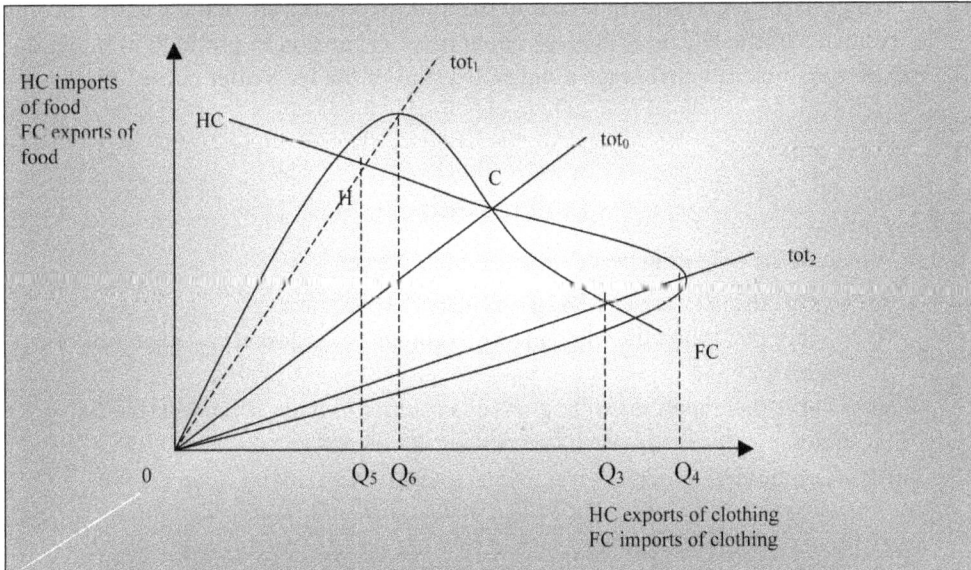

Figure 5.14: Multiple equilibrium using offer curves

Figure 5.14 illustrates this same instability via the use of offer curves. Let tot_2 represent a disequilibrium terms of trade. In this diagram, the HC wishes to export Q_4 units of clothing, but the FC is only willing to import Q_3 units. The gap $Q_4 - Q_3$ represents a surplus of clothing on the world market, and this encourages the price of clothing to fall and the terms of trade to move towards tot_0. Similarly, at the terms of trade tot_1, the HC only offers to export Q_5 units of clothing while the FC is willing to take up Q_6 units of clothing as imports, so that there is an excess demand for clothing of $Q_6 - Q_5$ units. The excess demand for clothing places pressure on the price of clothing to rise. The improvement in clothing prices relative to food encourages the terms of trade to drift towards tot_0. Point A in figure 5.13 corresponds to point C in figure 5.14.

It is possible to generalize and argue that an unstable equilibrium on the international trade market requires the offer curves of both the HC and FC to be highly inelastic.

5.3 Conclusion

This chapter provided an introduction to offer curves and an outline of how the equilibrium terms of trade could be determined. The discussion included the derivation of offer curves for both the HC and FC. The chapter also provided a practical illustration of the determination of the terms of trade.

Summary of Key Points

- Offer curves show the quantity of a product that can be exported or offered for every quantity of another type of product or import.
- The elasticity of demand for imports varies along the length of the offer curve. The elasticity of imports at any point is given by the slope of the curve at that point.
- The international terms of trade will settle where the two offer curves (OC^{HC} and OC^{FC}) intersect.
- A change in the HC's tastes in favour of the imported good, an increase in the income of residents of the HC or a resource boom or an expansion in production in the domestic economy can encourage a rightward shift of the HC's offer curve.

Multiple Choice

1. Which of the following best defines an offer curve?
   a) a curve that shows an exchange of exports for imports
   b) a curve that shows the willingness of a country to export at varying terms of trade
   c) a curve that shows the willingness of a country to trade at varying terms of trade
   d) all of the above

2. For a given improvement in the terms of trade, a more elastic offer curve results in which of the following:

   a) a fall in the amount of trade
   b) an increase in the amount of trade
   c) an improvement in a country's terms of trade
   d) a decline in a country's terms of trade

3. Assuming a two nation world, under which conditions can offer curves be used to determine the international terms of trade?

   a) The international terms of trade settles where the offer curves for both countries intersects.
   b) The international terms of trade can only be determined along the elastic portion of the curve.
   c) The international terms of trade cannot be determined using offer curves.
   d) none of the above

4. All of the following factors cause shifts of the offer curves except

   a) the home country experiencing a change it its preferences is biased towards imported goods
   b) a resource boom and expansion in the production levels in the economy
   c) an appreciation of the exchange rate
   d) an increase in the income of residents of the home country

5. Shifts of offer curves affect

   a) the amount of trade a country engages
   b) the exchange rate
   c) the price of imports relative to exports
   d) none of the above

Short Essay

1. Explain the concept of an offer curve. Show clearly how the elasticity of demand for imports varies along any offer curve.
2. Evaluate the factors that cause shifts of offer curves.
3. What are trade triangles? Show how the size of the triangle changes when the international terms of trade changes.

Key Trade Terms

- Offer curve
- Trade triangle
- Equilibrium terms of trade
- Price stability
- Multiple equilibrium

6.

A Basis for Trade

The Factor Proportion Hypothesis

Learning Objectives

a. Define the Heckscher-Ohlin (H/O) theorem and list its key assumptions.
b. Briefly describe the general equilibrium framework of the Heckscher-Ohlin theorem.
c. Understand what the factor price equalization theorem (FPET) postulates.
d. Define the Stolper–Samuelson (SS) theorem and list its main assumptions.
e. Algebraically derive the SS theorem.
f. Explain the Leontief Paradox.

6.0 Introduction

In chapter 3, we discussed how trade can be engaged at a terms of trade lodged between the relative prices of the home country (HC) and the foreign country (FC). These differing relative prices in each country reflect different opportunity costs, with each country having a comparative advantage in the production of one or more commodities. With free trade, each country would specialize in the production of those commodities in which it has a comparative advantage (the home country would produce and export those commodities in which its per unit cost is lowest and import those commodities in which it has a comparative disadvantage).[1]

In this chapter, the factor proportion hypothesis (also called the Heckscher-Ohlin theorem) is discussed and some of its shortcomings are outlined. The main purpose of the Heckscher-Ohlin theorem is to provide an explanation as to why relative prices differ before free trade. The Heckscher-Ohlin theorem commences by explaining the differences in the shape of the production possibility frontiers of the respective countries. The idea underlying the Heckscher-Ohlin theorem is that differing countries with differing factor endowments have differently shaped production possibility frontiers, and further, a country with an abundance of a particular factor of production will tend to have a relatively lower price for that factor of production. In contrast, a scarce factor of production will command a higher factor remuneration.

6.1 The Heckscher-Ohlin Theorem:
Two Countries, Two Factors, Two Commodities

The currently prevailing theory regarding what determines the pattern of trade that a nation engages in originated in Sweden, with the work of two noted Swedish economists, Eli Heckscher and Bertil Ohlin, in 1919. Bertil Ohlin, the student of Eli Heckscher, published a clear overall statement in the 1930s (see Ohlin 1933; Heckscher 1949). Ohlin's work was later supplemented by the work of Paul Anthony Samuelson,[2] who derived the various mathematical conditions under which the H/O theorem held.[3]

To explain the Heckscher-Ohlin theorem we make the assumption of two countries (HC and FC), two commodities (X and Y) and two factors of production (K and L). This is the 2 × 2 × 2 framework. Although simple, results from this analytical starting point are consistent with more realistic scenarios involving more countries, more commodities and more factors of production.

The other central assumptions of the Heckscher-Ohlin model are the following:

- Both factor and commodity markets are perfectly competitive, implying that price equals marginal cost and full employment exists in both industries.
- Factors are perfectly mobile intra-nationally but immobile internationally.
- Both countries have identical preference structures.
- No barriers to free trade exist and transport costs are zero internationally.
- Technology is internationally homogenous.
- Both industries are characterized by constant returns to scale.
- Both X and Y can be clearly ranked in terms of their relative factor intensities. Specifically, we shall assume X is always capital intensive and Y is always labour intensive, regardless of factor price ratios.

6.2 The Heckscher-Ohlin (H/O) Theorem:
Factor Proportions Are Key to Trade Patterns

Factor Abundance

In the literature, there are two main arguments concerning how the factor abundance of a country is measured: in terms of the physical stock of units and in terms of relative factor prices. To illustrate these two definitions, we shall assume that the FC is a capital-abundant country if the ratio of its stock of capital to its endowment of labour is greater than the corresponding ratio for the HC. This physical definition of factor abundance is couched not on the absolute availability of both factors of production but on their relative availability.

An alternative indicator of factor abundance is in terms of the relative cost of factors of production. More specifically, the HC is said to be more capital-abundant as compared to the FC if the cost of renting capital goods in the HC is less than the cost of renting capital goods in the FC (the cost of labour is considered to be the wage rate while the cost of capital is considered to be the rate of interest). Note that it is not the absolute rate of interest that determines the capital abundance status of the foreign country but the rate of interest in relation to the prevailing wage rate in that country – that is, the ratio of the factor price rental of capital and labour.

The Heckscher-Ohlin Theorem

The Heckscher-Ohlin theorem as expressed in Ohlin's own words argues, "Commodities requiring for their production much of [abundant factors of production] and little of [scarce factors] are exported in exchange for goods that call for factors in the opposite proportions. Thus indirectly, factors in abundant supply are exported and factors in scanty supply are imported" (Ohlin 1933, 92).

The essence of the Heckscher-Ohlin theorem is that countries export those commodities that intensively utilize their abundant factors of production and import those commodities that if produced would require the use of their scarce factors of production.

General Equilibrium Framework of the Heckscher-Ohlin Theorem

In the lower-right-hand segment of figure 6.1, the demand for final commodities is established by both the tastes of households and the distribution in the ownership of factors of production (or distribution of income). The demand for factors of production is derived from the demand for commodities. The derived demand for factors and the supply of factors together determine factor prices. Commodity prices are influenced by both the state of technology and the prices of factors of production. Since all the economic forces are illustrated as jointly determining the price of the final commodity, we say that this is a general equilibrium framework.

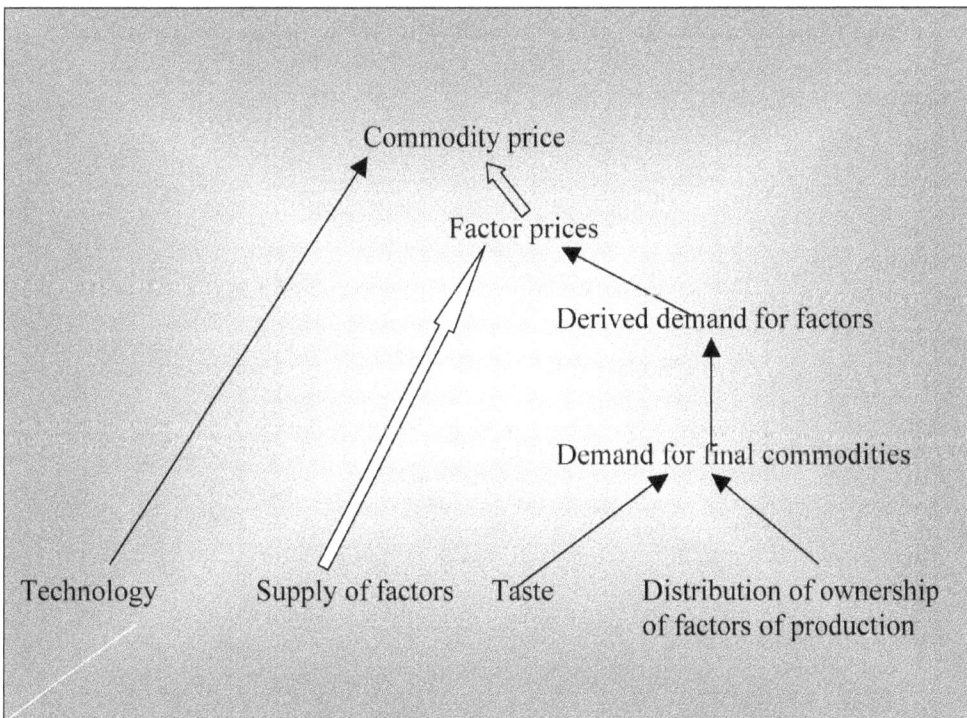

Figure 6.1: A general equilibrium illustration of the H/O model

The existence of identical preference structures and similar income distribution between the FC and the HC implies that the demand for final commodities is comparable. Assuming that trade partners have similar technologies provides the platform for one to argue that in the h/O model, the root of different relative factor prices in different nations are the differences in the factor endowments of the trading partners. Different relative factor prices in turn prompt different relative commodity prices, which in turn create the opportunity for trade among nations. Note that tastes, income distribution and technology need not be identical in the two countries; these assumptions simply facilitate greater clarity and graphical illustration of the H/O model.

Factor Intensity Relationship

A significant facet of the H/O theorem is that the factor intensity required at different relative prices does not influence the commodities produced. To see this we can make reference to figure 6.2. This figure shows differing factor intensity ratios, illustrated as $(K/L)_{s1}$, $(K/L)_{s2}$, $(K/L)_{c1}$ and $(K/L)_{c2}$. The ratio $(K/L)_{s2}$ represents a superior capital intensity to $(K/L)_{s1}$. Similarly, the ratio $(K/L)_{c2}$ represents a greater capital to labour ratio than $(K/L)_{c1}$. By construct, steel is capital intensive and cocoa is labour intensive. With a factor price ratio (or wage-rental ratio) of $(w/r)_2$, this economy would produce S_0 units of steel and C_0 units of cocoa, using the capital to labour ratios $(K/L)_{s2}$ and $(K/L)_{c2}$, respectively. Even when the factor price changes to $(w/r)_1$, steel will still be produced using a relatively capital-intensive process, $(K/L)_{s1}$, as compared to $(K/L)_{c1}$ for the cocoa sector. This illustrates that there is no factor intensity reversal even when factor prices change.

Is there a basis for trade when both countries share the same demand structure and technology? The answer to this question will be yes if both countries have relatively

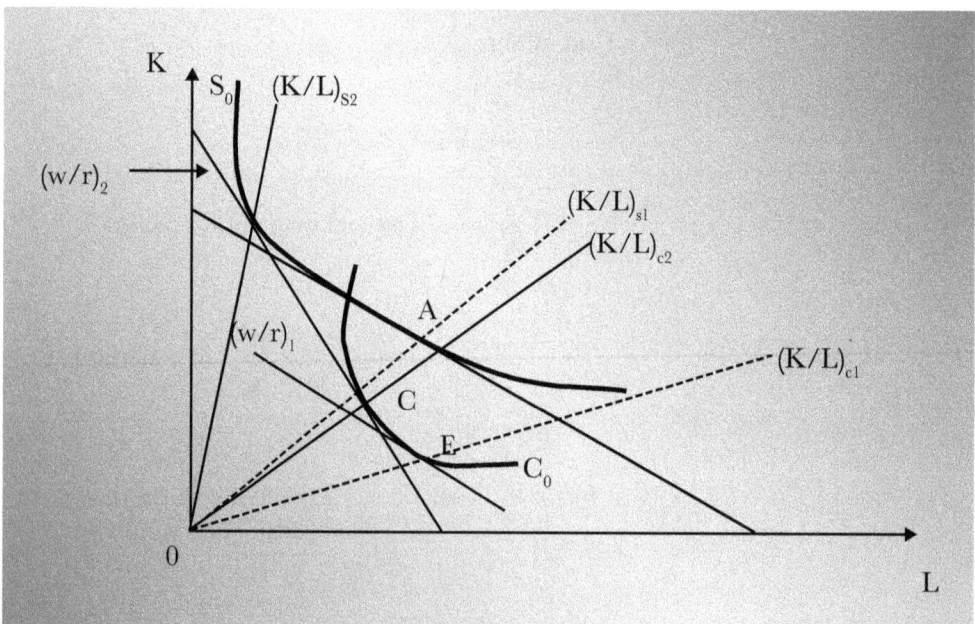

Figure 6.2: Commodity output and factor intensities

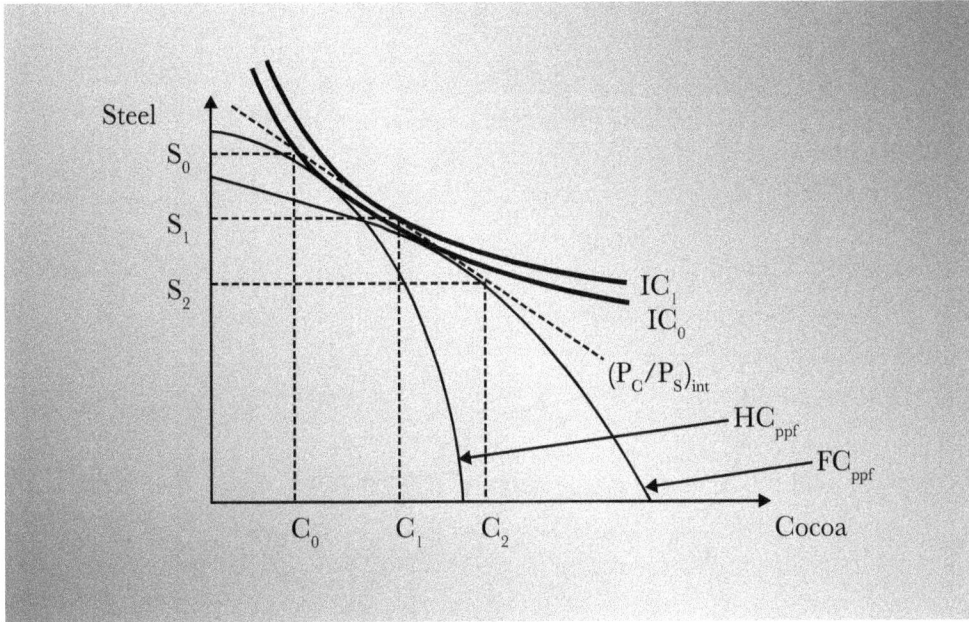

Figure 6.3: Gains from trade in two countries with identical technology and demands but different relative factor endowments

different factor endowments. The differing factor endowments are reflected in the alternative shapes of the production possibility curves of the HC and FC. Identical demand preferences are reflected in a homogenous set of indifference curves. By construct, in figure 6.3 we shall let the HC be the capital-abundant country and the FC be the labour-abundant country. The international terms of trade settles at an intermediate range between that of the HC and the FC, in this case $(Pc/Ps)_{int}$. With an international terms of trade of $(P_C/P_S)_{int}$, the HC specializes in steel and exports S_0S_1 units of this commodity, while the FC specializes in cocoa production and exports C_0C_1 units.

6.3 The Factor Price Equalization Theorem

One corollary of the Heckscher-Ohlin theorem is the factor price equalization theorem (FPET). The FPET postulates that free trade will eliminate relative and absolute differences in factor endowments. This section discusses the FPET.

In figure 6.4, the HC has a pre-trade factor price relative of $(w/r)_{HC}$ and produces S_{HC} units of steel at point M and C_{HC} units of cocoa. If the FC has a greater supply of labour, then the pre-trade factor price relative in the FC would be $(w/r)_{FC}$ and the FC would produce S_{FC} units of steel at point E and C_{FC} units of cocoa at point F on the isoquant.

Figure 6.5 shows the link between relative factor prices and relative product prices in the HC and FC. In the FC (under conditions of perfect competition), the abundance of labour leads to a low relative price of the labour-intensive good, cocoa. In contrast, in the HC, the relative scarcity of labour results in a high relative wage rate and thus a high relative price of the labour-intensive good in autarky conditions. Thus, if relative factor prices (w/r) are measured on the horizontal axis and relative product prices (P_C/P_S) are

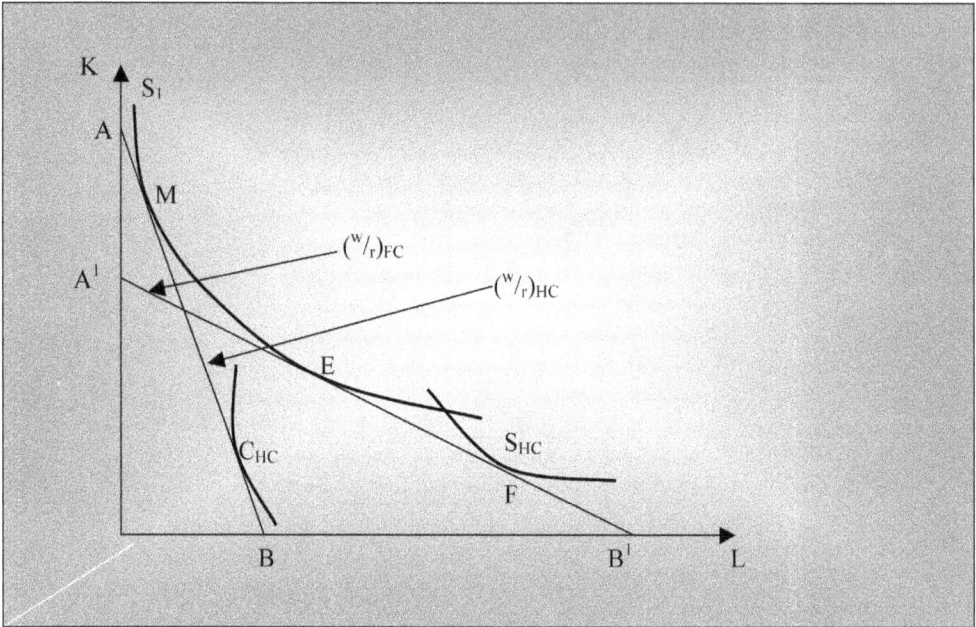

Figure 6.4: Relative factor prices and relative product prices

measured on the vertical axis, then a positive relationship such as that displayed in figure 6.5 would be observed.

The existence of different relative factor prices under autarkic conditions guarantees the achievement of gains from specialization and trade. With trade, the price of the product that uses the relatively abundant factor of production increases and the price of the product that uses the relatively scarce factor decreases. This occurs as a natural aspect of the adjustment process associated with free trade. Specifically, the HC will demand goods from the FC that are cheaper abroad than at home. As the demand for such goods

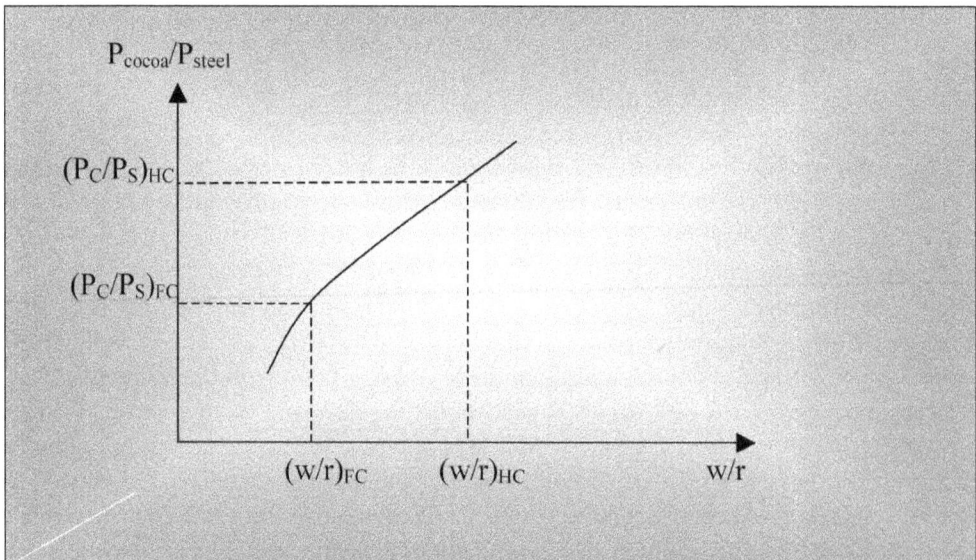

Figure 6.5: The relationship between relative factor prices and relative factor rewards

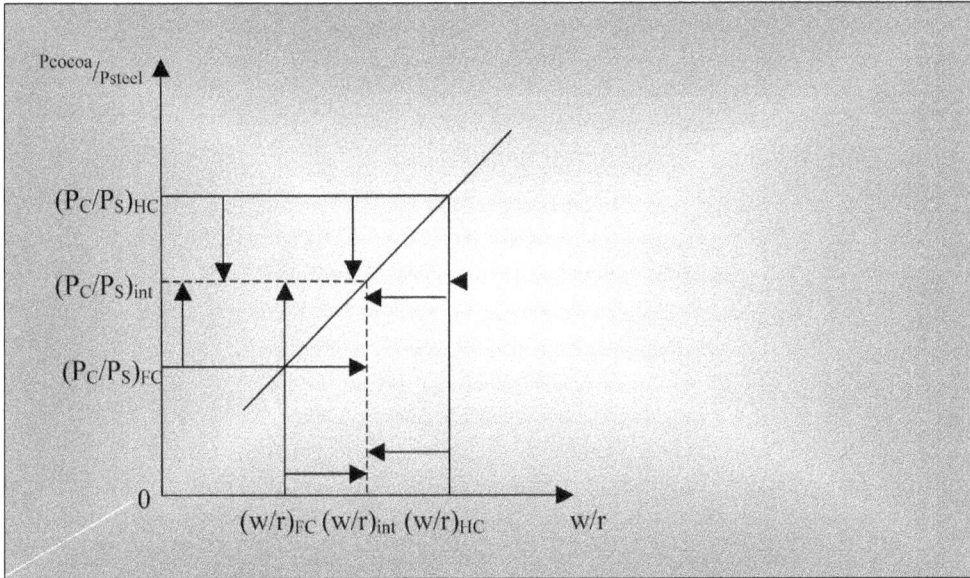

Figure 6.6: Factor price equalization with trade

increase, there is an increase in demand for the relatively abundant factor of production of the FC, and as a consequence its relative price increases. These factor price adjustments continue within both the FC and the HC until both face identical relative factor prices – this is the factor price equalization theorem (see figure 6.6). The factor price equalization theorem states that as free trade enables the product prices in each country to converge, so too will factor prices (capital and labour) between countries. Figure 6.6 provides a summary of the relative movement in product prices and factor prices.

6.4 Intra-CARICOM Single Market and Economy (CSME) Nurses' Salaries and the Factor Price Equalization

In the context of the CARICOM Single Market and Economy (CSME) and the formation of a unified trading bloc, it is expected that there will be a convergence of wages. This section discusses the salaries of nurses in the CSME context and the extent of equalization of regional nursing wages.

Figure 6.7 shows the salaries of staff nurses in various CARICOM economies. There is a clear disparity in nursing staff salaries for 2003, with the salary of nurses in Barbados being 578 per cent more than that in Guyana, 480 per cent that in Jamaica and 204 per cent that in Trinidad and Tobago. With the formation of a regional integration arrangement in the form of the CSME, which involves the uninhibited intra-regional movement of factors of production, a narrowing of wage differentials across labour markets can be expected as wages increase in low-wage countries and fall in high-wage countries. The factor price theorem explains how free trade equalizes factor prices among trading partners.

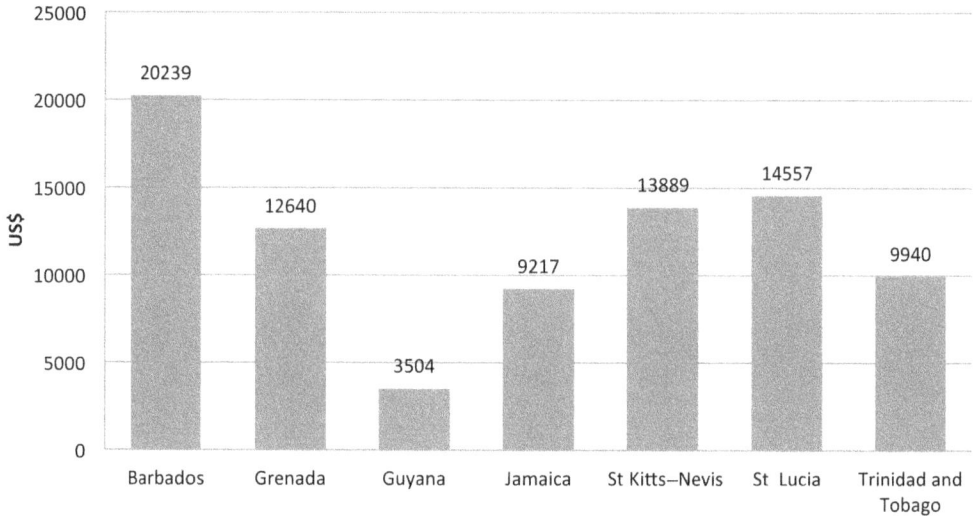

Figure 6.7: Comparison of yearly salary of nurses in seven CARICOM economies, 2003
Source: Clive, Hosein and Yan (2005).

6.5 The Stolper–Samuelson Theorem

This section is devoted to an illustration of the Stolper–Samuelson (SS) theorem,[4] which asserts that abundant factors of production benefit from trade while scarce factors lose.

There are several versions of the SS theorem in the literature including the original SS theorem and the specific factor model. The specific factor version of the SS theorem provides different results to the original Stolper–Samuelson model.[5] The specific factor model is not discussed here, but a good illustration of this model is available in Jones (1965).

The Stolper–Samuelson Theorem

The standard assumptions of the Stolper–Samuelson theorem are as follows:

1. Two countries (HC and FC) are engaged in balanced trade with perfectly competitive product and factor markets, with households and firms characterized by rational behaviour.
2. Both countries carry a homogenous pattern of consumption preferences.
3. Each country has two factors of production, typically labour and capital, but here treated as skilled and unskilled workers to determine if trade liberalization precipitated a greater degree of wage inequality.
4. There are two goods produced in the economies (X_1 and X_2), which are produced using the same technology (the production function used to produce these goods are linear homogenous, twice differentiable and strictly concave).
5. No factor intensity reversals occur – that is, regardless of the price level, one of the goods will always be intensive in the input of factor i. (Assumptions 2, 3, 4 and 5 outline the supply side attributes of the Heckscher-Ohlin model.)

6. Of the two trading partners, one is relatively abundant in unskilled labour and the other is relatively skill endowed (full employment is assumed to hold in the economy).
7. There are no costs attached to international trade in goods.

The Stolper–Samuelson theorem evaluates the effect of opening trade in an environment where factors are immobile internationally but perfectly mobile between industries.

Under this list of assumptions, the relationship between factor prices and commodity prices are given by equations 1a and 1b, and the full employment conditions are given by equation 2a and 2b:

$$P_1 = a_{S1} W_S + a_{u1} W_u \tag{1a}$$

$$P_2 = a_{S2} W_S + a_{u2} W_u \tag{1b}$$

$$L_S = a_{S1} X_1 + a_{S2} X_2 \tag{2a}$$

$$L_U = a_{U1} X_1 + a_{U2} X_2 \tag{2b}$$

where

a_{S1}, a_{S2} = unit skilled labour requirements for X_1 and X_2, respectively;
a_{U1}, a_{U2} = unit unskilled labour requirements for X_1 and X_2, respectively;
W_S = wage rate of skilled workers;
W_U = wage rate of unskilled workers.

X1 and X2 are the final commodity outputs. Equations 3 and 4 are the zero-profit conditions and they link prices to costs. "Any trade induced change in a country's product prices alters the relative profit opportunities facing its price taking firms, who respond by shifting their resources towards the industry whose relative profitability has risen" (Blanchflower and Slaughter 1998, 76). Totally differentiating equations 1 and 2 and dividing the results by prices and factor endowments, respectively, provides the following results:

$$\hat{P}_1 = \theta_{S1}\hat{W}_S + \theta_{U1}\hat{W}_u \tag{3a}$$

$$\hat{P}_2 = \theta_{S2}\hat{W}_S + \theta_{U2}\hat{W}_u \tag{3b}$$

$$\lambda_{S1}\hat{X}_1 + \lambda_{S2}\hat{X}_2 = \hat{L}_S + \delta_S\left(\hat{W}_S - \dot{W}_U\right) \tag{4a}$$

$$\lambda_{U1}\hat{X}_1 + \lambda_{U2}\hat{X}_2 = \hat{L}_U + \delta_U\left(\hat{W}_S - \hat{W}_U\right) \tag{4b}$$

The Stolper–Samuelson effects can be determined by solving equations 3a and 3b with respect to relative wages:

$$(\hat{W}_S - \hat{W}_U) = \frac{1}{|\theta|}(\hat{P}_1 - \hat{P}_2) \tag{5}$$

The Stolper–Samuelson theorem asserts that an increase in the relative price level of the skilled-labour-intensive good will result in an increase in the real return to skilled labour and a fall in the real return to unskilled labour. In this formulation,

$$|\theta| = \theta_{s1} - \theta_{s2} = \theta_{u1} - \theta_{u2},$$

and this is assumed to be positive.

Because θ is a fraction, the change in the relative price of the skilled-labour-intensive good in relation to the unskilled-labour-intensive good would have a magnification effect on the difference between W_S and W_U:

$$\hat{W}_s > \hat{P}_s > \hat{P}_u > \hat{W}_u \qquad (6)$$

Expression 6 states that the size of the effect is magnified relative to the cause.

Graphical Illustration of the Simple SS Theorem

To illustrate the Stolper–Samuelson scenario graphically, we can make reference to figure 6.8. With the opening up of trade, let us assume that there is an increase in demand for the skilled-labour-intensive good (X_1) as produced by the home economy (assume that the home country is skilled-labour abundant). It follows that in the HC there will emerge an increase in the demand for skilled labour and a fall in demand for unskilled labour. As figure 6.8 illustrates, the increase in demand for skilled labour boosts the wage rate of skilled labour upwards, while the decrease in demand for the unskilled-labour-intensive good leads to a decline in the demand for unskilled labour.[6]

As a consequence of the opening up of trade and the increase in the production of good X and decrease in the production of good X_2, there will be a change in the demand for skilled and unskilled labour. The increase in the demand for skilled-labour-intensive good X will lead to an increase in the amount of skilled labour demanded and a rise in the wage rate of labour from w^s_0 to w^s_1. The fall in the demand for unskilled labour leads

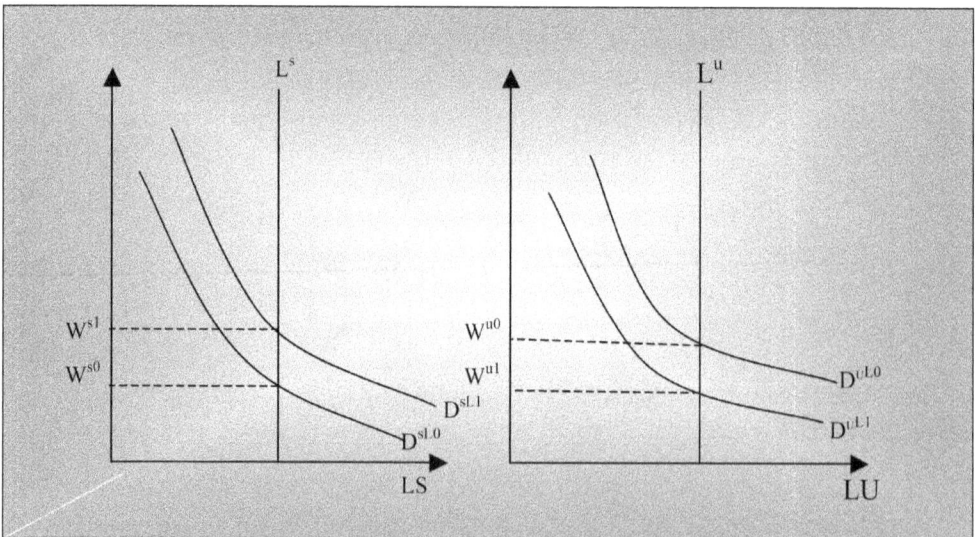

Figure 6.8: Free trade and factor demand in a labour-abundant economy

to a decline in the price of unskilled labour from w^u_0 to w^u_1. The wage structure before the price change and after the price change is w^s_0/w^u_0 and w^s_1/w^u_1.

The Stolper–Samuelson theorem makes the important contribution of explaining one of the controversial elements of trade policy. Starting from autarky, an opening up of trade results in a change in relative commodity prices, which in turn leads to a change in relative factor rewards. This in turn sometimes creates friction as owners of the abundant factor tend to support free trade as the commodity using the abundant factor of production benefits, and hence factor rewards improve. Owners of the scarce factor lose out as free trade reduces domestic demand for this commodity, and so its price falls and with it the rewards offered to those factors of production deployed in the sector.

This section proceeds to investigate the existence of the SS theorem.

Wages of Skilled and Unskilled Factors of Production: Petroleum and Agriculture

Table 6.1 shows the trends in the implicit deflators for various sub-sectors of the Trinidad and Tobago economy. Using 1993 as the base year, observe that there was a 166 per cent increase in the price of crude oil. In the same interval of time, the implicit gross domestic product (GDP) deflator for export agriculture contracted by 50 per cent, and there were only small improvements in the implicit price levels for export agriculture and domestic agriculture.

Table 6.1: Implicit deflators for various sections of the Trinidad and Tobago economy (2000 = 100)

	Export agriculture	Domestic agriculture	Sugar	Petroleum
1993	100.0	100.0	100.0	**100.0**
1994	51.7	97.7	80.0	**165.8**
1995	57.8	117.5	79.1	**159.1**
1996	50.8	127.6	121.6	**170.4**
1997	47.6	115.1	62.6	**150.4**
1998	37.3	123.1	89.7	**105.4**
1999	85.7	126.2	69.9	**121.8**
2000	71.1	121.3	97.7	**181.0**
2001	76.4	122.0	56.6	**174.0**
2002	44.8	133.9	52.4	**141.6**
2003	47.2	120.8	58.1	**186.9**
2004	51.4	151.4	113.8	**201.3**
2005	60.6	128.1	71.6	**247.7**
2006	50.3	127.4	123.8	**266.1**
% change	−49.7	27.4	23.8	**166.1**

Source: Computed from data in the *Review of the Trinidad and Tobago Economy* (various years).

Table 6.2: Trends in some key variables in the crude oil sector, 1956–2009

Year	Crude oil production (1,000 barrels per day)	Price per barrel of crude oil (US$), West Texas Intermediate	Government oil revenues (US$mn)	Oil exports (US$mn)	Real GDP (US$mn)
1956	79.0	1.98	25.7	53.66	n.a.
1957	93.9	2.08	32.0	64.91	n.a.
1958	102.3	1.83	40.8	69.78	n.a.
1959	112.1	1.56	37.9	74.61	n.a.
1960	115.7	1.5	39.7	80.5	n.a.
1961	125.4	1.45	41.2	101.15	n.a.
1962	133.9	1.42	42.3	101.25	n.a.
1963	133.4	1.4	45.3	107.77	n.a.
1964	135.9	1.33	50.5	117.49	n.a.
1965	133.9	1.33	49.8	115.36	n.a.
1966	149.59	1.33	49.7	124.8	n.a.
1967	178.05	1.33	50.7	141.78	n.a.
1968	183.28	1.33	54.9	103.7	n.a.
1969	157.3	1.28	54.3	143.2	3,694.03
1970	139.84	1.3	56.4	134.1	3,746.05
1971	129.15	1.65	70.1	117.92	3,666.90
1972	140.28	2.7	75.6	145.41	4,142.57
1973	170.44	3.14	96.1	220.1	4,175.77
1974	186.65	11.2	410.1	724.42	4,432.08
1975	217.14	10.6	514.8	869.39	4,665.78
1976	212.76	11.83	593.4	946.56	5,196.05
1977	229.06	12.84	737.7	1,103.38	5,440.82
1978	229.49	12.95	722.3	1,089.13	6,116.60
1979	214.35	29.22	988.0	1,562.08	6,563.59
1980	214.53	36.68	1,723.5	2,474.79	6,973.33
1981	189.34	35.27	1,772.1	2,360.33	7,244.75
1982	177.03	32.45	1,364.3	1,943.46	8,066.94
1983	159.81	29.66	1,025.6	1,714.46	7,646.82
1984	169.55	28.56	1,149.9	1,764.88	8,116.25
1985	177.84	27.31	1,002.9	1,706.49	7,781.91

Year	Crude oil production (1,000 barrels per day)	Price per barrel of crude oil (US$), West Texas Intermediate	Government oil revenues (US$mn)	Oil exports (US$mn)	Real GDP (US$mn)
1986	169.82	14.23	469.6	969.83	7,526.72
1987	156.06	18.15	543.9	996.31	7,183.21
1988	152.13	14.72	400.6	827.45	6,901.76
1989	149.34	17.84	471.58	934.99	6,844.74
1990	152.23	22.97	545.15	1,275.41	6,947.96
1991	144.08	19.33	639.29	1,061.9	7,134.29
1992	135.69	19.03	425.6	992.8	7,016.78
1993	122.19	16.8	317.9	832.3	6,915.11
1994	128.77	15.9	322.98	750.36	7,161.42
1995	131.78	17.16	430.5433	1,108.9	7,732.17
1996	129.04	20.42	510.9683	1,125.6	8,037.33
1997	123.56	18.8	331.168	1,087.13	8,254.70
1998	121.1	11.1	271.7994	922.79	8,896.02
1999	126.8	19.3	318.66	1,523.20	9,286.43
2000	130.46	30.3	712.68	2,789.57	9,856.06
2001	113.52	26.1	596.29	2,653.38	9,872.55
2002	130.62	26.0	611.16	2,315.19	10,541.97
2003	134.2	31.07	1,097.97	3,494.40	11,931.59
2004	123.25	41.49	1,218.77	3,923.77	12,670.16
2005	144.5	56.59	2,134.25	6,746.98	12,141.57
2006	142.8	66.02	3,405.30	10,718.06	13,173.89
2007	120.0	72.20	3,187.17	8,850.19	13,898.57
2008	114.59	100.06	4,838.18	13,047.48	14,385.02
2009	107.17	61.92	2,549.74	6,917.78	14,255.55
1956–72	131.94	1.58	48.05	105.73	3,812.39
1973–82	204.08	19.62	892.23	1,329.36	5,887.57
1983–89	162.08	21.5	723.44	1,273.49	7,428.77
1990–2000	131.43	19.19182	438.79	1,224.54	7,930.75
2001–9	125.63	53.50	2,182.09	6,518.58	12,541.21

Source: CSO data, World Bank, IMF.

6.6 Growth and Changing Factor Endowments in Trinidad and Tobago

The economic growth process in Trinidad and Tobago has historically (especially in the last century) been conditioned by trends in the crude oil exploration and production sub-components of the petroleum sector.[7] Table 6.2 illustrates the trends in the production and price of crude oil for Trinidad and Tobago in the period 1956–2009. The output of crude oil from Trinidad and Tobago began to fall by 1971; however, the discovery of a huge pool of hydrocarbon reserves by American Oil Company (AMOCO) in the early 1970s reversed this trend, with production levels peaking in 1978 at 229,490 barrels per day (bpd). Around the same time, the oil price on the international market increased significantly from $1.3 in 1966 to $36.7 per barrel by 1980 (see table 6.3). The consequence of this twin increase in both the price and production of crude oil was a rapid increase in the Trinidad and Tobago government's oil revenues, equipping the government with the necessary resources to become the "prime mover" of the Trinidad and Tobago economy. The boom in the price and production of crude oil also favourably affected the level of economic activity, as the average rate of economic growth for the period 1973–82 was 5.5 per cent per annum as compared to 4.6 per cent in the period 1956–72, at constant prices. The Trinidad and Tobago economy, a net exporter of crude oil and petroleum products, prospered during the oil boom period. Export revenues earned on the standard international trade classification section SITC 3 account (mainly hydrocarbons) increased sharply from $145.4 million in 1972 to reach $2,474.8 million by 1980, an increase of 1,601.2 per cent at current prices.

The Trinidad and Tobago government spent heavily during the boom years on building up its human and infrastructural capital. For example, expenditure on education (an important factor in creating human capital) increased considerably from $27.4 million to $55.7 million between 1976 and 1983, an increase of 103 per cent, with health expenditures (an important factor in maintaining human capital) increasing from $.5 million to $24.4 million between 1977 and 1983. Concerning infrastructural capital, expenditure on electricity increased from $7.8 million in 1976 to $17.3 million in 1980, with housing expenditure increasing substantially from $7.8 million to $191.8 million over the period 1976–82. Other important infrastructural capital areas such as roads, national transportation, water and telecommunications also benefited substantially, as indicated in table 6.3.

Apart from these direct long-term development investment outlays, a plethora of subsidies were granted. For example, between 1973 and 1983, the basic food subsidy increased from $1.6 million to $92.5 million, with subsidies to various basic utilities increasing during the same interval of time from $10.7 million to $369.3 million. No doubt, these trends in government expenditure and government subsidies helped to alter the factor endowment portfolio and by extension the comparative advantage position of the Trinidad and Tobago economy. Some relevant trends in this regard are provided in table 6.4.

The first two columns of table 6.4 show the trends in gross capital formation (GCF) and foreign direct investment (FDI) inflows. Over the period 1966–2008, the cumulative amount of money expended on the capital formation process amounted to

Table 6.3: Funds allocated to long-term development projects in Trinidad and Tobago, 1976–1983 (US$mn)

	Education	Health	Electricity	Housing	Roads	National transport	Water	Tele-communications
1976	27.39		7.80	0.47	6.11	9.11	7.24	1.93
1977	19.62	0.50	9.11	6.67	19.36	9.28	26.46	13.70
1978	22.20	1.22	8.07	37.09	22.88	13.74	64.58	18.66
1979	27.58	6.82	9.27	49.45	55.85	9.12	78.19	25.76
1980	17.23	4.89	15.92	86.05	98.91	22.23	44.76	29.17
1981	27.37	10.07	17.34	111.18	16.09	13.22	45.24	29.57
1982	47.39	13.13	3.61	195.10	189.48	8.64	34.98	41.81
1983	55.70	24.35	3.61	191.80	172.1	87.67	38.0	42.0

Source: Accounting for the Petrodollar (1983).

$57,731.6 million. If 10 per cent depreciation per annum is assumed, then this stock was worth $51,958.4 million. To glean a clearer idea of the enormity of the change in the capital formation stock between 1966 and 2008, one only has to compare the 1966 flow of $166.9 million with the cumulative figure through 2008 of $51,958.4 million. The cumulative inflow of FDI between 1966 and 2000 was $6.71 billion.

Primary school graduates are used in table 6.4 as an approximation for human capital. While it is very clear that there has been a fall in the flow of primary school graduates between 1966 and 2009, it must be understood that the stock of graduates in this time interval would have expanded considerably.[8] Infrastructural capital in Trinidad and Tobago also increased substantially between 1966 and 2009. For example, in 1970 there were 35,100 telephones in service in Trinidad and Tobago, but by 2008 the number of telephone lines in service increased considerably to reach 303,300. During the same interval of time, the annual amount of water produced in Trinidad and Tobago expanded by 344 per cent from 19,385 million gallons in 1966 to 86,057.9 million gallons in 2008. Similarly, rapid improvements were experienced in terms of electricity production, which expanded from 701 megawatts in 1966 to reach 7,750.7 megawatts in 2008. The natural resource endowment bundle of Trinidad and Tobago also changed between 1966 and 2009. For example, in 1966 the level of crude oil production was 55.6 million barrels, but by 2009 this fell to 39.1 million: a decline of 30 per cent. During the same interval of time, the production of natural gas expanded considerably from 3,367.6 million cubic metres in 1966 to reach 42,396 million cubic metres in 2009: an increase of 1,159 per cent. Finally, if we approximate the flow of entrepreneurial talent by the annual number of graduates from UWI, St Augustine, the flow of graduates increased from 100 students

Table 6.4: Trends in some aspects of the factor endowment portfolio of Trinidad and Tobago economy, 1966–2009

Year	Physical capital		Human capital	Physical labour	Infrastructural capital			Land resources			Entrepreneurs
	Gross capital formation (US$mn)	FDI (US$mn)	Primary school graduates	Labour force (thousands)	Telephone lines in service (thousands of connections)	Water (millions of gallons)	Electricity (megawatts)	Crude oil production (millions of barrels)	Marine production (thousands of barrels)	Natural gas production (millions of cubic metres)	UWI graduates with first degrees from the St Augustine campus
1966	166.9	24.9	216,063	351	n.a.	19,385.8	701.0	55.603	n.a.	3,367.6	100
1967	134.2	24.5	219,679	372	n.a.	19,923.7	731.1	64.995	n.a.	3,973.9	131
1968	150.3	25.5	223,164	361	n.a.	20,476.6	805.5	66.904	n.a.	4,288.4	163
1969	133.9	57.2	224,343	365	n.a.	21,044.8	892.2	57.406	n.a.	3,893.5	130
1970	212.5	83.2	227,254	364	35.1	21,422.3	907.3	51.043	25,692	3,428.0	133
1971	304.7	104.5	228,319	368	n.a.	21,741.5	955.8	47.144	22,933	3,109.6	189
1972	339.3	85.0	227,815	n.a.	n.a.	22,806.8	1,074.7	51.211	29,280	2,954.5	253
1973	339.7	62.6	222,928	383	41.12	22,070.5	1,017.3	60.67	40,504	3,397.4	283
1974	445.7	113.7	213,820	394	n.a.	23,310.1	1,121.0	68.136	49,346	3,632.8	268
1975	667.9	93.0	204,004	391	n.a.	23,331.1	1,124.2	78.621	63,525	3,580.2	288
1976	614.0	132.2	200,095	n.a.	n.a.	25,153.3	1,286.6	77.673	61,321	3,906.5	312
1977	836.5	83.5	190,155	428	43.4	25,504.0	1,430.7	83.609	67,135	4,236.2	308
1978	1,076.5	128.8	181,863	440	n.a.	25,024.7	1,527.6	83.809	97,206	4,471.3	368
1979	1,338.9	93.8	171,635	447	n.a.	26,993.0	1,679.9	78.209	61,096	4,805.4	329
1980	1,908.5	184.5	166,763	431	n.a.	32,269.1	1,892.9	77.608	60,510	5,601.0	388
1981	1,891.9	258.1	167,117	436	n.a.	37,228.7	2,169.3	69.109	52,316	5,604.1	360
1982	2,257.1	203.5	167,452	445	46.8	42,910.4	2,573.5	64.621	49,513	5,841.0	394
1983	1,996.0	114.1	169,886	453	66.3	45,982.6	2,790.0	58.34	44,567	6,318.0	376
1984	1,860.5	109.8	166,739	478	82.7	48,824.4	2,883.4	61.897	48,321	7,229.0	404

Year											
1985	1,384.0	-7.0	168,790	474.0	118.1	50,795.5	2,903.1	64.361	49,823	7,550	433
1986	1,035.5	-21.8	172,424	472.0	141.4	52,614.6	3,181.9	61.652	46,847	7,585	474
1987	927.3	35.0	176,544	475.0	158.8	52,637.2	3,351.9	56.383	41,941	7,672	796
1988	587.6	62.9	182,764	477.0	161.1	53,181.5	3,355.5	56.1	40,630	7,442	561
1989	716.5	148.9	186,566	469.1	158.2	54,355.7	3,331.7	55.8	40,777	7,244	537
1990	638.4	109.4	189,752	467.6	164.9	56,166.4	3,466.1	55.2	41,672	6,645	547
1991	865.8	169.3	193,632	492.6	173.9	56,165.0	3,642.4	52.6	40,018	7,411	589
1992	750.3	177.9	196,333	505.1	180.1	59,867.1	3,851.6	50.2	36,954	7,483	629
1993	657.0	379.2	197,012	504.5	188.7	57,315.0	3,816.9	44.6	32,858	7,077	568
1994	999.4	516.2	195,041	509.3	200.2	57,570.5	4,033.0	47.0	36,112	7,695	837
1995	1,107.5	298.9	191,641	521.0	205.4	55,158.0	4,228.6	48.1	36,746	7,757	1,268
1996	1,398.1	355.4	185,898	533.4	210.8	62,867.0	4,487.8	47.1	36,225	9,058	1,288
1997	1,727.9	999.3	181,003	541.0	232.5	59,322.0	4,841.0	45.1	33,464	9,137	1,287
1998	2,017.5	729.8	176,218	558.7	260.8	60,464.0	5,228.0	44.8	33,779	10,294	1,319
1999	1,430.6	379.2	169,540	563.4	270.0	62,950.0	5,190.9	45.6	35,409	13,240	1,652
2000	1,631.5	654.3	168,734	572.9	290.6	65,759.0	6,307.8	43.6	33,803	15,473	1,641
2001	2,357.4	684.9	154,201	576.5	307.0	64,044.0	5,688.3	41.4	32,151	16,485	1,624
2002	2,038.1	684.3	150,346	586.2	318.2	73,228.0	6,036.0	47.8	38,792	18,861	1,708
2003	2,847.7	583.1	146,587	596.6	319.8	72,591.0	6,424.0	50.2	39,992	26,794	1,817
2004	2,567.9	972.7	142,922	613.5	321.3	76,135.0	6,709.6	44.9	35,898	29,672	1,952
2005	4,609.3	598.7	139,349	623.7	324.0	77,405.0	7,036.1	52.7	43,876	33,053	2,256
2006	2,874.9	512.7	135,865	625.2	326.4	84,265.2	7,143.2	52.1	43,526	39,296	2,522
2007	2,804.1	830.0	132,468	622.4	306.6	80,906.0	7,713.1	43.8	35,765	41,250	2,522
2008	3,082.2	2,100.8	129,156	626.7	303.3	86,057.9	7,750.7	41.8	33,153	42,240	2,218
2009	n.a.	n.a.	125,927	620.9	n.a.	n.a.	n.a.	39.1	n.a.	42,396	2,802

Source: CSO data.

in 1966 to 2,802 in 2009. Let us assume (conservatively) that the average age of a graduate is twenty-four years; then, a graduate in 1970 would today be less than sixty-five years old and still be part of the pool of entrepreneurial talent in Trinidad and Tobago, assuming a retirement age of sixty-five years.

These changes in factor endowment capabilities have facilitated a change in the structure of production in Trinidad and Tobago, with agriculture, crude oil exploration, narrow manufacturing and services value added as a proportion of total GDP (at constant prices) contracting by 3.5, 8.5, 0.2 and 4.4 percentage points, respectively, between 1966 and 2008. Resource-based manufacturing has outstripped growth in all of the other listed sectors, expanding considerably by 12 percentage points in the same time interval (see table 6.5).

The discussion in this section helped to illustrate that the comparative advantage of an economy is not static and evolves as the economy's factor endowment bundle changes through investment or the discovery of new resources and so on.

6.7 Empirical Evidence on the Classical Model

MacDougall (1951) conducted a test of the classical model of international trade using data for the United States and United Kingdom with the rest of the world for 1937. Apart

Table 6.5: Snapshot summary of share of GDP in various sectors of Trinidad and Tobago economy, 1966–2008 (constant prices)

	Agriculture	Crude oil exploration and production	Narrow manufacturing	Resource-based industries	Broad manufacturing	Services
1966	4.2	30.3	8.6	3.2	11.8	**54.5**
1970	4.3	25.5	10.3	3.2	13.5	**56.5**
1975	3.3	30.3	9.6	1.4	11.0	**56.3**
1980	2.1	21.9	8.5	1.2	9.7	**66.7**
1985	2.3	20.9	7.5	2.0	9.5	**66.9**
1990	3.4	20.4	8.3	2.9	11.2	**64.1**
1995	3.3	16.8	8.3	4.2	12.5	**65.9**
2000	1.9	17.4	7.1	9.7	16.8	**60.7**
2005	0.6	22.7	7.5	13.4	20.9	**52.5**
2008	0.7	21.8	8.4	15.2	23.6	**50.1**
Structural change (1966–2008)	−3.5	−8.5	−0.2	12.0	11.8	−4.4

Source: National Income Accounts of Trinidad and Tobago (various years).

from exports, MacDougall also utilized data on the output of goods and the requisite amount of labour to produce these goods.

The gist of MacDougall's hypothesis was very straightforward. He argued that the United States, for example, would have a comparative advantage in the production of good i as compared to j, and in the production of good i as compared to the rest of the world (ROTW), if the following conditions applied:

$$APL_{i\ USA} > APL_{j\ USA} \tag{6a}$$

$$APL_{i\ USA} > APL_{i\ ROTW} \tag{6b}$$

where APL refers to the average productivity of labour.

Specifically, equation 6a indicates that the United States will have a comparative

Table 6.6: Results from MacDougall's test of the classical model

Industries	US output per worker/ UK output per worker	US exports/UK exports
Radios	More than 2	8.0
Pig iron	More than 2	5.0
Cars	More than 2	4.0
Glass containers	More than 2	3.5
Tin cans	More than 2	3.0
Machinery	More than 2	1.5
Paper	More than 2	1.0
Cigarettes	1.4–2	0.5
Linoleum	1.4–2	0.33
Hosiery	1.4–2	0.33
Leather footwear	1.4–2	0.33
Coke	1.4–2	0.2
Rayon weaving	1.4–2	0.2
Cotton goods	1.4–2	0.11
Rayon making	1.4–2	0.09
Beer	1.4–2	0.06
Cement	Less than 1.4	0.09
Men's woollens	Less than 1.4	0.04
Margarine	Less than 1.4	0.03
Woollen and worsted	Less than 1.4	0.004

Source: MacDougall (1951).

advantage in the production of those goods for which its average productivity of labour is highest. At the same time, the United States will have a comparative advantage in the production of good i if the average productivity of labour in the United States to produce this good exceeds that in the rest of the world.

When MacDougall outlined his study, the wage rate in the United States was virtually double that in the United Kingdom, and so for the classical model to carry weight in such an environment, it was necessary for the United States to have a productivity rate twice as high as in the United Kingdom. After adjusting for differences in wages, MacDougall explained that he expected the United States to export those goods, which adhered to the specifications of equation 6b.

To measure comparative advantage, MacDougall used the ratios of US output per worker to UK output per worker and US exports to UK exports.

As the data in table 6.6 illustrates, in those industries that produced radios, pig iron, cars and so on, the United States' labour productivity was more than twice as high as in the United Kingdom, and in these industries the United States clearly had a comparative advantage, as the associated US exports as a proportion of the UK exports (USA_x/UK_x) indicate – for example, radios have a $APL_{USA}/APL_{UK} > 2$ and an associated export ratio of 8.

In contrast, in those industries with a $APL_{USA}/APL_{UK} < 2$, the USA_x/UK_x was less than unity. Two observations are in order:

1. MacDougall's results provide general support that a relationship exists between the average productivity of labour and the export performance of economies.
2. MacDougall's estimates do not have to be taken as evidence of the classical model being valid. This can be explained using the following three basic reasons.
   a) The classical model was designed to study trade between two countries and not trade between two countries to a third country (the former was studied by Mac-Dougall). In the strictest sense, if the classical model is true, then either the United Kingdom or the United States should export the commodity but clearly not both.
   b) MacDougall's result does not rule out the possibility that other models may hold. Thus under certain common conditions, it may be possible to show that the H/O results hold.
   c) MacDougall's result allows a comparison between relative export levels and relative productivity levels. Other factors of importance such as transport and product differentiation are not considered, and these factors may be able to explain the patterns of trade observed by MacDougall.

6.8 Tests of the Heckscher-Ohlin (H/O) Model

The most prolific test in the trade literature on the H/O theorem was developed by Professor Wassily Leontief. Leontief's main theoretical tool was an input-output table. His analysis utilized data from two hundred different industries. In addition, Leontief also provided data on capital to labour ratios for these two hundred industries. Using data on US imports and exports for 1947, Leontief posed the following question: What would be the effect on the capital and labour requirements if the United States were to decrease its imports and exports by one million dollars each?

It would have been expected that Leontief would find that the United States, the most capital-abundant economy in the world, would produce and export capital-intensive goods. This would mean that by reducing exports by $1 million the United States would shed more capital than would be required to produce a $1 million expansion in import-competing goods.

Surprisingly, however, Leontief found just the opposite: the United States produced and exported labour-intensive commodities:

> To replace US$1mn of US imports by domestic output expansion would require 170 additional years per worker of labor and 3.1mn of capital. Reducing US exports by US$1mn would provide 182.3 years per worker of labor and US$2.6mn in capital. Thus, according to the experiment, US exports tend to be labor intensive relative to US imports. Because this finding was so unexpected, it has become known as the Leontief paradox. (Henegedara 2011)

6.9 Reconciling the Leontief Paradox

A number of explanations have been provided in the literature to explain Leontief's unexpected results.

Labour Productivity: Leontief attempted to reconcile the paradox by arguing that because American labour productivity was superior to its trade partners', it produced and exported labour-intensive goods. American labour productivity, Leontief argued, was higher than elsewhere because of the culture of entrepreneurship in the American economy and a superior American education system. If Leontief's education arguments are considered, then Leontief's empirical findings become consistent with the predictions of the H/O theory.[9]

Natural Resources: One researcher, Jaroslav Vanek, argued that because Leontief used a two-factor (capital and labour) model and ignored natural resources as a third factor of production, the results are not surprising. Vanek assumed that if the United States is a natural-resource-scarce economy but is abundant in capital and labour, then it should be a net importer of scarce natural resources. Since natural resource exploitation tends to be very capital intensive, if capital and labour are considered as the only two factors of production, then the paradox can be explained. However, even when Vanek's modification was considered, some aspects of the paradox still remained.

Tariff Structure: W.P. Travis, writing in the 1960s, found that a partial explanation of the Leontief paradox could be made by referring to the tariff structure that prevailed in the United States at the time. In particular, US tariffs on labour-intensive products tended to be high, typically in excess of 25 per cent. At the same time, tariffs on capital-intensive goods tended to be lower than on labour-intensive goods. Travis argued that in such an environment, there could be a distortion in the pattern of US trade to the extent of importing capital-intensive goods. Travis's comments may be true, but they would require collecting import data in the absence of tariffs, and this type of data is not easily available.

Tastes: A fundamental assumption of the Heckscher-Ohlin model is that tastes are the same among trading partners. If tastes are not the same among trading partners, then trade does not have to follow the H/O channels. In this regard, it is necessary to investigate the consumption patterns of trading partners.

Figure 6.9 highlights consumption data for 1975 that was published by the United

Food	Tobacco	Clothing & shoes	Rent, fuel, power	Furniture	Medical care	Transportation & communication
HIGH India (59.7)	HIGH Sri Lanka (6.6)	HIGH Ghana (14.2)	HIGH Israel (20.7)	HIGH Belgium (15.0)	HIGH Netherlands & France (11.2)	HIGH Cyprus (19.6)
AVG 33.3	AVG 2.9	AVG 8.8	AVG 13.6	AVG 8.4	AVG 4.9	AVG 11.2
LOW US (14.4)	LOW France (0.9)	LOW Jamaica (4.3)	LOW Sri Lanka (6.8)	LOW Korea (3.2)	LOW UK (1.0)	LOW US (2.2)

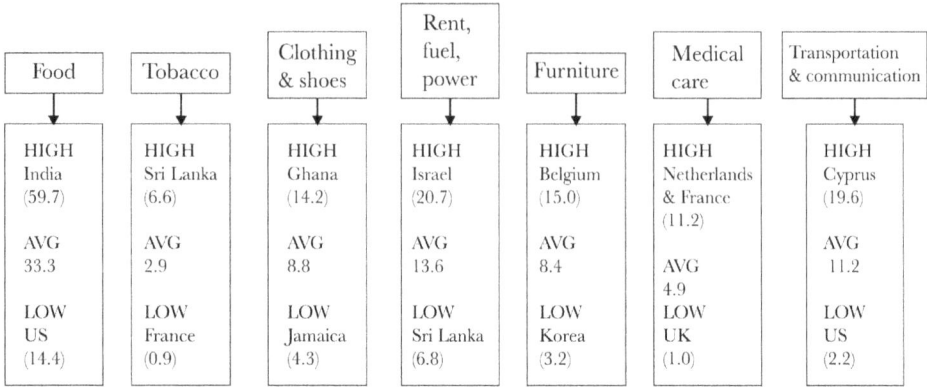

Figure 6.9: Consumption patterns across countries (percentages of total private consumption devoted to each category)

Nations. This preliminary information indicates that the expenditure pattern of households was in fact different, providing indicative evidence that the assumption of similar tastes among households may be misleading.

Technologies: In performing his calculations, Leontief assumed that the home country utilized the same technology in exporting industries and import-competing industries. This assumption is consistent with the assumption of the H/O model pertaining to identical technologies between the HC and FC; however, it is only valid in the H/O model if there is the equalization of factor prices internationally or if the industries in the trading partners can substitute capital for labour as factor prices change. In the absence of these conditions, and assuming labour is more costly in the United States than in its trading partners, Leontief would have estimated US imports as being relatively capital intensive.

6.10 Conclusion

This chapter provided a detailed examination of the factor proportion hypothesis. The discussion included the Heckscher-Ohlin, factor price equilibrium and Stolper–Samuelson theorems. The chapter concluded with empirical evidence of the classical model of international trade using data for the United States and the United Kingdom with the rest of the world.

Summary of Key Points

- The essence of the Heckscher-Ohlin theorem is that countries export those commodities that intensively utilize their abundant factors of production and import those commodities that if produced would require the use of their scarce factors of production.
- There is a basis for trade when both countries share the same demand structure and technology if both countries have relatively different factor endowments.
- The factor price equalization theorem states that as free trade enables the product prices in each country to converge, so too will factor prices (capital and labour) between countries.

- The Stolper–Samuelson theorem asserts that abundant factors of production benefit from trade while scarce factors lose.
- The Leontief paradox was derived from the empirical finding that a capital-abundant economy, rather than producing and exporting capital-intensive goods, produces and exports labour- intensive commodities.

Multiple Choice

1. The H/O model of international trade illustrates that developing countries have a comparative advantage in the production of labour-intensive goods such as textiles for which of the following reasons?
   a) Developing countries tend to be relatively more labour abundant.
   b) Workers in developing countries tend to live closer to the points of production in these industries.
   c) The climate of developing countries is more facilitative of these types of industries.
   d) Workers in developing countries are more specialized in the techniques of production for these commodities.

2. Which of the following theories associated with the H/O model concludes that capital accumulation with favourable economic growth will require the importation of natural resources?
   a) the H/O theorem
   b) the Stolper–Samuelson theorem
   c) the Rybczynski theorem
   d) the factor price equalization theorem

3. The H/O theorem asserts an economy's comparative advantage in the production of a particular good is evidenced by
   a) the predominant employment of the abundant factor of production
   b) the predominant employment of the scarce factors of production
   c) the importation of raw materials
   d) the employment of a small amount of the abundant factors of production

4. The factor price equalization theorem claims that
   a) Countries will export goods in which they have a comparative advantage.
   b) Countries will import goods in which they have a comparative advantage.
   c) With international trade, eventually the returns to all factors of production will equalize.
   d) none of the above

5. The Leontief Paradox
   a) failed to validate the Ricardian theory
   b) failed to validate the H/O model
   c) supported the theory of comparative advantage
   d) supported the H/O model

Short Essays

1. Identify the core assumptions of the H/O model.
2. Show diagrammatically the gains from trade.
3. Show clearly how the gains from trade can occur in spite of identical demand functions between trading partners (n.b. the production functions are different between trading partners).

Key Trade Terms

- Factor proportion hypothesis
- Heckscher-Ohlin theorem
- Factor proportions
- Factor intensity
- Factor price equalization theorem
- Factor rewards
- CARICOM single market and economy (CSME)
- Stolper–Samuelson theorem
- Implicit deflators
- Classical model of international trade
- Leontief paradox
- Labour productivity
- Tariff structure

7.

Alternative Theories of Trade and Intra-Industry Trade

Learning Objectives

a. Explain the imitation gap theory.
b. Discuss the phases of the product cycle hypothesis.
c. Define the Engel effect and Linder's representative demand hypothesis.
d. Explain the concept of intra-industry trade (IIT).
e. Explain how vertical IIT differs from horizontal IIT.
f. List the explanations of IIT.
g. Explain the static and dynamic measures of IIT and their theoretical ranges.

7.0 Introduction

In this chapter, alternative trade theories to the Heckscher-Ohlin (H/O) theorem are presented. These theories deviate from those mentioned earlier by paying attention to some of the weaknesses in the H/O theorem. While the H/O theorem focused on the supply side, some of the theories considered in this chapter focus on the demand side. The H/O model also requires a perfectly competitive world, while some of the theories presented later relax this assumption. This chapter also explores developments in the theory of intra-industry trade.

7.1 Imitation Gap Theories of Trade

In previous discussions, no reference was made to the genesis of technological changes or how technological changes are transferred from one country to another. Posner (1961), in a seminal paper, explicitly demonstrated how technological changes and technology transfer can influence trade patterns.

In this work, Posner highlighted that technological change is a continuous process and that there are time lags between the adoption of the technology in one country and its utilization in another (this is called the imitation lag). Posner also identified a demand lag, which was described as the time period between the emergence of a new good and its demand abroad. His contention was that even among countries that are similar in the H/O context, technological changes can still sprout trade.

To illustrate the fundamentals of Posner's theory, let us assume that one country experiences a technological advancement. The new commodities that result from the technological improvement will have a time lag before they penetrate foreign markets: the demand lag. The length of the demand lag is conditioned by the similarity between the new good and its old substitutes. From the inception of the technological breakthrough, the producers in the FC can decide to adopt the new technology, but there may be a time lag if there is a patent in place or there is the need to learn the dynamics of the new blueprints. Whether or not sustainable trade is stimulated between the two trade partners hinges on the length of the demand lag and imitation lag.

If the time duration of the demand lag exceeds the imitation lag, then trade will not be stimulated by the technological innovation, as producers in the FC will adopt the technology before the good is imported. However, it is more likely that the length of the imitation lag will be greater than the demand lag, so the innovating country can realize some of the benefits of free trade.

To explore some of the main features of the imitation gap model, consider figure 7.1, which shows the trade balance of the innovating country. Let us treat the period $0-t_1$ as the time interval in which the blueprint for the product itself is developed. After the breakthrough in the innovation of the commodity, production commences. As consumers in the foreign country (FC) become aware of the new good and they start to demand it, their imports (i.e., the exports of the innovating country) will start to expand. Let us assume this starts at t_1. Note that in the time interval t_1-t_4, the exports of the home country (HC) continually improve, under the assumption that the imitation lag is greater than the demand lag. The time interval t_1-t_4 therefore represents the time interval in which consumers in the FC respond fully to the innovated good from the HC. Note that for ease of analysis we have assumed uniform growth in export.

Figure 7.1 shows the FC imitating the HC's production at time t_5. The consequence of this is that in the time interval t_5-t_7 the foreign economy will start to produce the innovated good in sufficient quantities to drive exports by the HC down to zero. The general standardization of the production process may even see the HC importing the commodity after t_7.

Two things should be noted at this point:

1. If the imitation lag is short, then at some time before the FC's market is fully penetrated their producers can take over the production of the commodity, causing the effect that would have occurred at t_7 to occur at t_2.
2. If at a point in time such as t_6 another innovation is made, then the HC can realize a new boost in its export revenues.

Table 7.1 shows the high-technology exports of several developed economies for 1990 to 2009. Clearly, the proportion of high-technology exports as a percentage of manufactured exports is significant and, between the indicated time periods, has increased for most of the listed developed economies.

In the 1960s, Professor Gary Hufbauer researched the length of imitation lags. By using a variety of synthetic products, Hufbauer estimated the first production dates in differing economies. He then used this information to estimate imitation lags in terms of the time lag between production in the innovating economy and the imitating economy.

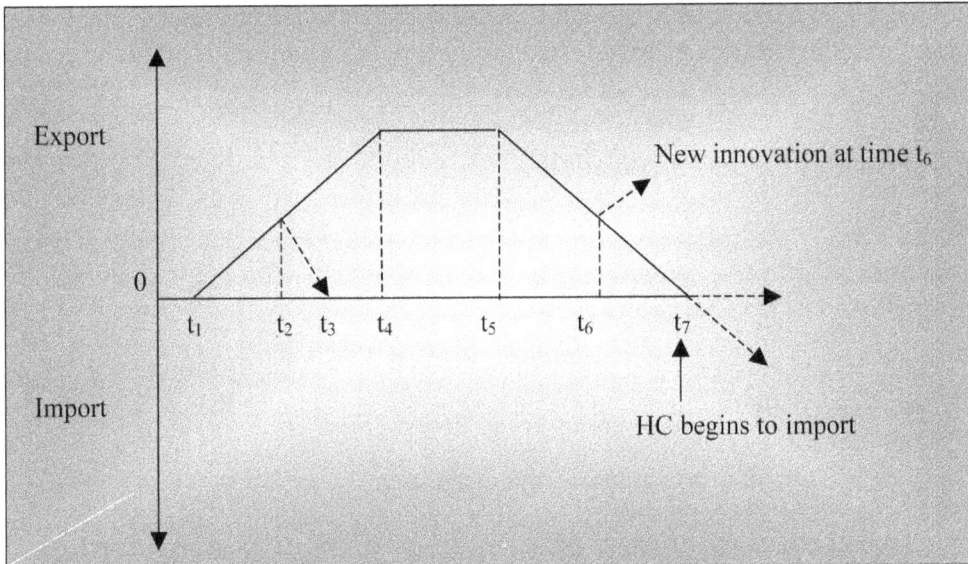

Figure 7.1: The imitation gap model

In general, imitation lags have tended to become smaller over time for the United States, Canada, Italy, Japan and Australia but relatively longer for Germany, the United Kingdom and France. Hufbauer explained that the reason for the experience in the latter group of countries was the fact that in the early years these countries were innovators but eventually became imitators. If imitation lags were to be calculated today, then the

Table 7.1: Exports of technology-intensive goods by developed countries

Countries	High-technology exports (% of manufactured exports)	
	1990	2009
Norway	12	20
Australia	8	13
Canada	14	18
Switzerland	12	25
United States	33	23
Japan	24	20
Netherlands	16	24
Denmark	15	18
United Kingdom	24	23
France	16	23
Germany	11	16
Republic of Korea	18	32

Source: World Development Indicators (various years).

general spread of multinational companies and the more widespread use of information communication technology would most likely result in shorter imitation time lags (see table 7.2).

7.2 Product Cycle Hypothesis

Many of the technological advances in production have emerged in a handful of developed economies. Some countries are able to make technological progress and rapidly innovate because they are characterized by

1. high levels of research and development (R&D) as a proportion of gross domestic product (GDP),
2. high levels of literacy,
3. high levels of university graduates and scientists,
4. high levels of physical capital,
5. high levels of "initial" technology, and
6. consumers more accustomed to trying new products.[1]

Table 7.3 shows the trends in R&D expenditures of various developed economies.

Two researchers, Vernon (1966) and Hirsch (1967), developed trade theories that attempt to explain why the production of new commodities tends to be concentrated in developed countries. These researchers argued that initial production will concentrate in developed countries, but production will eventually spread to other countries.

The innovation of a new good is a risky business and requires a substantial amount of investment. It also requires consumers with a willingness to experiment and deep enough pockets to carry the "cost" of the innovation. In general, Hirsch argued that innovations

Table 7.2: The length of the imitation gap for various economies

Countries	1930	1939	1950	1962
United States	5.7	6.8	4.6	3.1
Germany	1.5	1.2	2.5	4.7
United Kingdom	1.7	5.5	6.9	9.8
France	4.1	8.2	8.6	11.8
Canada	25.5	20.3	17.5	14.3
Italy	20.8	16.8	14.5	14.7
Japan	17.7	16.4	13.6	14.8
The Netherlands	16.3	19.8	19.7	20.7
Sweden	20.4	20.2	18.9	21.1
Australia	30.1	27.4	26.4	24.4

Source: Hufbauer (1966).

Table 7.3: Research and development attributes of various economies

	Researchers in R&D (per mn people), 2006[a]	Expenditures for R&D (% of GDP), 1996–2006[b]
Australia	4,224.33	1.69
United States	4,663.28	2.64
United Kingdom	4,193.33	1.77
Canada	4,260.42	1.91
France	3,431.31	2.17
Cuba	n.a.	0.49
Germany	3,396.20	2.41
Japan	5,568.35	3.10

Source: World Development Indicators (various years).

[a]Researchers in R&D refer to those professionals who engaged in the generation of new knowledge and products and the management of the products concerned.
[b]Expenditures on R&D refer to current and capital expenditures used up in the process of creating new knowledge.

will tend to be associated with countries that have an abundance of skilled labour and rapid information flows on consumer preference patterns and responses, which can be obtained by a firm close to the market. These characteristics suggest that innovation would therefore concentrate in the more richly endowed countries. As the production process becomes more standardized and the patents of innovating firms expire, other producers, some of whom may be located in other countries, will commence production of the commodity. If the production of the commodity still requires highly skilled labour and the good is still sufficiently costly so as to restrict its use to high-income economies, then what may transpire is that the original innovating firm may establish itself in other advanced nations where an abundant supply of skilled labour still exists. In the final analysis, what we would expect is that the number of goods exported from the original innovating country would gradually decrease (see figure 7.2, which is based on consumption and production in a typical developed economy). As time elapses and the production process becomes more standardized, other developed countries learn the relevant technology.

One possibility is that the dominant firm with the relevant blueprint may shift its production base to other developed countries that may possess the relevant factor endowments. In particular, as the technology required becomes more standardized in a manner consistent with greater labour employment, the production process is disseminated to more labour-abundant countries. Table 7.4 shows various characteristics of a product as it goes through the different phases of the product cycle (early, growth and mature).[2]

The product cycle hypothesis (PCH) does not have wide-ranging applicability. It provides an explanation of trade in a particular category of goods: manufactures, which require technical knowledge for production. A good example is information communication

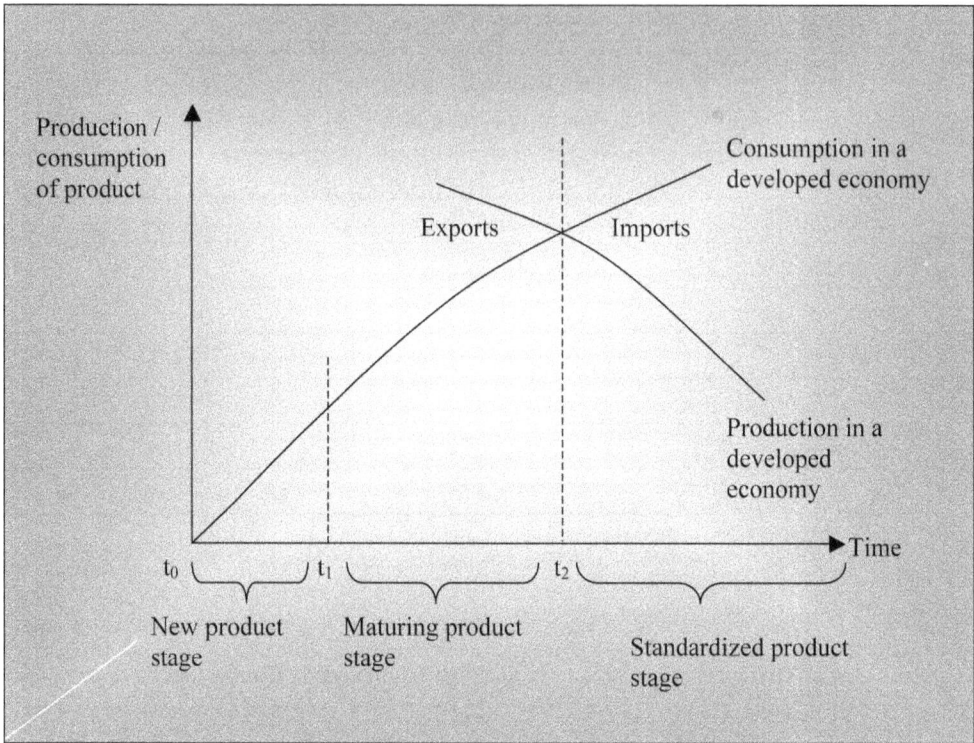

Figure 7.2: The trade pattern of a developed economy in the product cycle hypothesis

technology like colour television sets, which were first produced in the United States but later shifted to countries such as Japan, Taiwan and Korea. The PCH does not do well explaining other products like aircraft for which the United States still maintains a comparative advantage, even though it is now a relatively mature product. In fact, it is this inability of the model to provide an accurate gauge as to the timing of changes in the comparative advantage of an economy that represents its main deficiency.[3]

7.3 Increasing Returns, Imperfect Competition and International Trade

Increasing returns can be described as a situation where proportionate increases in the use of productive inputs result in greater than proportionate increases in output. For a firm, increasing returns to scale can either be internal or external. Internal economies of scale are a result of mass production within the firm, while external economies of scale occur on account of outside influences like location. Countries involved in international trade are able to expand production and achieve increasing returns to scale. Gains from international trade are obtained when a country specializes in the production of particular goods and trade these goods in the international market. In international trade, there is no definite method for determining the direction of specialization. In some cases, it is a simple historical accident. For example, an increase in demand for a particular commodity by an overseas customer signals to firms in the industry

Table 7.4: Product cycle phases

Characteristic	Early	Growth	Mature
Technology	Rapidly changing techniques; dependence on external economies	Mass production; methods gradually introduced; variations in techniques still frequent	Long runs and stable process; few innovations of importance
Capital	Low	High, due to high obsolescence rate	High, due to large quantity of specialized equipment
Industry structure	Entry is knowledge-determined; numerous firms	Growing number of firms; many casualties and mergers; growing integration	Market position and financial resources affect entry; number of firms declining
Critical human inputs	Scientific and engineering	Management	Unskilled and semiskilled labour
Demand structure	Sellers' market; performance and price of substitute goods determine buyers' expectations	Individual producers face growing price elasticity; competition reduces prices; product information spreads	Buyers' market; information easily available

Source: Johns (1985).

to increase production. As production increases, average costs eventually fall, and this induces further expansion.

It is possible that increasing returns may be internal to the firms within an industry. This usually occurs when investments are lumpy and cannot be easily broken down to facilitate different levels of production. In many cases, the cost of obtaining and installing a larger machine is lower per unit than the cost of a smaller machine. The consequence of this is that the per unit production costs of larger firms tend to be lower than that of smaller firms. This can eventually lead to market imperfection, as big firms crowd out small firms. The final outcome is a function of several factors including market size, the extent of product differentiation and the range of output for which the firm benefits from economies of scale.

Two of these factors, increasing returns to scale and imperfect competition, provide a basis for explaining intra-industry trade (IIT). An example of IIT involves the HC exporting and also importing refrigerators. In the presence of free trade, firms in both the HC and FC can expand their production. If we assume increasing returns to scale, then the HC or FC firm that expands first can corner the market in both countries, especially if they were producing identical products. Increasing returns to scale is illustrated in figure 7.3.

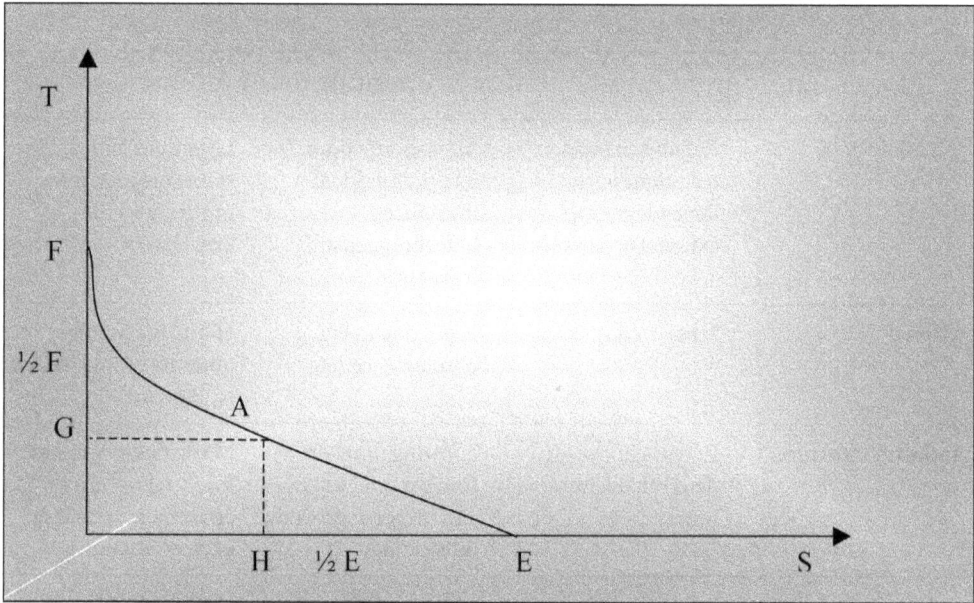

Figure 7.3: PPF of a country with increasing returns to scale industries

With increasing returns to scale, the production possibility frontier (PPF) takes the form illustrated in figure 7.4. Let us assume that both papaya and canned juices can be produced using the same proportion of capital and labour and both industries enjoy external economies of scale. In the diagram, points A and B represent the maximum amount of papaya and canned juices that can be produced, respectively, assuming in each case that all the economy's resources are deployed. If we were to commence production at A, for example, this would mean that all the resources are used to produce papaya. If we were to move from A to C, then we could produce E units of canned juices and D units of papaya. Let point C be defined as representing half of all the resources used to produce each commodity. Due to increasing returns to scale, the reduction in the employment of factors means that point D represents less than half of A. In the canned juices sector, the availability of resources in an environment characterized by increasing returns to scale can lead to an increase in output. However, this output level would be less than half of what it could have produced if it utilized all of the factors of production. Therefore, in order for the principle of increasing returns to scale to hold, the production possibility function must be drawn convex to the origin.

Where the PPF is tangential to the highest attainable community indifference curve or country indifference curve (CiC0) represents the autarkic equilibrium position.[4] This is represented by point M (this is also represented for convenience by point C). Since autarky is not a desirable level of production for the country, the country would be better off by specializing in the production of one good. In such a case, the gains from increasing returns to scale would be maximized. Additionally, the surplus production would be traded in the international market. Point N represents equilibrium in the international trade market. In this case, the gains from trade occur from specialization in industries where average cost falls, productivity rises and additional resources are utilized. Thus

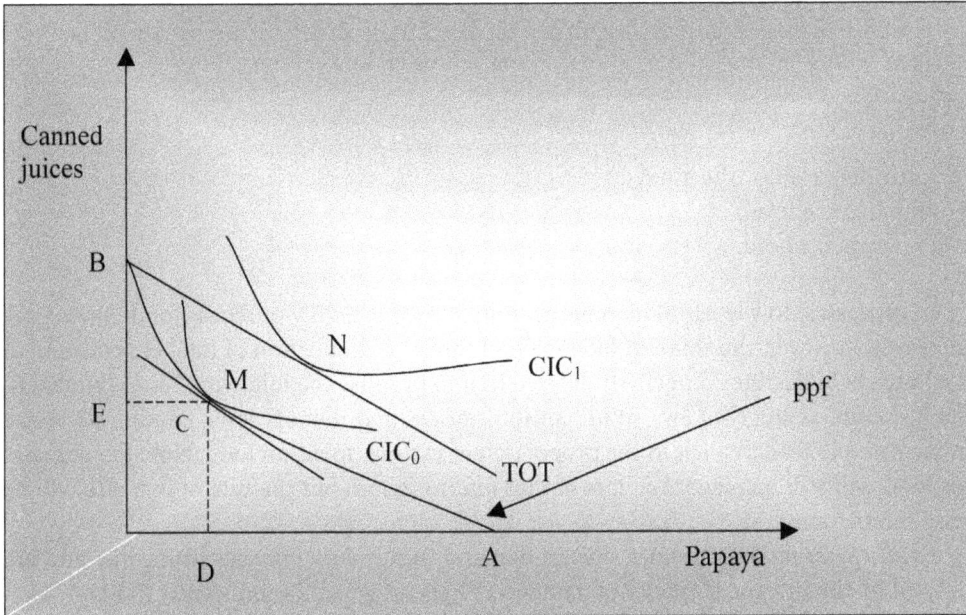

Figure 7.4: Increasing returns to scale and gains from trade

trade allows the country to expand production to achieve gains from increasing returns to scale, and so we have increasing returns to scale as a new basis for trade.

For countries that are similar in terms of factor endowments, there exist less incentive for inter-industry trade and a greater likelihood for intra-industry trade. Additionally, the welfare effects of free international trade can be explained by the theory of increasing returns and imperfect competition. The standard of living in both countries that engage in trade is improved. In some cases, trade can be harmful when free trade leads to a contraction in the production of goods that are subjected to increasing returns to scale. However, this situation is unlikely, and in most situations both countries gain from international trade.

7.4 Engel Effects

Changes in the real per capita incomes of economic agents influence the basket of goods and services they demand. In this section, two important theories associated with patterns of demand changes are discussed:

- Engel effects
- Linder's representative demand

Ernst Engel (1857), a German economist, pioneered the study of how a household's spending pattern changes as its income changes. Standard microeconomic theory teaches that the income elasticity of demand measures the responsiveness of the demand for a particular commodity (X) to change in the household's income.

$$YED_x = \frac{\%\ D_x}{\%\ Y\ of\ HH}$$

where

D_x = the demand for the good x,
Y = the income level,
HH = the household.

In general, at low levels of income, economic agents mainly purchase food. As income increases, however, the share of food expenditure as a proportion of total expenditure of the household declines. Engel's studies led him to propose the following "law" (known in the literature as Engel's Law): With constant prices and demographic conditions, a rise in income will lead to a fall in the proportion of income spent on food. Note the demand for food will still increase (i.e., it is not an inferior good, but the rate of increase will be less than income).

Engel effects refer to the net shift in demand induced by changes in income and are defined by the income elasticity of demand (YED) for good X minus unity ($YED_x - 1$).

In general,

$$YED_{CD} > 1$$

$$YED_F < 1$$

$$\Longrightarrow Engel\ Effect_{CD} > 0$$

$$\Longrightarrow Engel\ Effect_F < 0$$

where

CD = consumer durable,
F = food.

Out of all the "laws" that have been established by economists, this is one of the most rigorous. Engel effects can be observed when the focus is on the consumption patterns of households or entire nations over time. The law implies that as per capita income increases with economic growth, the demand for basic food staples increases but at a slower rate because of its low income elasticity of demand.

In a world of growing income, Engel's law suggests that those countries where production is concentrated on goods with high YED would benefit relative to those countries producing goods with low YED.

Engel's law also asserts that if there is an equal productivity growth in all industries, the resultant income growth will reduce the proportional demand for food, and this in turn will trigger a relative decline in food prices.

7.5 Linder's Representative Demand Hypothesis

Steffan Burenstan Linder (1961), a Swedish economist and politician, introduced the idea of a representative demand hypothesis. Linder's approach to how income affects demand and hence trade is cast in the following manner:

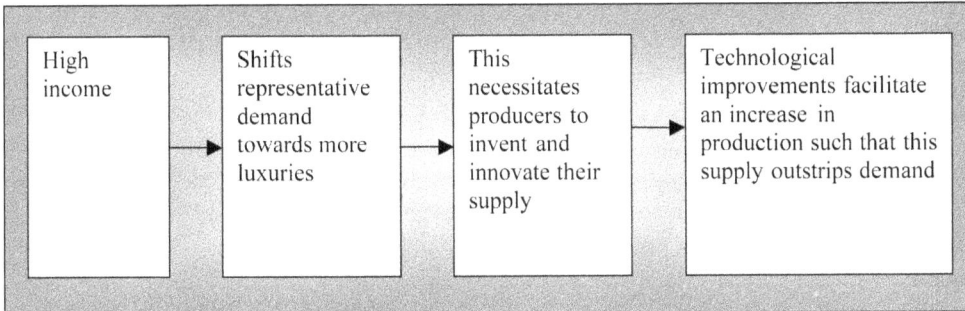

| High income | Shifts representative demand towards more luxuries | This necessitates producers to invent and innovate their supply | Technological improvements facilitate an increase in production such that this supply outstrips demand |

Figure 7.5: Linder's representative demand hypothesis

The implication of Linder's proposition is that we should expect to see countries exporting commodities they consume. Linder's hypothesis is not dependent on any single set of assumptions, but it would be facilitated if economies of scale or learning by doing existed in the manufacturing sector.

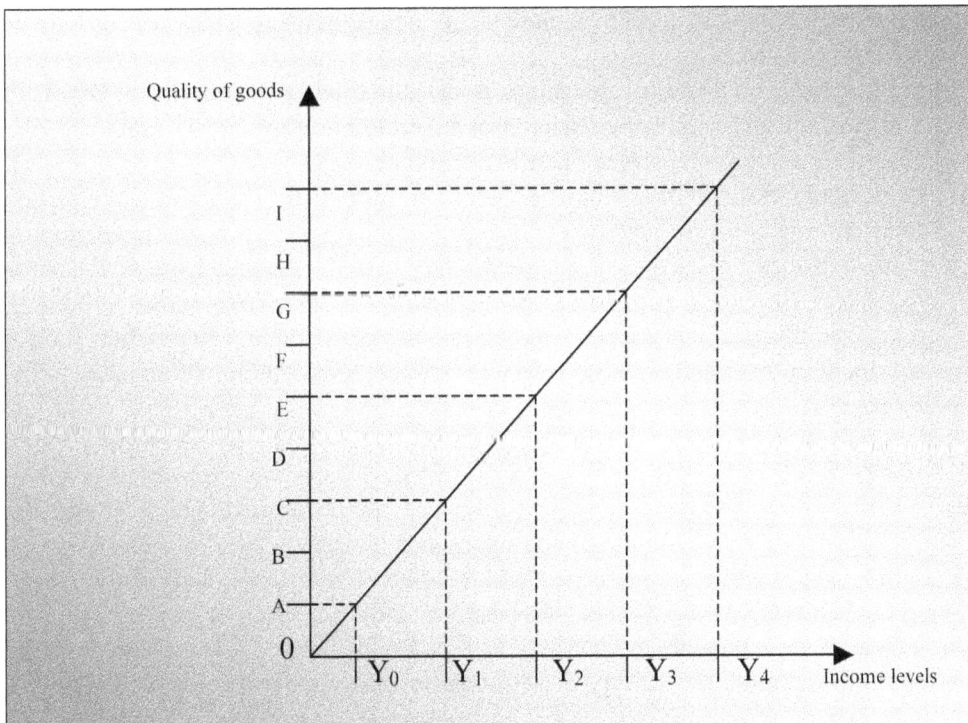

Figure 7.6: Overlapping demands in the Linder model

A to E = range of goods demanded and produced by country X,
C to G = range of goods demanded and produced by country Y,
E to I = range of goods demanded and produced by country Z,
Y_0 to Y_2 = country X's income range,
Y_1 to Y_3 = country Y's income range,
Y_2 to Y_4 = country Z's income range.

In figure 7.6, the vertical axis shows the quality of goods and the horizontal axis shows various income groups. Country X has a per capita income that allows it to cover a consumption pattern of goods A to E, while country Y has a per capita income ranging from Y_1 to Y_3, so that it will be interested in consuming goods in the quality range C to G. The wealthiest economy, Z, has a per capita income in the range Y_2 to Y_4 and attracts a quality of goods in the range E to I. With Linder's representative demand hypothesis, each country could produce the range of goods dictated by the income level per capita within its economy. As is immediately clear, goods of the quality C, D and E are demanded by both economies X and Y, so these goods would be produced by and traded between both economies. Country Z would trade good E with country X, but goods E, F and G with country Y.

Thus one can see that according to Linder's hypothesis there will be more intense trade between countries with similar per capita income than between countries with different per capita income.

Further points are relevant:

• Linder's hypothesis applies to trade in manufactured goods and therefore does not cover trade in raw materials (including agricultural output), which is explained by the H/O theorem.
• Linder's focus on manufactured goods revealed nothing paradoxical with Leontief's model, and it may simply be reflective of a consumption pattern by American consumers for capital-intensive manufacturing imports.
• Linder's model also forms a basis on which intra-industry trade can be explained. *Intra-industry trade* refers to two-way trade in similar goods. Simple explanations of comparative advantage theory exclude this type of trade pattern. However, if Linder's hypothesis that trade helps to satisfy the need for varieties of a similar product is true, then this can help explain why Americans, for example, buy products such as automobiles from Japan when American producers also bring automobiles to the market.

Linder's hypothesis has yet to be rigorously tested. However, its suggestion that countries export the various types of commodities that closely approximate those they are likely to be consuming seemingly fits the automobile market.

To provide a preliminary enquiry of Linder's hypothesis, we can look at the type of data provided in table 7.5. Observe that the high-income economies spend the greatest proportion of their income on services – that is, health care, education, and transport and communication. A similar type of importance is attributed to those service sectors in upper-middle-income countries. Note though the greater proportion of expenditure on food in all the other income categories as compared to high-income economies.

Table 7.5: Shares of various goods and services in household expenditures, selected countries, 1997

	Food	Clothing and footwear	Fuel and power	Health care	Education	Transport and communication	Other consumption
High-income economies							
Canada	9	5	4	11	9	11	51
France	12	4	3	21	8	12	40
Japan	11	5	2	17	8	9	47
United States	8	6	3	12	7	14	49
Upper-middle-income economies							
Botswana	25	4	1	7	22	21	19
Czech Republic	15	4	6	10	15	5	46
Mauritius	24	8	3	10	5	19	30
Turkey	23	7	4	5	9	7	44
Lower-middle-income economies							
Belize	28	10	10	5	10	11	34
Iran	23	7	7	13	11	11	23
Romania	24	7	7	6	15	4	39
Thailand	23	8	8	22	10	17	17
Low-income economies							
Kenya	38	8	8	5	22	10	16
Moldova	28	5	5	11	25	3	20
Pakistan	40	6	6	12	7	4	27
Zambia	47	8	8	3	12	10	19

Source: World Development Indicators (1999), 228–29.

Given these various expenditure outlays, one would expect that overlapping demand would exist between the high-income economies and the upper-middle-income economies in the service and "other consumption" sectors, while among the lower-middle-income and low-income economies there would be greater overlap in the area of food consumption.

7.6 Intra-Industry Trade

Intra-industry trade (IIT) involves the exchange of products from the same industry. In such a case, the same products are both imported and exported. Cars, foodstuff, beverages and computers are examples of products that fall under the category of intra-industry trade.

Vertical and Horizontal IIT

Before delving into the various reasons for IIT, a distinction must be made between vertical and horizontal IIT. Vertical intra-industry trade involves exchanges of varieties of goods that belong to different levels of quality, and as such, consumers can be assumed to rank alternatives according to product quality. Horizontal intra-industry trade involves exchanges of goods that are horizontally differentiated – in other words, trade that involves exchanges of alternative varieties of a particular commodity that differ in their actual or perceived characteristics. With horizontal differentiation, preferences for alternative varieties of a given quality differ between consumers, and no unique ranking would be agreed by all consumers. For example, all consumers may rank Toyotas as qualitatively superior to Mitsubishis, but not everyone would prefer black Toyotas over red ones. Horizontal IIT is determined by industry-based factors such as scale economies and product differentiation. With horizontal IIT, the general presumption is that higher prices reflect higher quality. On the other hand, levels of vertical IIT are determined by country-based factors like differences in relative factor endowments.

Explanations of IIT

Product Differentiation: Product differentiation is a situation in which firms across national borders produce similar goods that are distinguished from one another by brand or by other subtle differences. Product differentiation plays a key role in explaining trade between countries with similar income but diverse preference structures. Where there is similarity in demand between countries and consumers have a desire for varied products and services, product differentiation generates intra-industry trade between the relevant economies (Venables 1987). Product differentiation may occur in three forms: horizontal, vertical and technological. Horizontal differentiation occurs when commodities have different attributes, vertical differentiation occurs on account of a difference in quality and technological differentiation occurs because of a technological breakthrough (Greenaway 1984).

Economies of Scale: Gray (1973) showed that one of the factors influencing the occurrence of IIT was that of product differentiation coupled with increasing returns to scale over some segment of a firm's supply curve.[5] He highlighted that economies of scale can be experienced when varieties of a given product are produced. This specialization may also result in a reduction in the per unit cost of production. A firm may, however, choose to specialize in a particular variety. Economies of scale arise from three principal sources: the size of firms, the size of plants and the length of the production runs. If any of these are large enough, then a firm may produce a selected variety of a product rather than all the possible varieties (Grubel and Lloyd 1975, 6).

Economic Development: Developed economies generally have enough capacity and technological potential to create new and differentiated products. A high level of development means a high level of personal income and a greater degree of variety in demand. If two economies are identical in many regards, including income and factor endowments, then their IIT will be very high. As the economic development gap between two trading partners widens, there is a fall in the level of IIT.

Technological: Firm-specific conditions, such as technological expertise, are an important source of comparative advantage in the international trading arena. Research- or technology-intensive industries can trade in differentiated goods. IIT therefore arises in technologically sophisticated manufactured goods that require substantial amounts of research and development expenditure.

Foreign Direct Investment (FDI): Greenaway and Milner (1994) have argued that if a situation exists in which there is a demand for different varieties of the same product and the production of these products are subject to economies of scale, there may be the tendency for a greater amount of FDI to be associated with a greater amount of IIT. At the same time, it should be noted that if the purpose of FDI flows are to fragment the production process into geographic blocs according to different stages, then the tendency will be for a greater amount of inter-industry trade as compared to intra-industry trade.

Location: Intra-industry trade in homogeneous products can be explained by transportation costs and seasonal trade. Figure 7.7 illustrates the case associated with a difference in transportation costs. These homogenous goods include items that are heavy or expensive to transport. The two firms in figure 7.7, F^A in country A and F^B in country B, are spatially located. The two consumers, C^A and C^B, purchase the products produced by firms F^A and F^B. In order to minimize cost, consumer C^A deals with firm F^B and consumer C^B deals with F^A. This arrangement occurs because of the location of firms and consumers. The result is that economy A and economy B both import

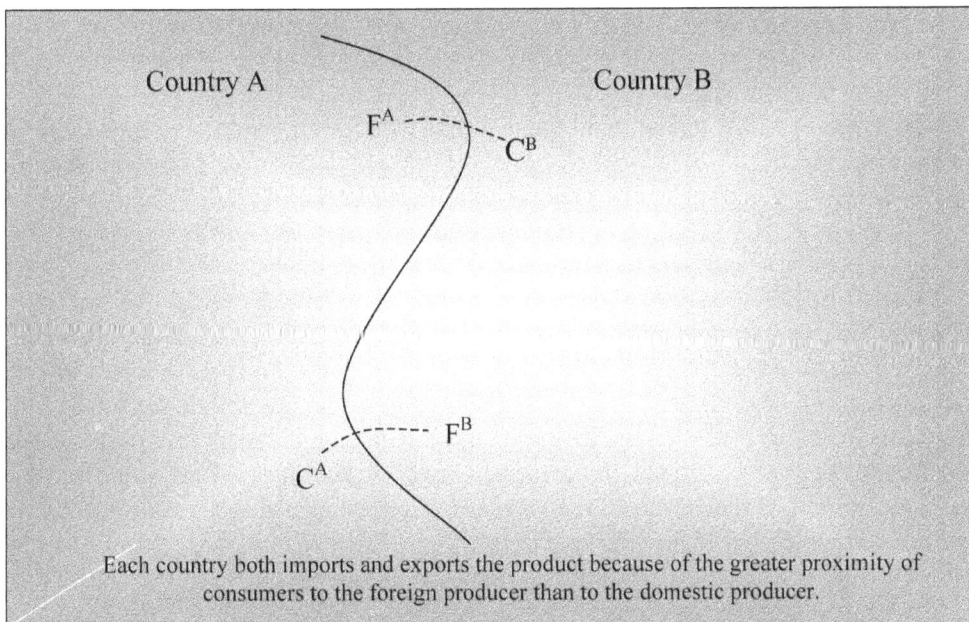

Each country both imports and exports the product because of the greater proximity of consumers to the foreign producer than to the domestic producer.

Figure 7.7: The influence of location can cause intra-industry trade in homogeneous goods

and export the same good. In a like manner, seasonal considerations can also cause intra-industry trade.

Regional Integration: The literature does not carry any systematic concrete body of information regarding the link between economic integration and the extent of IIT. It would be expected that with the formation of an economic integration arrangement, especially a customs union, there would be a decrease in the amount of intra-customs-union barriers, and this in turn may prompt an increase in the volume of intra-union trade. This intra-union trade can adopt either an intra- or inter-industry format. The exact nature of the resultant trade hinges on the type of market structures that existed in the various economies making up the integration arrangement prior to its formation (Drabek and Greenaway 1984).

For an economic integration arrangement to stimulate a greater degree of IIT than would occur with multilateral trade liberalization, a number of factors have to be present. One key factor is that there must be a greater degree of trade overlap. Specifically, if before the integration arrangement the economies were characterized by both similar production and consumption patterns, then with the formation of a customs union there would be a greater likelihood of intra-industry trade as compared to inter-industry trade. As Drabek and Greenaway (1984, 448) note, "Insofar as countries with similar factor endowments and similar levels of income per capita form customs unions, this will be an important basis for the formation of intra-industry exchange".

It is critical for the production structures in existence between trading partners to be competitive rather than complementary for IIT. If production structures were complementary, then this would tend to promote H/O-type trade. If production structures are competitive, then this will trigger the type of changes necessary to motivate the allocation of scarce factors of production to be used by least-cost producers.

Another requirement for economic integration to prompt a greater amount of IIT is that consumers within the customs union arrangement have a high propensity to import from intra-bloc member states as compared to extra-bloc trading partners. If economic agents have a high propensity to purchase extra-bloc, then economic integration will not be sufficient to sprout high amounts of IIT.

The widening of the markets and the ability to plan longer production runs result in decreasing costs for the manufacturing sector. If there is a taste overlap among member states, then with decreasing costs there can be an expansion in IIT.

Staffan Linder (1961) has identified that as the per capita income in an economy increases, there is also an increase in its demand for variety.

Country Specific Factors: These also influence the extent of the IIT that a country engages. Two types of country specific factors are (a) natural trade barriers and (b) artificial trade barriers. Natural trade barriers like high transportation costs shape an inverse relationship with IIT; higher degrees of IIT tend to be associated with lower transportation costs. Artificial trade barriers tend to trigger a reduction in the total amount of trade in the range of products traded. In the presence of artificial trade barriers, some tradable goods may become non-tradable. In this regard, it may be argued that the lower the level of barriers to trade, the higher the level of IIT.

Measurement of IIT

The whole issue of IIT was posted in the literature by Verdoon (1960), who proposed that it occurred between countries that possessed similar factor endowments. In two subsequent pieces of research, Kojima (1964) and Balassa (1965) provided further discussions on IIT, though it was not a principal focus of their analysis. The IIT indices proposed by Grubel and Lloyd (1975) prompted a more elaborate discussion on IIT.

Many indices have been put forward by various scholars to provide a quantification of IIT. These indices were initially developed to calculate static intra-industry trade and have evolved to capture dynamic or marginal intra-industry trade. The rest of this section outlines various measures of static IIT.

Balassa Index

The first person to initiate a rigorous formulation to quantify intra-industry trade was Balassa (1966). Balassa proposed a measure of the extent to which the absolute amount (by value) of the exports of a commodity (X_i) is offset by imports (M_j) at a given level of aggregation. The Balassa indices can be represented as

$$\beta_i = \frac{|X_i - M_i|}{(X_i + M_i)} \tag{1}$$

$$\beta = \frac{1}{n} \sum_{i=1}^{n} C_i \tag{2}$$

These in turn can be generalized to give $\beta = \sum_{j=1}^{n} W_j \beta_j$

where

X_i = exports of commodity i,
M_i = imports of commodity i,
W_j = industry j's share of total trade.

Summing across industries and taking the arithmetic mean leads to a measure (C) of the degree of a country's inter-industry specialization.[6] Observe that if exports and imports have the same value, then this index will carry a score of zero. According to Balassa, this signifies a low degree of inter-industry trade and a high degree of intra-industry trade. On the other hand, observe that if X_i and M_i are very different, then the index tends towards unity. This type of index has very specific weighting characteristics. First, since net trade is expressed as a proportion of gross trade in a particular commodity grouping (i), the index can take on a specific value for markedly different absolute values of imports and exports. For example, $C_i = 0$ if $M_i = X_i = \$100$ or $\$100$ million.

Note also that net trade is measured relative to gross trade and not domestic production and sales. A high level of industry trade, therefore, as indicated by this measure, does not necessarily involve a high level of specialization. From a statistical perspective, C_i is a weighted average of any sub-group only if the signs on the trade imbalances at the sub-group level are all the same (and therefore the same as that at the more aggregate level). But if there are opposite signs on sub-group trade balances, this weighting effect is lost.

Grubel-Lloyd (G/L) Index

The Grubel-Lloyd (1975) index is by far the most widely used measure of intra-industry trade. At the time it was introduced, it represented the most rigorous attempt to quantify intra-industry trade and even until today is still widely deployed by many researchers to measure IIT.

On a multilateral basis, the G/L index measures the extent of the absolute amount of commodity exports in a particular industry (j) or commodity grouping that is offset by imports in the same grouping, and it expresses this intra-industry trade as a proportion of the total trade in this commodity. For commodity i, the G/L index is measured by

$$G/L = 1 - \frac{|X_i - M_i|}{(X_i + M_i)} = 1 - \beta_j \quad (3)$$

where GL is the value of the IIT, and X_i and M_i are the values of exports and imports of industry i, or a given country for a given period. Theoretically, the range of this index resides between 0 and 1; the closer the value to unity, the higher the rate of IIT in that industry.

Brülhart (2002) identifies the following issues with the G/L measure of IIT: categorical aggregation, trade imbalance and scale invariance.

Categorical Aggregation: IIT is described by Grubel and Lloyd (1975, 86) as "trade in differential products which are close substitutes". It is generally accepted that substitutability is in reference to production rather than with consumption industries.[7] In this format, the G/L index carries problems associated with categorical/sub-aggregation issues. These issues adopt two principal forms that bias the index towards unity: (a) the grouping together of commodities that don't fall into the same classification and (b) trade imbalance. To explain the problems associated with the wrongful grouping of commodities, consider the data in table 7.6.

Table 7.6 shows aggregated data at the Standard International Trade Classification (SITC) three-digit level with two sub-groups at the five-digit level. It is understood that statistical product classifications are hardly likely to be perfect and are driven by the effort to group together commodities that require similar factor inputs. The most appropriate level of statistical aggregation is therefore a bit ambiguous, and most studies tend to use

Table 7.6: Simple aggregation bias in the G/L index

Category	X_i	M_i	$[X_i - M_i]$	$(X_i + M_i)$	G/L index
Three digit	140	160	20	300	0.93
Sub-group five digit	0	160	160	160	0.00
Sub-group five digit	140	0	104	140	0.00

three-digit data, with the principal purpose typically being speed. When the G/L index is calculated at the three-digit level, the G/L scores a value of 0.93, indicating high IIT. But when it is calculated at the five-digit level, we get no IIT (even if we take the average of the two five-digit sub-group levels).

Trade Imbalance: The aggregation bias in table 7.6 occurs because of the trade-imbalance bias. In this particular example, observe that at the five-digit level, $(X_i + M_i) - (X_i - M_i) = 0$; gross trade and net trade carry the same values. To further explore this point, let us assume that the industry, i, is characterized by only two commodities, i_1 and i_2. Then we can formulate

$$|X_i - M_i| / (X_i + M_i) = |(X_{1i} - M_{1i}) + (X_{2i} - M_{2i})| / (X_{1i} + X_{2i} + M_{1i} + M_{2i})$$

If the particular economy we are considering was a net exporter or net importer in both sub-groups, then the weighting effect is lost and the G/L index will have a different value. To see this clearer, consider table 7.7.

In the upper part of table 7.7, the economy is a net importer of both commodities, while in the lower part, the economy is a net importer in one commodity and a net exporter in the other. Given that the G/L index is not considerate of the direction of trade, the G/L scores are the same at the sub-group level. But when the groups are aggregated to the three-digit level, the G/L in the lower part of table 7.7 (which includes the one net-exporter case) is higher than the G/L in the net-importer case. A corrected version of this expression, which facilitates aggregation of the G/L index across industries by deploying a weighted average, can be expressed:

$$G/L_j = 1 - \sum_{i=1}^{n} |X_i - M_i| / \sum_{i=1}^{n} X_j + M_j$$

In general, if an economy is a net surplus exporter/importer in both goods, the G/L = G/L_j^i. Brülhart (2002, 6) noted that "given the difficulty in estimating equilibrium trade imbalances, the professional consensus has been to work with unadjusted G/L indices".

Table 7.7: Trade imbalance bias in the G/L index

Category	X_i	M_i	$|X_i - M_i|$	$(X_i + M_i)$	G|L Index
Three digit	180	310	130	490	0.735
Sub-group five digit	80	160	80	240	0.667
Sub-group five digit	100	150	50	250	0.800
Three digit	230	260	30	490	0.939
Sub-group five digit	80	160	80	240	0.667
Sub-group five digit	150	100	50	250	0.800

Scale Invariance: The G/L index for industry i is not connected to the size of imports and exports, the size of the industry nor the level of production and consumption in the industry.

7.7 Marginal Intra-Industry Trade

The G/L index has been criticized as a static measure that is unable to reflect the dynamic changes in the IIT of a particular country. Some researchers – for example, Caves (1981) and Hamilton and Kneist (1991) – have identified that if there is a proportional increase in exports and imports within an industry motivated by trade liberalization or any other cause, this will raise the quantity of total trade, although the proportion of IIT as measured by the G/L index would not change. When focusing on structural adjustment, however, what is important is the structure of change in the pattern of trade.

An increase in the value of the G/L index indicates an increase in intra-industry trade, while a fall indicates a tendency towards inter-industry trade. The index, however, is limited by virtue of the fact that it cannot be effectively used to analyse trade-induced economic adjustments. For example, an increase in the G/L index in a given year can be the result of either a falloff in net exports or the balancing of a sector-specific deficit.

This is not to say that G/L indices in a time series format are not useful. The point is that if the intention is to focus on the structure of trade at differing points in time, then the G/L index is certainly adequate. The problem with using the G/L index emerges when the objective of the analysis is to evaluate the dynamic nature of trade. In this case, it is the changes in the structure of trade that is the object of analysis; if a dynamic type of analysis is to be undertaken, then using G/L indices as a basis for evaluation is insufficient. A comparison of G/L indices at differing points in time is really an exercise in comparative statistics rather than an evaluation of the dynamic structure of trade.

Because of the various concerns associated with the G/L index in measuring IIT over time, Hamilton and Kneist (1991) suggested the calculation of a MIIT index. The index proposed by Hamilton and Kneist (1991) adopts the following format:

$$\text{If } M_t - M_{t-n} > X_t - X_{t-n} > 0, \text{ then MIIT} = (X_t - X_{t-n}) / M_t - M_{t-n}$$

$$\text{Or if } X_t - X_{t-n} > M_t - M_{t-n} > 0, \text{ then MIIT} = (M_t - M_{t-n}) / (X_t - X_{t-n})$$

$$\text{If } X_t < X_{t-n} \text{ or } M_t < M_{t-n}, \text{ then MIIT is undefined.}$$

where

X_t = the exports of a particular country in time period t,
M_t = the imports of a particular country in time period t.

In this formulation, n is the number of years between the two successive periods of measurement. However, Greenaway, Hine, Milner and Elliot (1994) found this index to have deficiencies of its own. Using data for the United Kingdom, these researchers found as much as 32 per cent of UK trade at the five-digit SITC level was classified as undefined by this index. Greenaway et. al also identified that this index, expressed in its current nominal format, can create an upward bias.

Although Greenaway et al. proposed their own MIIT index (hereafter the GHME index), it was subsequently illustrated by Brülhart (1994) that this index was characterized by the same trade imbalance issue attached to the G/L index.[8] To measure MIIT, Brülhart (1994) proposed the following index (referred to as the A index):

$$MIIT_i = A_i = 1 - |(X_{i(t)} - X_{i(t-n)}) - (M_{i(t)} - M_{i(t-n)})| / (|X_{i(t)} - X_{i(t-n)}| + |M_{i(t)} - M_{i(t-n)}|)$$
$$= 1 - (|\Delta X - \Delta M| / |\Delta X| + |\Delta M|)$$

where

$X_{i(t)}$ and $M_{i(t)}$ = the flow of export and import, respectively, in year t for industry i,
$X_{i(t-n)}$ and $M_{i(t-n)}$ = the corresponding figures for year t-n.

Brülhart's A index carries a score between zero and one. Low values of the index reflect that trade in a particular sector changes disproportionately, indicating in part that the change in trade is more of an inter-industry trade type. A relatively high value indicates that marginal trade is more of the intra-industry type.

This A index can be summed by using the representation

$$A_{tot} = \sum_{i=1}^{k} w_i A_i$$

$$\text{Where } W_i = (|\Delta X_i| + |\Delta M_i|) \setminus \sum_{i=1}^{k} (|\Delta X|_i + |\Delta M|_i)$$

In this expression, A_{tot} is the weighted average either over all sub-industries or over all industries. The strength of this A index is that it indicates changes in the structure of the change in trade flows (exports and imports). Though similar to the Hamilton and Kniest index, the A index is defined in all cases and carries all of the statistical attributes of the G/L index (Brülhart 1994, 605).[9]

Table 7.8 shows the trend in the G/L indices between the Trinidad and Tobago economy and the listed CARICOM states. Note the following:

1. For each of the bilateral trade partners, the extent of IIT is small.
2. In each case, the extent of IIT is declining, indicating that over time intra-CARICOM trade involving the Trinidad and Tobago economy is becoming increasingly inter-industry. This is not surprising, given the complementary nature of the production structures.

Marginal Intra-Industry Trade (MIIT) in the CARICOM

The marginal intra-industry trade (MIIT) index also reveals that IIT is very low between Trinidad and Tobago and its bilateral regional trading partners. More so, this bilateral MIIT has been declining persistently in the listed time period.

Table 7.9 shows the MIIT of Trinidad and Tobago with several CARICOM economies. With each of the bilateral integration partners, the level of MIIT is low and effectively indicates that no significant amount of adjustment would follow such trade changes.

Table 7.8: G/L indices between Trinidad and Tobago and the listed bilateral trade partners

	Barbados	Guyana	St Lucia	Jamaica
1991	0.30	0.05	0.09	**0.26**
1992	0.31	0.08	0.06	**0.26**
1993	0.25	0.08	0.05	**0.22**
1994	0.24	0.10	0.07	**0.18**
1995	0.20	0.11	0.10	**0.17**
1996	0.24	0.08	0.08	**0.18**
1997	0.20	0.07	0.08	**0.14**
1998	0.17	0.06	0.08	**0.10**
1999	0.12	0.07	0.07	**0.10**
2000	0.07	0.05	0.03	**0.09**
2001	0.06	0.05	0.05	**0.06**
2002	0.07	0.06	0.08	**0.07**
2003	0.06	0.03	0.08	**0.06**
2004	0.04	0.03	0.07	**0.06**
2005	0.02	0.02	0.06	**0.03**
2006	0.02	0.01	0.04	**0.03**
2007	0.04	0.02	0.06	**0.05**
2008	0.02	0.03	0.04	**0.03**
2009	0.04	0.04	0.07	**0.04**
Change	−0.26	−0.01	−0.03	**−0.21**

Source: Computed from COMTRADE database.

Altogether, the results from the static G/L and dynamic Brülhart indices on IIT are not surprising. The small economies of the CARICOM sphere don't have a sufficiently high level of per capita GDP, and their income structures are complementary, especially between Trinidad and Tobago and the other member states, so that more inter-industry and less intra-industry trade is practised.

7.8 Conclusion

This chapter emphasized the alternative trade theories to the H/O model. These trade theories include the imitation gap model, product cycle hypothesis, and Linder's representative demand hypothesis. The chapter also reviewed the theory of intra-industry trade and provided an explanation and discussions of how it is calculated.

Table 7.9: MIIT between Trinidad and Tobago and the listed bilateral trading partners

	Barbados	Guyana	UK	USA	St Lucia	Jamaica	China
1992	0.075401	0.079384	0.0279	0.034607	0.054133	0.188289	**0.0060**
1993	0.092533	0.078835	0.028959	0.038736	0.035676	0.022587	**0.0006**
1994	0.132436	0.044053	0.052344	0.049721	0.04561	0.065575	**0.0008**
1995	0.059034	0.079221	0.026349	0.089939	0.049251	0.025184	**0.0000**
1996	0.146505	0.039371	0.024385	0.042583	0.005618	0.073389	**0.0013**
1997	0.079446	0.028348	0.059091	0.064312	0.043061	0.044285	**0.0035**
1998	0.057212	0.014844	0.052872	0.078997	0.011276	0.082657	**0.0022**
1999	0.034619	0.0246	0.081112	0.083312	0.016778	0.036794	**0.0009**
2000	0.035855	0.028799	0.071389	0.027158	0.006767	0.029117	**0.0057**
2001	0.032911	0.033001	0.114592	0.179746	0.03805	0.050885	**0.0144**
2002	0.016616	0.043299	0.08487	0.096531	0.007262	0.048437	**0.0150**
2003	0.024185	0.010612	0.086719	0.021939	0.040246	0.011702	**0.0136**
2004	0.030358	0.015765	0.020425	0.017036	0.062101	0.011319	**0.0074**
2005	0.00622	0.007576	0.054553	0.02399	0.025619	0.003872	**0.0178**
2006	0.010658	0.010428	0.048249	0.022446	0.021397	0.015765	**0.0152**
2007	0.006841	0.00972	0.04592	0.03768	0.028716	0.005575	**0.0138**
2008	0.00589	0.022191	0.040421	0.019721	0.008399	0.004499	**0.0131**
2009	0.008909	0.012432	0.107594	0.035384	0.004901	0.004037	**0.0145**

Source: Computed from COMTRADE database.

Summary of Key Points

- The imitation gap theory is primarily based on the assumption that technological change is a continuous process and that there are time lags between the adoption of technology in one country and its utilization in another (this is called the imitation lag).
- According to the product life cycle hypothesis, a product goes through different phases of the product cycle (early, growth and mature).
- Engel's law asserts that if there is equal productivity growth in all industries, the resultant income growth will reduce the proportional demand for food, and this in turn will trigger a relative decline in food prices.
- According to Linder's hypothesis, there will be more intense trade between countries with similar per capita income than between countries with different per capita income.
- Intra-industry trade (IIT) involves the exchange of products from the same industry.

- Vertical intra-industry trade involves exchanges of varieties of goods that belong to different levels of quality, and as such, consumers can be assumed to rank alternatives according to product quality. Horizontal intra-industry trade involves exchange of alternative varieties of a particular commodity that differ in their actual or perceived characteristics.
- The Grubel-Lloyd index has been criticized as a static measure that is unable to reflect the dynamic changes in the IIT of a particular country. Thus Brülhart pioneered the marginal IIT index.

Multiple Choice

1. The import and export of similar goods is known as
   a) intra-industry trade
   b) the life cycle hypothesis
   c) trade dynamics
   d) an integration arrangement

2. Linder's hypothesis of overlapping demand illustrates which of the following:
   a) the product life cycle hypothesis
   b) the H/O model
   c) trade due to differences in tastes among countries with similar income levels
   d) the imitation gap theory

3. Which of the statements regarding the H/O theorem is true?
   a) The H/O model provides a thorough explanation of why developing countries trade.
   b) The H/O model explains intra-industry trade.
   c) The H/O model is premised on the Ricardian theory of comparative advantage.
   d) none of the above

4. An industry characterized by increasing returns is facilitative of
   a) perfect competition
   b) lower levels of exports
   c) comparative advantage
   d) a reduction in the average cost of production as the size of the industry increases

5. The Grubel-Lloyd index is characterized by a theoretical range of
   a) 0 to 1
   b) 1 to ∞
   c) $-\infty$ to ∞
   d) 0 to ∞

Short Essay

1. Discuss the various indices used to measure intra-industry trade.
2. Illustrate the product life cycle hypothesis and evaluate how it affects trade.
3. Illustrate the imitation gap theory and evaluate how it affects trade.

Key Trade Terms

- Intra-industry trade
- Imitation gap theory
- Product cycle hypothesis
- Increasing returns to scale
- Imperfect competition
- Engel effects
- Linder's representative demand hypothesis
- Vertical intra-industry trade
- Horizontal intra-industry trade
- Product differentiation
- Economies of scale
- Economic development
- Homogeneous good
- Regional integration
- Natural trade barriers
- Artificial trade barriers
- Balassa index
- Grubel-Lloyd index
- Categorical aggregation
- Trade imbalance
- Marginal intra-industry trade
- Brülhart index

8.

Economic Growth and International Trade

Learning Objectives

a. Illustrate the production and consumption effects of economic growth.
b. Explore the effects of changes in technology on the production possibility frontier (PPF).
c. Define the Dutch Disease.
d. Explain the immiserizing growth theorem.
e. Define the Rybczynski theorem.

8.0 Introduction

Increases in real income affect both consumers and producers alike. Producers respond to changing demand signals by changing the mode of production or the very nature of the commodity supplied. Consumers in turn, as was noted with Engel's law, spend proportionately larger amounts of money on non-food commodities as their income level increases. The various responses of producers and consumers have implications for the amount of trade a country engages.

This chapter discusses several aspects of the impact of economic growth on international trade.

8.1 The Pre-growth Scenario

Figure 8.1 illustrates the production and consumption position of the home country (HC) before the inception of economic growth. At this stage, the HC is engaging AC units of exports and BC units of imports. The HC produces at point A and consumes at point B.

8.2 The Production Effects of Growth

The production permutations available to a country that has experienced consistent growth are such that the growth can be protrade biased, ultra-protrade biased, antitrade biased, ultra-antitrade biased or trade neutral. These permutations are illustrated in figure 8.2.

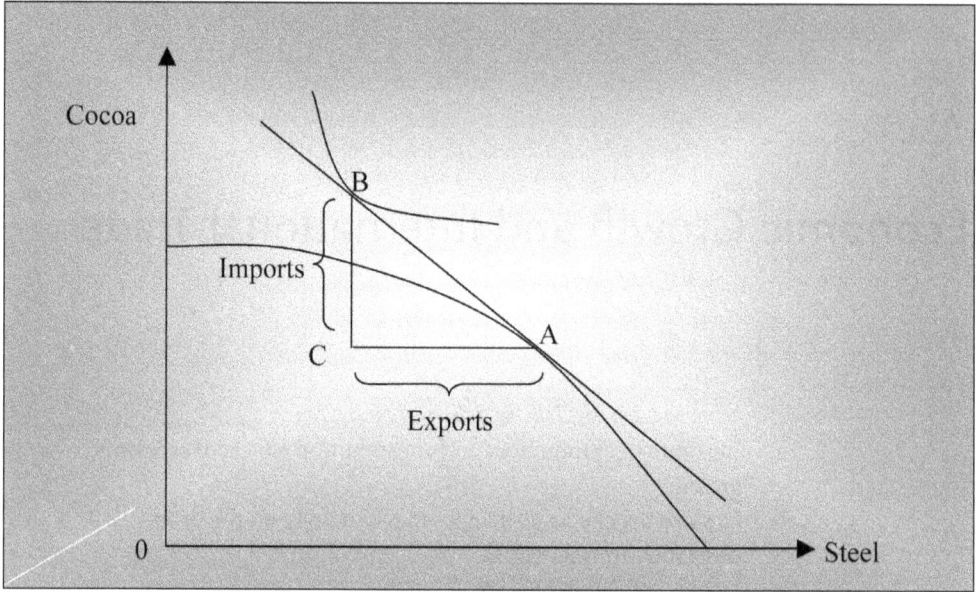

Figure 8.1: Imports and exports in the HC prior to economic growth

For simplicity, let us assume that the economy uses its endowment of factors of production to produce two goods: a petroleum good (P) and a non-petroleum good (NP).

More specifically, let A_0B_0 represent the initial production function, and let growth push this production function to A_1B_1. We may define the five production permutations economic growth facilitates in terms of an angle such as θ_i. At point P, we insert mini axes in order to identify the potential effects growth has on the structure of production in an economy. If the economy produces the same proportion of non-petroleum and

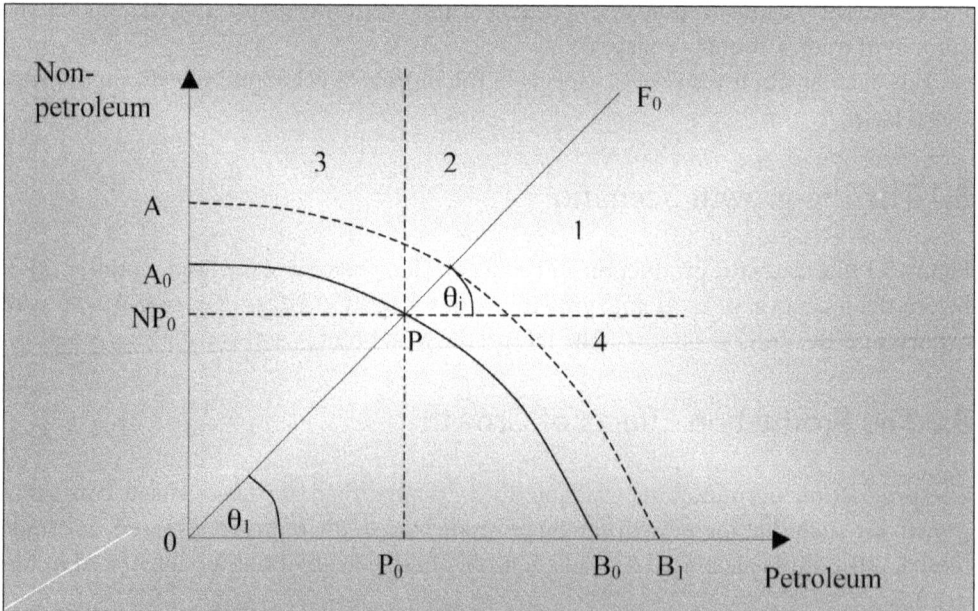

Figure 8.2: The production effects of economic growth

petroleum goods with economic growth, then θ_i, the angle between the relative amount of petroleum and non-petroleum goods produced, is the same as θ_1. It follows:

$$0 < \theta_i < \theta_1: \text{pro-trade-biased production – Zone 1}$$

$$\theta_1 < \theta_i < 90: \text{anti-trade-biased production – Zone 2}$$

$$90 < \theta_i < 270: \text{ultra-anti-trade-biased production – Zone 3}[1]$$

$$270 < \theta_i < 360: \text{ultra-pro-trade-biased production – Zone 4.}[2]$$

By way of distribution, figure 8.3 shows the trends in the output of petroleum and non-petroleum sectors of the Trinidad and Tobago economy in the period 1990–2003. In this time period, petroleum output increased by 48.9 per cent from TT\$4,376.1 million in 1990 to TT\$6,516.2 million in 2003. In the same interval of time, the value added in the non-petroleum sector increased from TT\$11,578.8 million to TT\$19,424.7 million, an increase of 65.2 per cent. The less-than-proportional increase in the production of petroleum goods (treated here as the exportable good) as compared to the non-petroleum output (the non-exportable good) is reflected in the graph, with the ratio of petroleum value added to non-petroleum value added in output decreasing from 34.7 to 33.5 per cent between 1990 and 2003.

The production of the exportable petroleum good increased but less than proportional to the non-petroleum good; consequently, the production impact of economic growth may be classified as antitrade. This is indicated in figure 8.4 where $\theta_i > \theta_1$. θ_1 is 70.8° and θ_i is 72.5°.

The overall production effect of economic growth appears as antitrade biased. This reads counterintuitive to the predictions of standard trade theory (the Heckscher-Ohlin theory). Indeed, a closer investigation of this period reflects that while the general trend from 1990 to 2003 has been more in favour of the production of the non-petroleum good, as time progressed it became clearer that the growth was originating more from the comparative advantage in the petroleum sector (see table 8.1). Note that after 1994 the growth performance was pro-trade biased.

A similar type of decomposition can be made concerning the effects of growth on consumption. Again, we shall commence with an illustrative diagram. In figure 8.5, let the initial point of consumption be C. With growth, the country has a similar array of

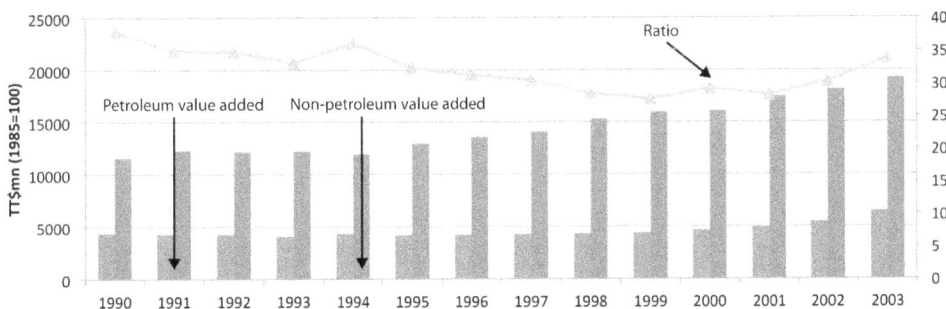

Figure 8.3: Relationship between petroleum and non-petroleum production, 1990–2003

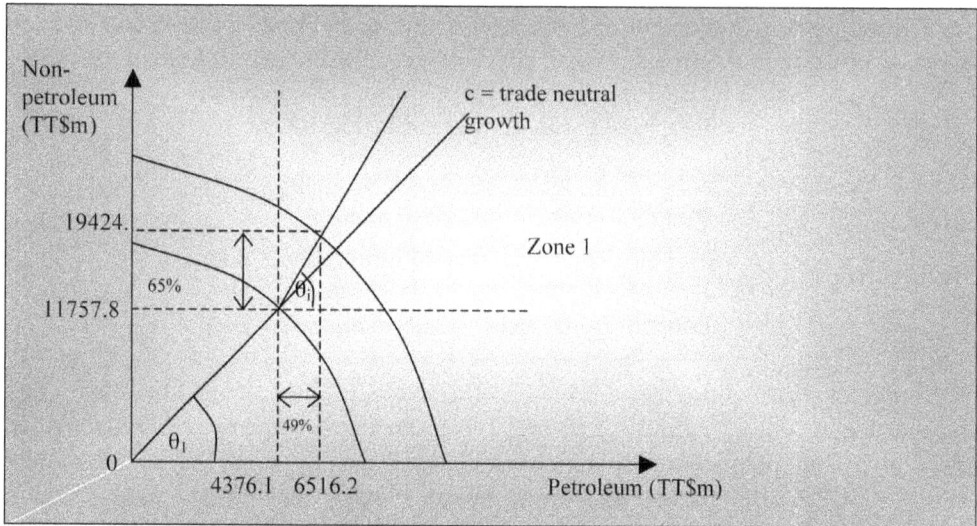

Figure 8.4: Production effects of growth on trade

Table 8.1: Growth of petroleum and non-petroleum value added (at constant prices) in total value added for the identified time periods

	Petroleum	Non-petroleum	Difference
1990–2003	48.90	65.21	−16.30
1991–2003	47.90	59.72	−11.82
1992–2003	54.10	60.99	−6.89
1993–2003	65.50	60.27	5.24
1994–2003	52.00	57.38	−5.38
1995–2003	51.43	49.60	1.83
1996–2003	48.53	43.22	5.31
1997–2003	48.42	38.10	10.32
1998–2003	42.14	26.91	15.23
1999–2003	27.45	24.12	3.34
2000–2003	21.12	17.05	4.07
2001–2003	20.39	13.09	7.31
2002–2003	9.46	5.86	3.60

Source: Central Bank of Trinidad and Tobago, own derivations.

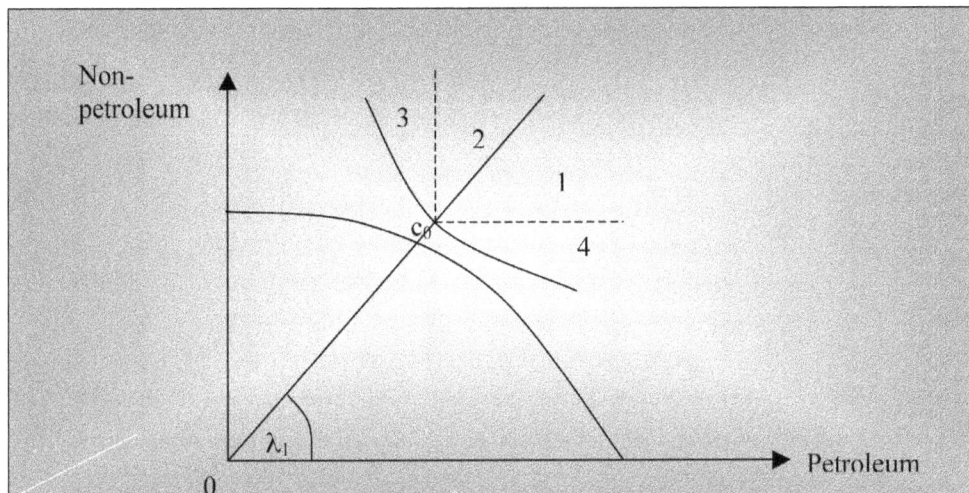

Figure 8.5: Consumption effects of growth

consumption permutations available to it. Specifically, the country can consume the same proportion of tradables and non-tradables as occurred prior to the growth experience, or it can consume in either of the zones indicated.

Observe that in 1990 the Trinidad and Tobago economy produced TT$4,376.1 million worth of petroleum goods and TT$11,757.8 million of non-petroleum goods (at constant prices). In this same year, the economy exported TT$3,787.4 million of petroleum products and imported TT$3,565.1 million of non-petroleum goods.[3] In this regard, we can locate the consumption bundle of the Trinidad and Tobago economy in 1990 as consisting of TT$588.7 million of the exportable good and TT$15,323.6 million of non-traded goods plus imports. By 2003, the Trinidad and Tobago economy progressed onto a consumption bundle consisting of TT$179.1 million of the exportable good and TT$25,065.2 million of the non-exported good plus imports, of which TT$9,075.2 million were imported. This therefore reflects that consumption of the importable good increased more than proportional to the consumption of the exportable good (this actually decreased) and the amount of trade that the economy engaged as a consequence of its trade liberalization policy expanded.

The information in figure 8.6 can be used to construct the size of λ_2 in figure 8.7. Note that the consumption preferences of Trinidad and Tobago in 2003 are located in the protrade zone, implying that the economic growth of the Trinidad and Tobago economy facilitated an increase in consumption of the import good but not at the expense of the consumption of the "other good". The specific sizes of λ_1 and λ_2 are 79° and 80°, respectively.

With trade liberalization, Trinidad and Tobago has moved towards a greater degree of specialization in the production of exportable commodities that it does not consume and the importation of those goods that it does not produce but chooses to consume.

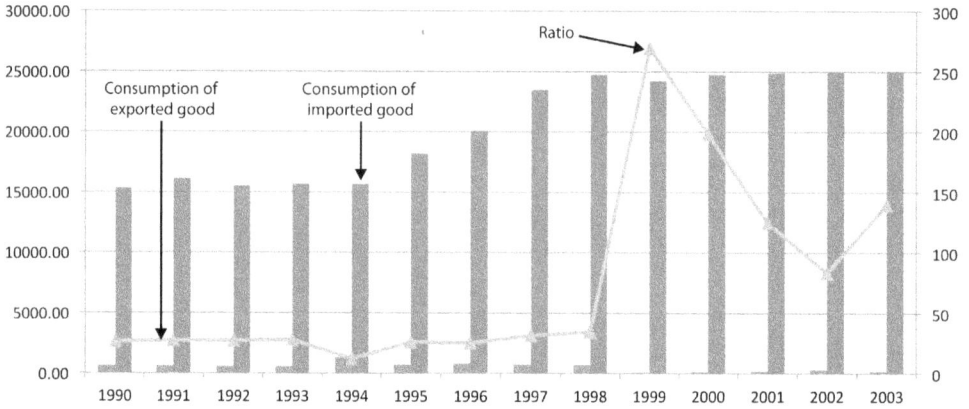

Figure 8.6: Relationship between the consumption of the imported and exported commodities, 1994–2003

8.3 Labour Growth and Capital Accumulation over Time

If the endowment of the labour and capital of an economy increases, then the production possibility capabilities of that country would expand, and this in turn would manifest itself in a rightward movement of the production possibility curve of the economy. The nature of the shift in the production possibility frontier depends on the extent of the increase in the factor endowment capabilities of the country, in that if the stock of capital increases at a greater than proportional amount to the stock of labour, it would mean that the country would be able to produce proportionately more of the capital-intensive good. If the proportional increase in the stock of the capital and labour of the country is equivalent, then the production possibility frontier would shift rightwards in a parallel fashion. This is an example of balanced growth.

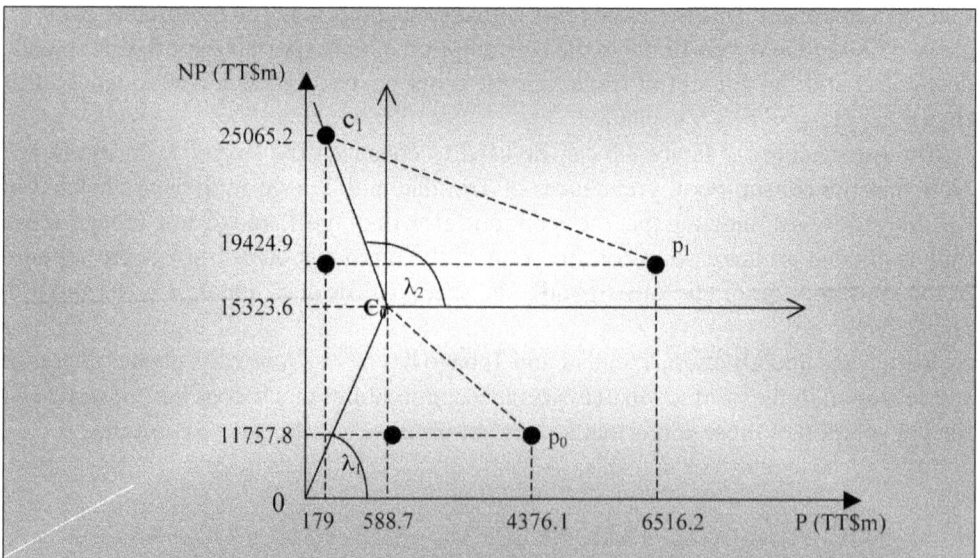

Figure 8.7: The consumption effect of growth on trade in constant prices

8.4 Technical Progress, Trade and Welfare

Improvements in the technological capabilities of a country imply that the country would be able to produce more goods and services using its existing factor endowment capabilities. Technological improvements may be commodity specific or neutral. If technological progress is commodity specific, then the production possibility frontier would shift outwards only along the axis of the commodity favoured by the technological shift.

In relation to figure 8.8, we see that technology can be biased either in favour of cocoa, leading to a pivoting of the PPF outwards on the cocoa axis from S_0C_0 to S_0C_1 (the pivot point is on the steel axis), or it can be biased towards steel, in which case the PPF would move from S_0C_0 to S_1C_0. These potential effects are displayed in figure 8.8 panel a. In panel b, the effect of neutral technological changes is shown, with an equi-proportionate expansion in the output of both cocoa and steel (i.e., the PPF expands from S_0C_0 to S_1C_1).

8.5 The Dutch Disease

The term *Dutch Disease* refers to the negative effects that a booming tradable resource has on other traditional export sectors. The term was first used to refer to the experience of the Dutch manufacturing sector on account of the natural gas discoveries of the 1960s. In the Dutch economy, the discovery of a massive pool of gas resources in the Schlochteren area motivated a higher real exchange rate, triggered principally by appreciating nominal wages in the Dutch economy, especially in relation to wages in Germany. The export boom caused an appreciation of the Dutch currency (the guilder) significantly above levels attained prior to the discovery of natural gas, and in so doing it decreased the level of competitiveness of the Dutch industrial sector as the real exchange rate appreciated.[4]

To outline the mechanics of the Dutch Disease, let us subdivide the production structure of the economy into three sectors: non-booming tradable (NBT), booming tradable

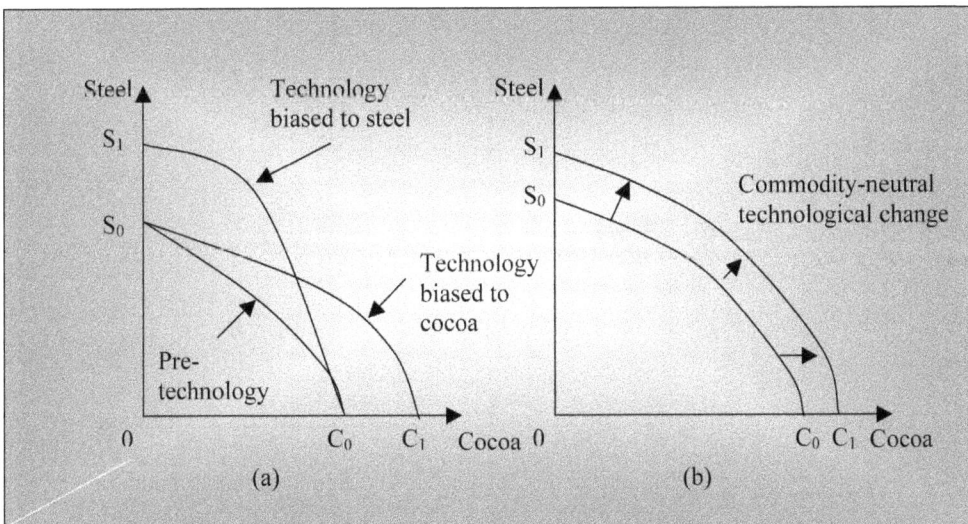

Figure 8.8: Effect of change in technology on the production possibility frontier

(BT) and non-tradable (NT). The benefitting economy is a small price-taking economy, and its firms are price takers in the NBT and BT sectors in the respective international commodity markets in which they participate. For simplicity, we assume a two-factor model with each sector having a specific factor intensity and with labour (L) being the mobile factor.[5]

Typically, traditional export sectors such as cocoa, coffee, sugar, beef and so on from developing economies are price-taking sectors in their various international export price markets. A boom in the BT sector pushes wage rates up in that sector, and mobile factors of production flow out of the NBT sector, the result of which is that the supply curve of this sector shifts leftward from S^0_{NBT} to S^1_{NBT}. The overall consequence of all this is a fall in output in the NBT sector from Q_1 to Q_0 (see figure 8.9).

With an oil boom or any other kind of commodity boom, there is an increase in domestic demand (providing all of any increase in income is not expended on imports) and this in turn inflates the real (effective) exchange rate.[6] This appreciation occurs irrespective of the economy's exchange rate regime.

Specifically, with a boom, the increasing marginal productivity of labour motivates an increase in wages in the booming sector. This is even more pronounced in small economies where labour costs are a small fraction of operating costs and the sector is dominated by multinational companies (MNCs) wishing to minimize conflicts with the indigenous population. The rise in wages in the booming sector creates labour shortages in the non-booming sectors (the resource movement effect). Even if incomes are kept constant, the resource movement effect, which manifests itself as a decline in the supply of non-tradable goods from S_0 to S_1, leads to an increase in the equilibrium price level in this market from P_0 to P_1. With increasing income, domestic expenditure rises on account of expanding wages in the booming sector. Rising incomes trigger even further excess demand in the non-tradable sector, the consequence of which is a further increase

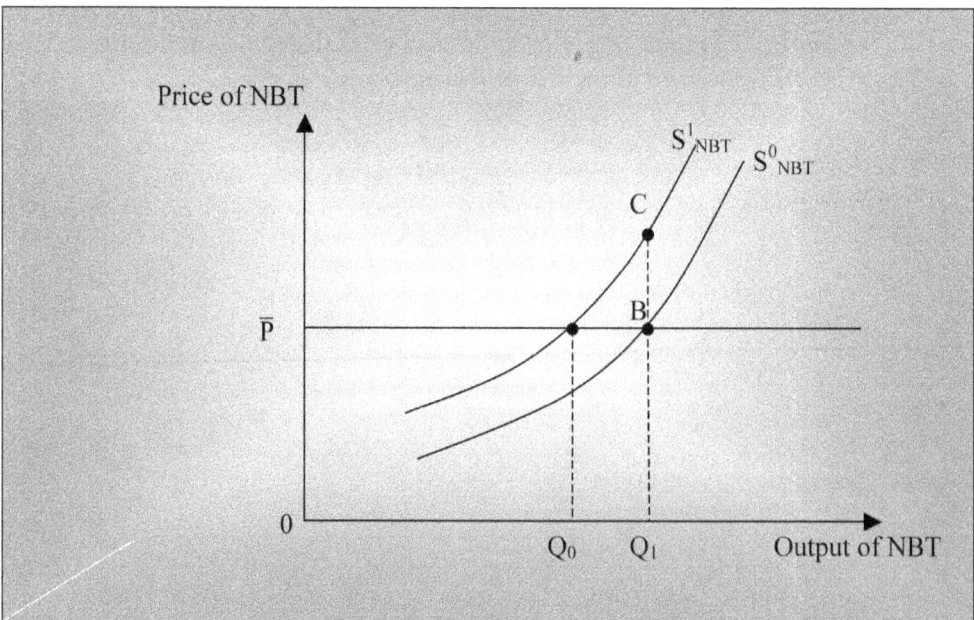

Figure 8.9: Dutch Disease effect on output in the NBT sector

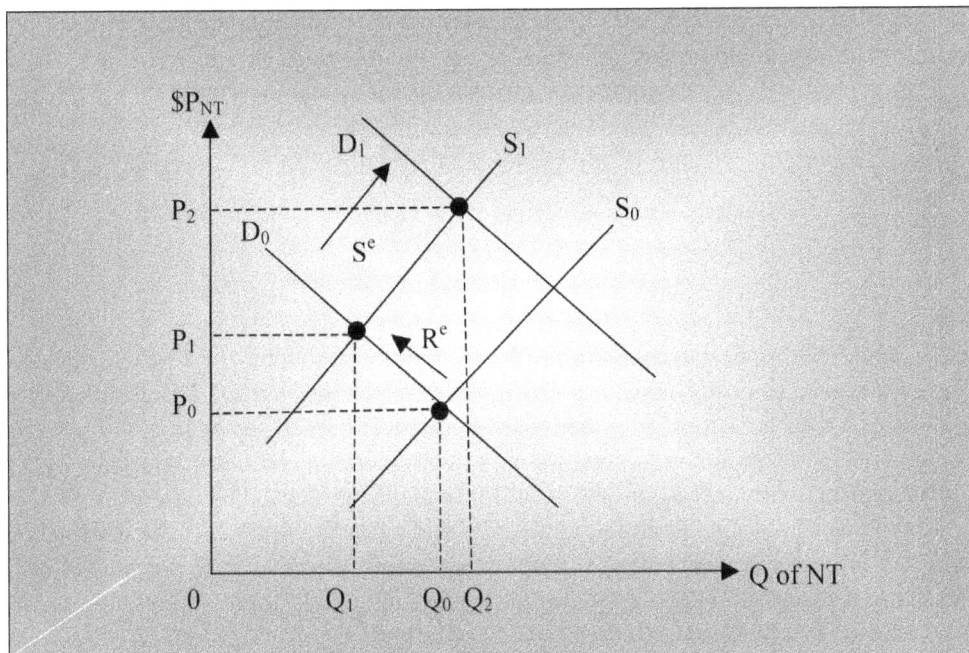

Figure 8.10: R^e and S^e as a result of an oil boom in the NT sector

in the price of non-tradable goods and services from P_1 to P_2 (the spending effect; see figure 8.10).

Q_2 is likely to be higher than Q_0 because the income elasticity of demand for non-tradable goods (usually services) is typically in excess of unity.

In summary, with the Dutch Disease, the resource movement should lead to an increase in the output of the booming tradable good, a fall in the output of the non-booming tradable good (the resource movement effect) and an increase in the output of the non-tradable sector (spending effect outstripping resource movement effect). The net implication is that a boom in a tradable good leads to an increase in the price of non-tradable goods (P_{NT}) and hence the overall domestic price level manifesting itself as an appreciation of the (real effective) exchange rate.

8.6 The Dutch Disease and Deindustrialization

Deindustrialization refers to a contraction in the size of the manufacturing sector in terms of a fall in the share of the manufacturing sector in total value added and a fall in the share of manufacturing employment in total employment. The early literature on deindustrialization was germinated by Baumol (1967) but was coherently and rigorously argued by Rowthorn and Wells (1987), who highlighted the notion that deindustrialization may not be an undesirable feature but may occur as a natural consequence of the economic development process.

To illustrate some of the fundamental attributes of deindustrialization, this section proceeds as follows. Let A_0 = share of agriculture in total output, M_0 = share of manufacturing in total output, S_0 = share of services in total output, Y_L = low income economies, Y_M = middle income economies and Y_H = high income economies.

Prototypically, in the developmental process, the following relations hold:

$$\text{For } Y_L, A_0 > [M_0, S_0] \tag{1}$$

$$\text{For } Y_M, M_0 > [A_0, S_0] \tag{2}$$

$$\text{For } Y_H, S_0 > [M_0, A_0] \tag{3}$$

A similar pattern holds regarding employment in the agriculture, manufacturing and services sectors. Thus, in the natural process of development, the manufacturing sector undergoes a transformation from being an economically small sector in a Y_L economy (expression 1) to a dominant sector in a Y_M economy. In a Y_h economy, the share of the manufacturing sector falls again (figure 8.11 provides a graphical illustration).

Clearly, as an economy matures, a natural pathological feature is that the share of the manufacturing sector will contract. Observe that in this natural process the gap between the share of manufacturing output and manufacturing employment widens. In this regard, Rowthorn and Ramaswammy (1998, 7) observed,

> Productivity growth in the manufacturing sector is typically much faster than in most other sectors of the economy. In the earlier stages of development, the labor saving effects of productivity growth are more than offset by the explosive growth of manufacturing output, so that employment in the manufacturing sector increases, both absolutely and as a share

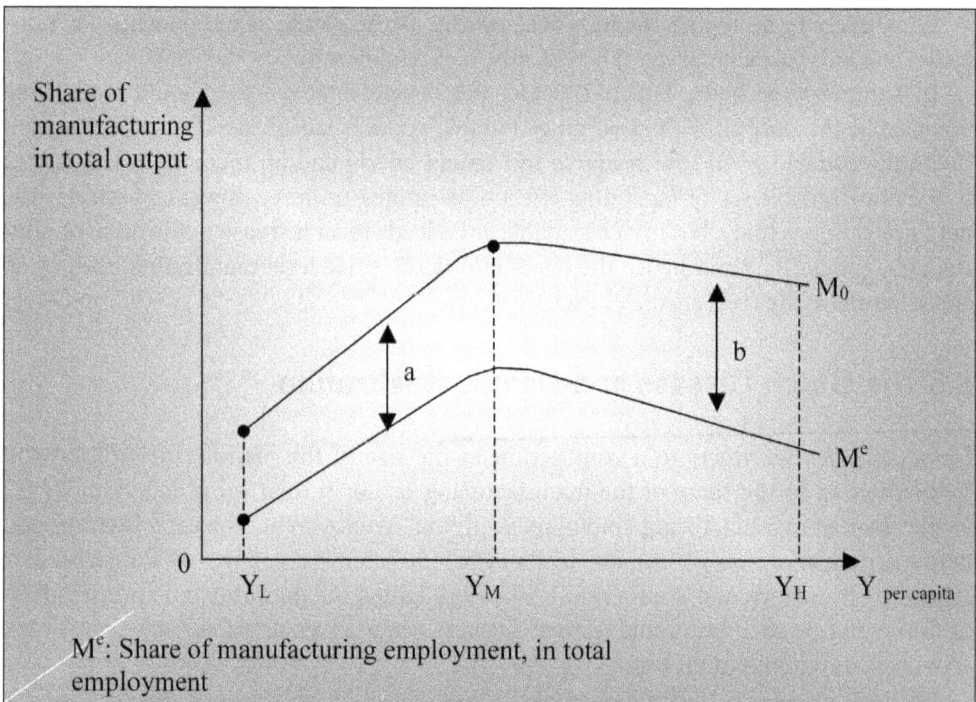

Figure 8.11: Share of manufacturing output and employment in their respective totals

of total employment. Later on, as the demand for manufactured goods slows down, productivity growth is no longer offset by mushrooming demand so that employment in the manufacturing sector starts to fall as a share of the national total.[7]

When deindustrialization occurs naturally, it is associated with rising living standards. However, when deindustrialization occurs unnaturally, as with a resource boom, industrialization may be delayed, and as a consequence the rate of urbanization may also slow. The resulting effect is a decline in the dependency/worker ratio, as may occur with a competitive industrialization strategy. In this context, the savings and investment ratio of the overall economy would improve much slower than it may have been able to otherwise, and in the aftermath of the resource boom, the long-term growth prospects of the economy may have been compromised.

Table 8.2: External competitiveness of the Trinidad and Tobago economy, 1990–2006

Year	Nominal exchange rate (1995 = 100)	Real effective exchange rate (1995 = 100)
1990	71.4	118.7
1991	71.4	119.1
1992	71.4	121.6
1993	89.9	109.9
1994	99.5	102.4
1995	100.0	100.0
1996	100.8	101.8
1997	105.0	102.2
1998	104.8	107.3
1999	104.8	110.2
2000	104.8	115.3
2001	103.5	123.2
2002	103.6	127.9
2003	104.7	126.2
2004	104.6	123.6
2005	104.9	126.1
2006	105.1	125.3

Source: Annual Economic Survey of Trinidad and Tobago (various years).

8.7 Empirical Investigation of the Dutch Disease and Deindustrialization in the Trinidad and Tobago Economy

The Trinidad and Tobago economy realized a hydrocarbon boom in the period 1994–2006. In particular, after 1994 there was a rapid increase in the price of crude oil from the Trinidad and Tobago economy. Also during this period, there was a clear and persistent increase in the value of the real effective exchange rate for the Trinidad and Tobago economy. The gap between the nominal exchange rate and the real effective exchange rate reflects the relatively higher inflation rate of the Trinidad and Tobago economy in relation to its main trading partners (see table 8.2).

The dominance of the petroleum sector and the increase in the price of crude oil since 1998 points to a build-up of economic rents and the accumulation of an economic windfall. Economic windfall may be calculated using this formula:

$$EW_t = TO_t (XP_t - BP_t)$$

where

TO_t: total output of crude oil,
XP_t: export price of crude oil,
BP_t: the budgeted price of crude oil.

For the period 1990–2005, the cumulative economic windfall in Trinidad and Tobago was $2,305.5 million. Economic rents earned by the Trinidad and Tobago government in the time interval 1990–2005 was $6,455.1 million (see figure 8.12).[8]

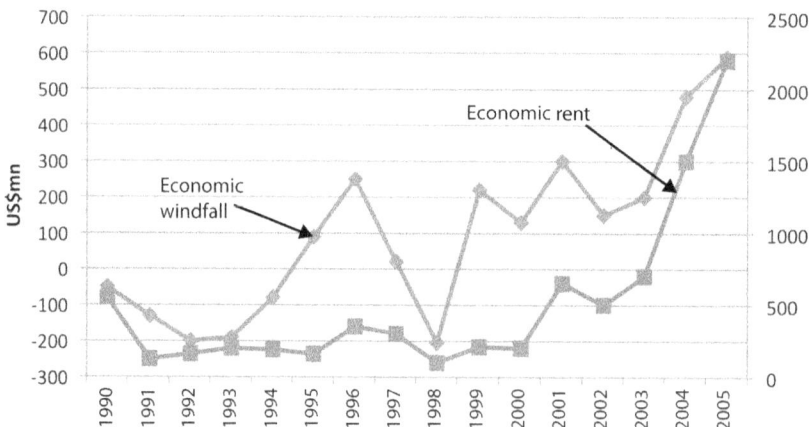

Figure 8.12: Economic windfall and economic rent for Trinidad and Tobago, 1990–2005

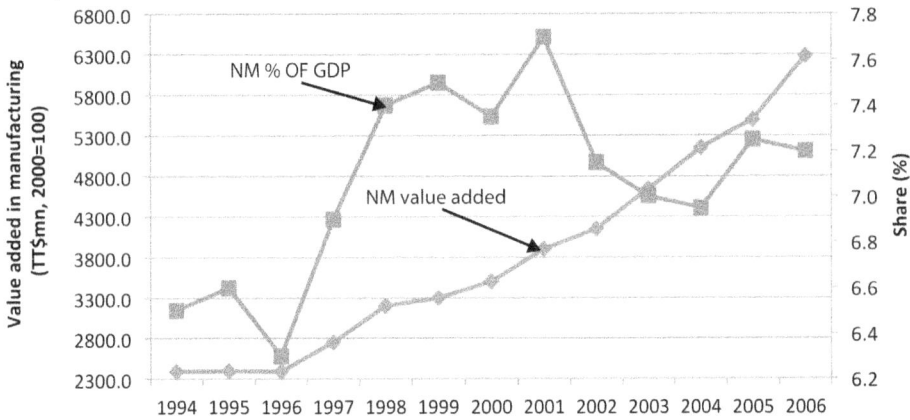

Figure 8.13: Value added and percentage contribution as the narrow manufacturing sector

Deindustrialization with the Second Oil Boom

This section provides an analytical discussion of the effect of the Dutch Disease on the narrow manufacturing sector of the Trinidad and Tobago economy.

Value added in the narrow manufacturing sector of the Trinidad and Tobago economy increased from TT$2,388.2 million in 1994 to TT$6,280.3 million in 2006: an increase of 163 per cent at constant prices. In terms of the share of the narrow manufacturing sector in total output, this increased from 6.5 per cent in 1994 to 7.7 per cent in 2001, but it thereafter declined to 7.2 per cent in 2006. The narrow manufacturing sector excludes the energy sector. After 2001, the price of oil and natural gas rose significantly; thus revenues from this sector rose as well. So the share of the narrow manufacturing sector in total output fell as the contribution of the energy sector rose.

From a labour perspective, there was an increase in the amount of workers employed in the narrow manufacturing sphere from 40,400 in 1994 to 59,100 in 2005: an increase

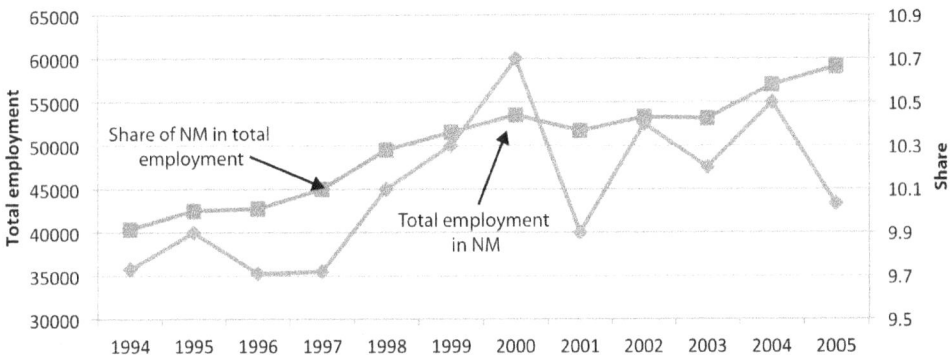

Figure 8.14: Total and sectoral share of employment in the narrow manufacturing sector, 1994–2005

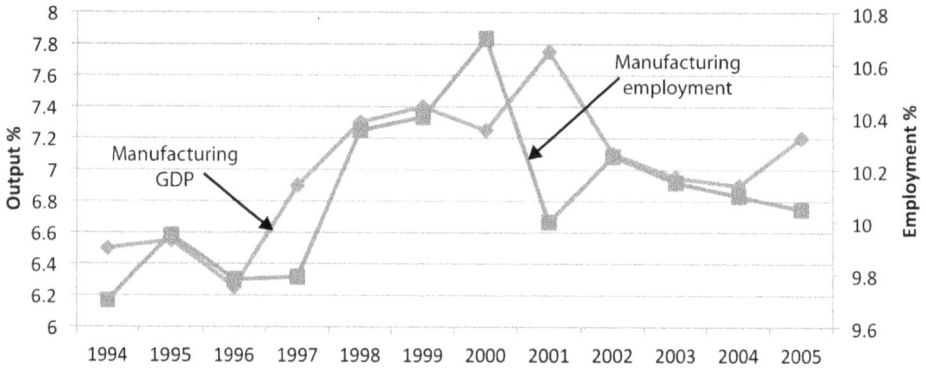

Figure 8.15: Share of manufacturing in total output and employment, 1994–2005

of 46 per cent. In the same interval, there was a rise in the share of the narrow manufacturing sector in total employment from 9.73 per cent in 1994 to 10.7 per cent in 2000. Thereafter, however, the share of narrow manufacturing workers as a proportion of total employment decreased marginally to 10.03 per cent in 2005.

These two measures of deindustrialization, manufacturing gross domestic product (GDP) and manufacturing employment, display a high degree of co-movement and carry a correlation score of 67 per cent. This indicates that statistically both indicators of deindustrialization provide a similar type of information.

Surprisingly, figure 8.16 shows that in the context of the Trinidad and Tobago economy, there was an increase in narrow manufacturing value added as a percentage of GDP. This result may be explained as follows: Although the real effective exchange rate for the Trinidad and Tobago economy increased, the increase in the purchasing power capability of economic agents in that economy facilitated an increase in the amount of narrow manufacturing goods that could be sold and hence produced.

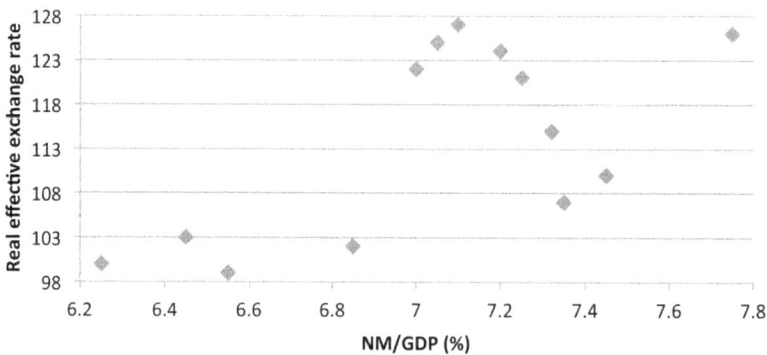

Figure 8.16: Scatter plot of the real effective exchange rate and NM/GDP (%)

8.8 Immiserizing Growth

Jagdish Bhagwati (1958) introduced the idea that a large country can actually become worse off with an expansion in the output of one of its goods. Consider a large country like Brazil, which enjoys the leading production and export market share of coffee. If Brazil were to increase its output of coffee, then it could adversely affect the international terms of trade for coffee to such an extent that it would eventually be worse off.

It is indeed possible that an expansion in the production levels of a particular commodity can so adversely affect its terms of trade such that the net change in export revenues is negative. For example, see commodity C, at terms of trade tot_0, in figure 8.17.

$$P_0 X_0 = R_0$$

Export price (P_0) times export volume (X_0) gives export revenues (R_0).

Assume a higher volume is now produced; $X_1 > X_0$. If the effect of this $X\Delta$ is such that it proportionally lowers the export price (P_1) more than the export volume was raised, then $P_1 X_1 = R_1 < R_0$. It is in this regard that an export diversification agenda may be considered as a fruitful development strategy for countries with extreme commodity concentration.[9]

The source of immiserizing growth is a strongly negative change in the country's terms of trade, and as such this problem is confined to those countries whose size in the export commodity is sufficiently large to significantly influence world prices (see figure 8.17).

Although immiserizing growth is perhaps unlikely, it is still very possible that expansion in the growth of some primary commodities can worsen the international terms of trade for some less-developed countries, especially those that are major players in the supply of the commodity.

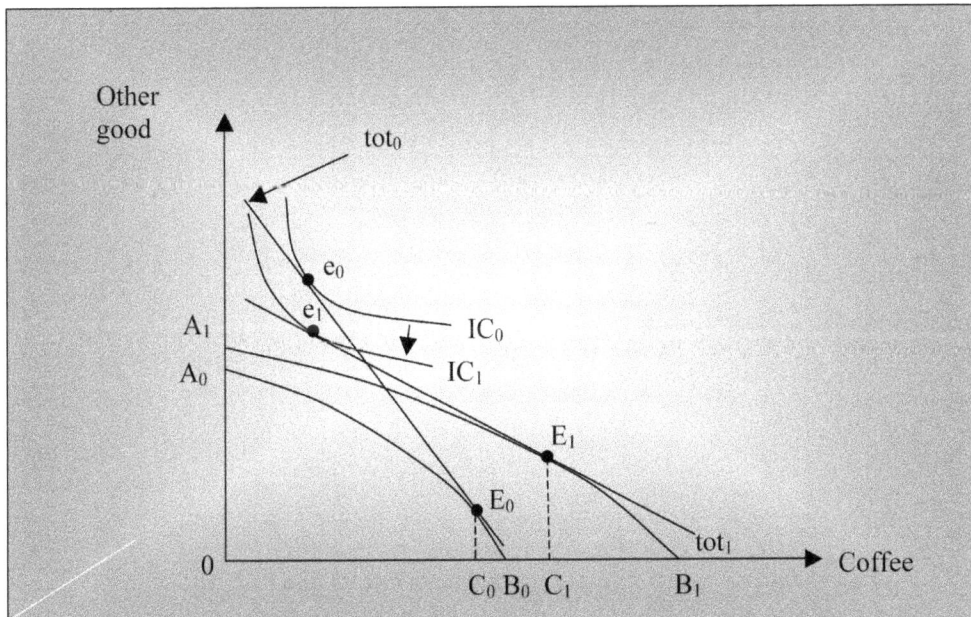

Figure 8.17: Illustration of immiserizing growth

8.9 The Rybczynski Theorem: Growth of Production Alone

The Rybczynski theorem was introduced into the literature in 1955 by Thaddeus Rybczynski. The theorem shows how the structure and volume of output produced by an economy may change when its factor endowment changes. Let us for simplicity assume we are dealing with a small country with two factors of production: labour (L) and capital (K).[10]

Assume that the HC experiences an increase in its stock of labour because of a change in regional immigration laws. The net effect of this increase in the availability of labour will lead to

1. an increase in the output of the labour-intensive good and
2. a reduction in the production of the capital-intensive good (see figure 8.18).

With the increase in labour, the benefiting economy will produce more of the labour-intensive good. To facilitate this, the production of the capital-intensive good will need to contract, as the required factors of production to expand the labour-intensive sector will come from the capital-intensive sector. Given a constant endowment of capital, an outflow of capital from the capital-intensive sector will lead to a contraction of that sector.

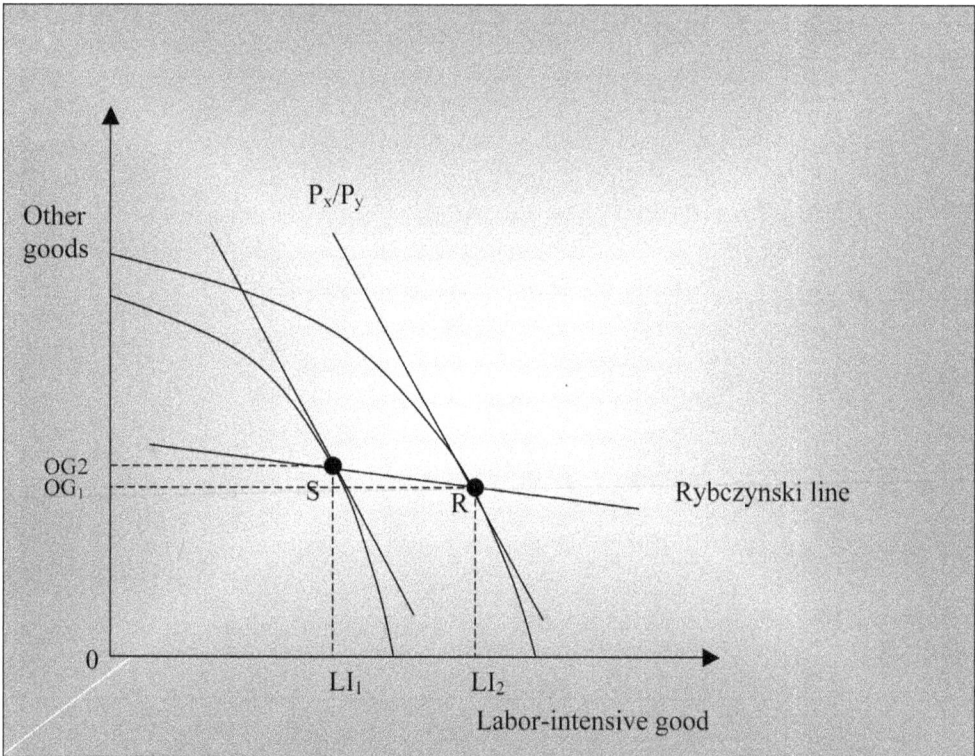

Figure 8.18: Illustration of the effects of a growth in one factor only

8.10 Conclusion

This chapter continued the discussion on Engel's law, focusing on the link between economic growth and international trade. The chapter also reviewed the Dutch Disease together with its application to the economy of Trinidad and Tobago.

Summary of Key Points

- The production permutations available to a country that has experienced consistent growth are such that the growth can be pro-trade biased, ultra-pro-trade biased, anti-trade biased, ultra-anti-trade biased or trade neutral.
- Technological improvements may be commodity specific or neutral. If technological progress is commodity specific, then the production possibility frontier shifts outwards only along the axis of the commodity favoured by the technological shift.
- The term *Dutch Disease* refers to the negative effects that a booming tradable resource has on other traditional export sectors.
- The net implication of the Dutch Disease is that a boom in a tradable good leads to an increase in the price of non-tradable goods and hence the overall domestic price level manifesting itself as an appreciation of the (real effective) exchange rate.
- *Deindustrialization* refers to a contraction in the size of the manufacturing sector in terms of a fall in the share of the manufacturing sector in total value added and a fall in the share of manufacturing employment in total employment.
- The immiserizing growth theorem is based on the idea that a large country can actually become worse off with an expansion in the output of one of its goods.
- The Rybczynski theorem shows how the structure and volume of output produced by an economy may change when its factor endowment changes.

Multiple Choice

1. As a result of a boom in a resource, profits in the manufacturing sector fall. This is known as

    a) deindustrialization
    b) immiserizing growth
    c) an export-led strategy
    d) none of the above

2. The Stolper–Samuelson theorem can be used to show the impact of trade on

    a) output
    b) wages
    c) prices
    d) none of the above

3. Balanced growth is evidenced by which of the following changes of the PPF:

    a) a parallel shift of the PPF
    b) a shift along the x axis only
    c) a shift of along the y axis only
    d) none of the above

4. Trade openness can result in which of the following situations:

    a) a decline in the incentive to innovate
    b) a decline in the long run growth capability of an economy
    c) improvements in technology
    d) all of the above

5. Which of the following statements is true:

    a) A fall in the output of the non-booming tradable sectors results in an increase in the wages of workers in the non-booming sectors.
    b) An appreciation of the real effective exchange rate causes an increase in the level of domestic demand.
    c) A resource movement effect results in a fall in output in the booming sector.
    d) none of the above

Short Essay

1. Discuss in detail, using diagrams, the theory of immiserizing growth.
2. What is the Dutch Disease?
3. Discuss the experience of any one country that has experienced the Dutch Disease.
4. What can be done to eliminate some of the negative effects associated with the Dutch Disease?
5. Discuss the concept of deindustrialization and describe the experience of any economy that was characterized by the Dutch Disease and deindustrialization.

Key Trade Terms

- Economic growth
- Real income
- Pro-trade biased
- Ultra-pro-trade biased
- Anti-trade biased
- Ultra-anti-trade biased
- Trade neutral
- Consumption effect
- Dutch Disease
- Competitiveness
- Real exchange rate
- Non-booming tradable (NBT) sector
- Booming tradable (BT) sector
- Non-tradable (NT) sector
- Resource movement effect
- Spending effect
- Deindustrialization
- Economic windfall
- Economic rent
- Oil boom
- Narrow manufacturing sector
- Value added
- Immiserizing growth
- Rybczynski theorem

9.

International Factor Flows

Foreign Direct Investment

Learning Objectives

a. Compare the trends in foreign direct investment (FDI) flows between developed and developing countries.
b. Evaluate the welfare impact of international capital flows.
c. Identify the factors that influence FDI flows.
d. Briefly discuss various avenues through which FDI can effect (or affect) economic growth.

9.0 Introduction

This chapter discusses the international movement of factors of production with emphasis on foreign direct investment (FDI) flows.

FDI includes all capital transactions that are made to acquire a lasting interest (usually 10 per cent or more of voting stock) in an enterprise operating in a country other than that of the investor. FDI is the sum of equity capital, reinvested earnings and other long-term and short-term capital as shown in the balance of payments. It can also be defined as investment of long-term duration from a foreign country into a domestic "host" country that may take the form of a "composite bundle of capital stocks, know-how and technology". The implication of this long-term investment is that there exists a long-term relationship between the investor and the host country's enterprise. Direct investment comprises not only the initial amount of investment between the investor and the enterprise but also all subsequent transactions.

Almost a century ago, Vladimir Lenin (1916) wrote an essay titled "Imperialism, the Highest Stage of Capitalism". In this piece, he argued that capitalists in the Western world, in order to forestall the likelihood of a workers' revolt at home, would commence exporting their capital so that they could extract profits from the labour force of the less-developed countries (LDCs). Many LDC governments have in the past taken heed of this type of advice and have sought to restrict their inflows of FDI. However, by the start of the 1980s as the international debt crisis deepened, most developing countries began to rethink their approach to FDI, since most western banks were not disposed to granting additional loans to these countries.[1] In such an environment, developing countries chose to woo and fawn over private foreign capitalists. As the Berlin Wall fell and the process of globalization intensified – fuelled by a neoliberal ideology of free trade, free investment flows, democracy and markets – the global rate of investment rose dramatically.

This increase in FDI flows acted as the engine of growth for several developing countries. Economies where FDI fuelled growth include Taiwan, Singapore, Indonesia and China. CARICOM member states have also realized the importance of FDI in the development process and attempts have been made to maintain the competitiveness of the regional economies in terms of attracting FDI.

9.1 The Significance of FDI Flows

Table 9.1 indicates that FDI flows as a percentage of gross capital formation (GKF) increased between 1970 and 2008 for all of the economies listed. Observe that after 2000, FDI/GKF fell for most of these economies. Within CARICOM, all economies had an FDI/GKF ratio in excess of 15 per cent in 2003 and 18 per cent in 2008. Note that in all the economies listed, only Antigua and Barbuda, Bahamas, Barbados, and Jamaica had percentages less than 30 per cent for 2008, while for all other economies, more than 40 per cent of the GKF was accounted for by FDI inflows in 2008.

In terms of the stock of FDI as a percentage of gross domestic product (GDP), there have been persistent improvements for both developed and developing economies. By 2008, all CARICOM economies had stocks of FDI as a percentage of GDP that were in excess of 25 per cent. Antigua and Barbuda, Bahamas, Dominica, Grenada, Guyana, St Kitts and Nevis, St Lucia, and St Vincent and the Grenadines carried FDI stocks in excess of 100 per cent of GDP (see table 9.2).

9.2 Welfare Effect of International Capital Flows

To evaluate the welfare impact of capital flows, this chapter makes reference to figure 9.1.

In figure 9.1, the total stock of capital between the home country (HC) and the foreign country (FC) is 00`. The distribution of capital between the HC and FC is such that the HC has OA units while the FC has O`A units. The curves VMPK$_{HC}$ and VMPK$_{FC}$ indicate the values of the marginal product of capital in the HC and FC, respectively. The VMPK curve, under conditions of competition, illustrates the return to capital.

If there are barriers to the free movement of capital, then the HC would invest all of its capital stock at home at a return of OC. The total product of capital, in this context, is given by the area under the curve OFGA, with OCGA accruing to the HC's capital and CFG accruing to other factors. In a similar regard, the FC invests its O`A units of capital for a total product of capital of AMJO`, of which MJH accrues to the owners of other factors of production besides capital in the foreign country and AMHO` accrues to the owners of capital.

If there is now a greater degree of capital mobility, then capital will move from the HC, where capital is abundant and cheaply priced, to the FC, where capital is much scarcer and much more expensively priced. Capital to the magnitude of AB will flow out of the HC into the FC. In the HC, total output decreases to OFEB, which when added to the returns on investments in the FC (BERA) gives a total national product of OFERA:

$$OFERA = OFEB + BERA$$

Table 9.1: Inward FDI flows as a percentage of gross fixed capital formation, by host region and economy, 1970–2008

	1970	1975	1980	1985	1990	1995	2000	2001	2002	2003	2004	2005	2006	2007	2008
World	2.5	2.4	2.3	2.4	4.5	5.4	22.0	12.8	12.2	7.5	7.5	9.4	12.6	14.8	12.3
Developed countries	2.2	2.0	2.7	2.4	4.8	4.5	25.0	12.7	12.3	6.7	6.1	8.0	11.8	15.7	11.4
Developing countries	4.5	3.8	1.2	2.5	3.6	8.0	13.4	13.1	10.5	10.0	10.5	12.8	13.8	12.6	12.8
Latin America and the Caribbean	5.2	4.3	3.2	4.8	4.2	9.2	20.7	19.8	14.6	10.2	15.5	16.8	15.0	18.0	15.5
Antigua and Barbuda	0.0	0.0	51.1	27.8	47.7	17.3	10.4	23.6	17.9	22.3	24.1	29.9	45.7	70.0	28.4
Bahamas	0.0	23.3	2.4	-7.9	-2.6	15.3	38.8	15.7	31.2	22.6	10.5	20.3	38.2	57.7	29.7
Barbados	18.3	29.9	1.5	2.6	3.5	4.5	4.1	3.5	3.4	24.0	9.7	31.7	5.6	6.4	18.4
Belize	0.0	0.0	0.0	21.8	17.9	15.5	10.7	27.4	11.8	18.0	81.7	54.4	27.5	45.5	83.1
Dominica	0.0	0.0	0.0	10.7	19.0	78.4	12.9	18.7	25.3	23.6	24.9	37.4	45.1	54.6	51.3
Grenada	0.0	0.0	-0.1	11.4	16.6	22.6	21.2	46.1	38.7	40.1	20.0	13.4	65.4	60.0	88.2
Guyana	0.0	0.5	0.3	1.9	4.7	26.4	42.3	36.7	27.4	16.5	26.5	39.5	36.4	31.5	63.6
Jamaica	14.7	9.2	7.2	-1.9	15.0	9.0	22.3	26.1	17.7	21.8	24.0	20.8	24.1	22.9	18.5
St Kitts and Nevis	0.0	0.0	5.5	33.8	55.3	19.2	63.3	45.0	52.4	30.7	31.4	26.1	94.3	59.3	41.6
St Lucia	0.0	0.0	67.5	37.2	47.6	24.1	27.8	13.2	20.4	19.0	65.1	67.3	62.7	66.2	41.1
St Vincent and the Grenadines	0.0	0.0	4.7	6.4	13.1	38.4	32.0	20.5	30.0	37.3	38.7	21.5	47.1	57.3	42.2
Trinidad and Tobago	48.4	18.6	10.5	0.1	15.7	30.0	47.4	41.7	47.4	36.9	43.0	42.5	28.0	25.4	53.0

Source: World Investment Report (various years).

Table 9.2: Inward FDI stock as a percentage of gross domestic product, by host region and economy, 1980–2008

	1980	1985	1990	1995	2000	2001	2002	2003	2004	2005	2006	2007	2008
World	6.6	8.34	9.3	10.23	20	21.2	22.3	22.9	21.7	22.7	24.8	27.9	24.5
Developed countries	4.85	6.21	8.22	8.9	17.1	17.9	17.9	20.7	20.5	21.4	24.2	27.2	24.7
Developing countries	12.45	16.32	14.7	16.3	30.9	33.4	36.0	31.4	26.4	27.0	26.7	29.8	24.8
Antigua and Barbuda	21.26	46.47	74.48	88.57	83.8	88.8	99.7	94.4	139.6	144.1	150.7	190.3	187.3
Bahamas	40.99	23.41	18.86	21.18	32.9	34.0	37.6	39.2	39.9	44.6	63.7	125.5	101.7
Barbados	12.06	10.46	10.02	12.48	11.8	11.8	13.8	18.4	15.9	17.3	14.4	15.9	25.1
Belize	6.36	9.36	22.12	26.46	34.6	38.4	43.2	43.5	66.2	57.7	56.4	65.2	75.5
Dominica	0.14	10.73	42.88	89.87	100.4	107.5	117.1	123.1	130.7	141.2	149.7	141.5	153.4
Grenada	1.54	9.83	31.74	60.71	83.8	90.9	100.2	124.5	141.2	139.3	159.7	195.6	204.9
Guyana	4.18	8.57	10.63	71.59	93.3	116.8	120.0	125.9	120.9	126.5	125.4	119.7	125.8
Jamaica	21.28	25.02	18.65	29.84	44.8	50.5	56.7	62.4	66.4	65.1	68.8	76.6	65.7
St Kitts and Nevis	2.08	40.51	100.6	105.5	154.2	166.6	192.1	189	202.9	189.3	228.7	212.6	230.2
St Lucia	70.08	104.3	80.21	92.1	112.9	114.1	119.4	125.7	162.9	151.9	143.5	174.2	182.5
St Vincent and the Grenadines	1.99	7.53	24.33	67.89	146.5	144.3	146.4	155.4	169.8	168.2	172.4	182.8	167.9
Trinidad and Tobago	15.66	23.3	41.29	68.77	95.6	80.1	87.6	92.4	83.3	72.7	62.4	65.1	66.2

Source: World Investment Report (various years).

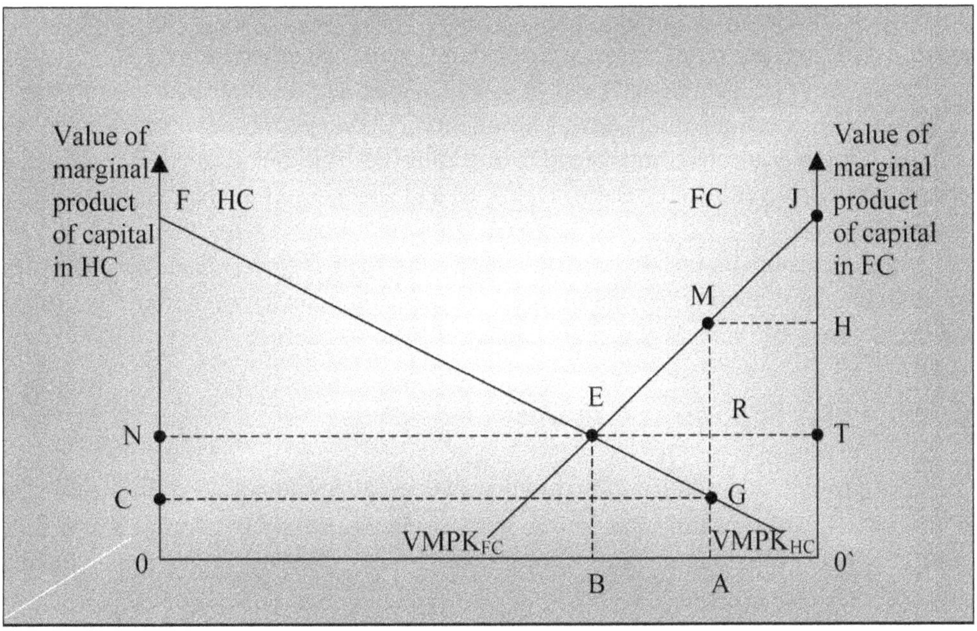

Figure 9.1: Output and welfare effects of international capital transfer

Alternatively, total national product = total domestic product + the returns on FDI in the FC.

Because of FDI, the overall return to capital in the HC increases from OCGA to ONRA. At the same time, there is a decline in the return to the other factors of production to EFN in the HC.

From a FC perspective, the inflow of AB units of K will expand the domestic product to BE JO`. The return on capital will decrease to O`T (i.e., the same as in the HC so that there is no further incentive for capital to flow from the HC to the FC). A significant portion of the increase in domestic product in the FC from BEMA to BERA goes to owners of capital in the HC, so that effectively, national product only expands by EMR.

As a result of the liberalizing capital flows, the total product of the world economy expands by ERG + ERM = EGM.[2] Thus the liberalization of capital flows increases the return to scarce factors of production and enhances world output levels.

9.3 Determinants of FDI Flows

Corporations invest abroad for several reasons. First, they may intend to exploit technological, managerial, financial or marketing strengths. Second, they may invest to exploit natural resources, usually employing specialized and often technologically sophisticated methods. Third, they may seek to take advantage of low wages but sufficiently skilled labour to serve as a base for exporting to other countries. Finally, they may want to sell services, in which case a local presence is normally required.[3]

The traditional theories on FDI assume that a firm operating in a foreign country must have comparative advantage in certain factors to counterbalance the additional costs that arise from differences in culture, language, legal system and other factors such as increased costs for communication and lack of knowledge of local conditions.

The degree of political stability and government intervention in the host economy also influences the extent of FDI flows to any economy.[4] In addition, economic factors also affect the attractiveness of a country to FDI, including the trade and investment regime, the extent of openness of the country and the level and adequacy of the basic infrastructure in the country.

Other determinants include institutional factors such as government subsidies, tax breaks, alien land holding regulations and the provision of warehouses and other infrastructural amenities such as electricity and water.

9.4 FDI and Economic Growth

The relationship between FDI and economic growth has prompted a significant amount of research (theoretical and empirical) in both the developed and developing world. This section discusses various avenues through which FDI can effect (or affect) economic growth.

FDI and the Stock of Physical Capital: The small economies of the CARICOM sphere are characterized by high levels of structural unemployment, indicating that the existing capital stock is insufficient to absorb the entire labour force. In these small, capital-starved developing economies, an increase in the physical capital stock is always a welcomed development. FDI in these economies can lead to an increase in the stock of physical capital per capita.

FDI, Human Capital and Organizational Skills: Foreign firms usually make substantial contributions to the host economy in terms of helping to improve its stock of human capital. Many multinational corporations (MNCs) now practise corporate social responsibility, routinely offering scholarships and bursaries to deserving students from the geographical area in which their productive operations are located. These foreign companies also offer staff upgrade opportunities. Labour training and skill acquisition are supposed to improve the stock of knowledge in the host economy. FDI also facilitates the introduction of alternative (superior) managerial and organizational practices. De Mello and Sinclair (1995) have also noted that even in the absence of significant amounts of physical capital accumulation with FDI, licensing and other such quasi-investment arrangements tend to promote knowledge transfers.

FDI and Technology: An important facet of the economic development process involves the transfer of best practices across sovereign borders. Before the industrial revolution took place in Europe, it took almost 350 years for per capita incomes in Britain to double. With the onset of the industrial revolution, however, Britain took sixty years to double its per capita income. Towards the end of the twentieth century, Botswana, Chile, China, Ireland, Japan and Thailand took just about ten years to double economic activity. This type of rapid growth is in part possible through the transfer of foreign technology associated with FDI inflows.

FDI also improves the extent of technical progress in the host economy via a "contagion effect". There are two main ways in which FDI helps to transfer technology from the FC to the HC: backward linkages and labour mobility. When foreign MNCs engage in backward linkages with local firms along their value chain, they often assist these firms in utilizing the appropriate technology. FDI also helps to transfer foreign technology to the host economy via labour mobility. Specifically, when a worker is employed with an MNC, they may be encouraged to adopt superior management practices and also benefit from the knowledge of superior technology. When employees leave these MNCs for other firms within the domestic economy, some of the technological knowledge embodied with the movement of the human capital spills over to the new firm.

In the short run, when an MNC sells a product in the host economy's market, there may be crowding out of domestic firms. This can result in the development of a negative correlation between the sales revenue of domestic firms and FDI.

At the same time, competition from MNCs may force domestic firms to upgrade their technology, knowhow, and research and development in order to survive in a more liberalized environment. Foreign investment and competition may therefore help to promote the output of domestic firms.

FDI also represents an important conduit for the spillover of research and development from developed to developing economies. Technological spillover to host economies occurs through staff training and the production specifications required by backward- and forward-related industries.[5]

FDI and Domestic Investment: FDI can have two predominant types of effects on domestic firms: competition effect and spillover effect. Foreign firms are generally more efficient than domestic firms and thus can penetrate domestic markets even though there may be a cadre of existing domestic firms. The presence of these foreign firms may actually force local firms to search for avenues to reduce inefficiency. In the short run, as foreign firms start to sell in the domestic economy, sales of local firms in the same industry often fall. In turn, as local firms invest and innovate, foreign firms may be forced to bring in more investment dollars.

The net effect of FDI on domestic investment therefore remains an empirical matter.

FDI and Market Access: In 1949, Sir Arthur Lewis emphasized that every enquiry into industrialization must commence with the market. Lewis argued that one of the most difficult tasks for a new firm was to find and penetrate foreign markets and thus that Caribbean firms practise an *industrialization by invitation strategy*. By expanding market access and exports, FDI can lead to economic growth through the operation of the multiplier.

Lewis also advocated that these goods should be sold to the developed world or extra-regional market. He emphasized dependence on the foreign market because the domestic market was too small to support economies of scale and while an intra-regional integration arrangement could serve as a launching pad, the longer-term emphasis needed to be on the foreign market. Lewis went on to note that in order to get access to foreign markets, foreign firms with established distributional outlets in extra-regional markets must be attracted.

FDI and Trade: The literature reflects that MNCs engage in a greater degree of trade (both with and without their parent companies) than indigenous firms. This occurs because most MNCs, especially in developing economies, operate in trade-intensive sectors. Furthermore, the marginal propensity to trade of MNCs is usually higher than indigenous firms operating in the same industry.[6]

FDI and Financial Crises: FDI also carries the advantage, when compared to other types of capital flows, of offering protection against financial crises in the global economy, and this in turn reduces the extent of volatility experienced in the growth process.[7]

FDI and Poverty Reduction: FDI can influence the economic growth performance of an economy, and as such, it carries serious implications for the reduction of poverty. Specifically, FDI can help to generate economic returns for the government, which in turn could be used to build up safety nets for the poor. By helping to reduce poverty, FDI creates room for benefiting economic agents to invest greater amounts in their stock of resources by improving their health and educational status, both of which could lead to an improvement in individual productivity and hence national productivity.

FDI in Trinidad and Tobago

Table 9.3 shows the trends in the inflows of FDI to Trinidad and Tobago. From 1989 to 2008, the amount of FDI flowing into Trinidad and Tobago expanded from $149 million to $2,800.8 million. The data also shows that some countries (e.g., Germany and India) are beginning to make investments in the Trinidad and Tobago economy. However, the two most consistent sources from which FDI flows to the Trinidad and Tobago economy remain the United States and United Kingdom. Of these two, the United States has been the largest single source. The last two columns of table 9.3 show the share of FDI originating from the United States, with an average during the period 1989–2008 of 63 per cent.

Table 9.4a shows the FDI investment income that foreign firms receive from their investment efforts in Trinidad and Tobago. Between 1989 and 2008, Trinidad and Tobago received $14,138.5 million in FDI flows from abroad. During this period, FDI income amounted to $9,448.7 million, of which $5,375.1 million were remitted abroad. Of the investment income flows remitted abroad, more than 40 per cent went as profits. One therefore has to be careful, in accessing the contribution of FDI, to take stock of remittances.

Table 9.4b shows the various sectors that are targeted by FDI in the Trinidad and Tobago economy. On average, for the period 1989–2008, the petroleum industries accounted for more than 75 per cent of all the inflows of FDI to the Trinidad and Tobago economy, the majority of which were directed at the mining, exploration and production refineries and petrochemicals sub-component of the petroleum industries sector.

9.5 FDI Flows in Other CARICOM States

Table 9.5a provides data on the position of CARICOM member states with respect to net FDI inflows. Among the countries for which data is available, the CARICOM region received a total of $345 million in net FDI inflows in 1990 as compared to $2,662 million in 2008: an increase of 672 per cent at current prices. In 1990, the recipient of the largest amount of foreign direct investment was Jamaica, which received $138 million. By 2008, the largest recipient of net FDI in the CARICOM region was again Jamaica, which received $789 million as compared to the paltry $60 million received by Dominica. Total net FDI inflows for the nineteen-year period to the CARICOM bloc of countries amounted to $21,564 million.

One of the more important contributions made by FDI to the overall process of

Table 9.3: FDI inflows to Trinidad and Tobago, by countries of origin, 1989–2008 (US$mn)

Country	USA	UK	Canada	Germany	Japan	India	Others	Total	Share of region in Trinidad and Tobago FDI	
									USA	Non-USA
1989	95.9	0.4	58.1	0.0	0.0	0.0	-5.4	149.0	64.36	35.64
1990	65.5	0.2	49.2	0.0	0.0	0.0	-5.8	109.0	60.09	40.00
1991	98.5	0.1	38.5	22.8	0.1	0.1	-16.0	144.0	68.40	31.67
1992	123.0	40.4	0.1	0.0	0.0	0.0	7.4	171.0	71.93	28.01
1993	339.0	31.0	0.2	3.7	0.1	0.0	-1.7	373.0	90.88	8.93
1994	398.0	8.7	0.0	47.0	0.0	70.1	-2.8	521.0	76.39	23.61
1995	275.0	15.9	1.2	6.6	0.0	0.0	-3.4	296.0	92.91	6.86
1996	328.6	21.6	0.8	10.1	0.0	0.0	-4.8	356.3	92.23	7.77
1997	483.0	55.2	159.0	116.0	0.0	150.0	36.9	1,000.0	48.30	51.71
1998	525.0	99.6	10.9	11.9	0.0	34.0	50.7	732.0	71.72	28.29
1999	274.6	232.1	9.3	7.5	0.1	57.0	62.7	643.3	42.69	57.31
2000	315.9	254.7	1.8	14.0	0.0	11.1	82.0	679.5	46.49	53.51
2001	372.3	307.1	7.1	36.5	0.1	20.8	91.1	834.9	44.59	55.42
2002	352.7	290.9	7.2	34.8	0.1	19.8	85.2	790.7	44.61	55.39
2003	375.8	297.4	11.7	35.6	0.2	20.1	67.5	808.3	46.49	53.51
2004	697.5	169.9	2.6	42.5	0.1	24.2	51.3	998.1	69.88	29.12
2005	693.8	164.5	1.4	41.4	0.2	16.4	22.0	939.7	73.83	26.17
2006	626.7	150.1	2.6	37.6	0.2	26.5	39.0	882.7	71.00	29.00
2007	574.4	159.1	2.9	43.1	0.2	21.2	29.1	830.0	69.20	30.80
2008	403.4	145.8	2,194.0	30.4	0.2	15.9	11.1	2,800.8	14.40	85.60

Source: Balance of Payment Yearbook of Trinidad and Tobago (various years).

Table 9.4a: Remittances on FDI inflows to Trinidad and Tobago, 1989–2008 (US$mn)

	FDI	FDI investment income	Total	Interest	Dividends	Profits	Retained profits
1989	148.9	206.8	115.5	23.2	7.6	84.7	91.3
1990	109.4	242.6	168.0	36.1	9.4	122.5	74.6
1991	144.1	256.9	139.8	5.3	15.6	118.9	117.1
1992	171.0	289.2	153.1	8.8	29.6	114.7	136.1
1993	372.6	202.4	110.9	24.6	23.9	62.4	91.5
1994	521.0	301.2	111.6	36.6	5.8	69.2	189.6
1995	295.7	309.8	155.0	56.1	18.6	80.3	154.8
1996	356.3	284.3	115.0	18.9	32.0	64.1	169.3
1997	999.6	289.0	163.9	70.2	33.7	60.0	125.1
1998	731.9	270.2	184.5	90.8	49.1	44.6	85.7
1999	643.3	338.9	187.4	108.2	49.4	29.8	151.5
2000	679.5	403.4	387.5	158.6	163.6	65.3	145.8
2001	834.9	467.8	300.2	142.7	106.3	51.2	167.6
2002	790.7	393.7	229.1	98.8	90.2	40.1	164.6
2003	808.3	614.5	248.6	125.4	86.8	36.9	365.9
2004	998.1	327.3	174.4	156.1	67.0	51.3	152.9
2005	939.7	741.6	349.4	182.5	167.8	99.1	292.2
2006	882.7	1,005.5	599.1	283.8	202.7	112.6	406.4
2007	830.0	1,000.7	704.1	336.3	267.3	100.5	296.6
2008	2,880.8	1,272.5	778	368.9	248.8	160.3	494.5
Cumulative sum	14,138.5	9,218.3	5,375.1	2,331.9	1,675.2	1,568.5	3,873.1

Table 9.4b: FDI inflows in private sector enterprises by sector of activity, 1989–2008

	A	B	C	D	E	F	G	H	Total	%
1989	86.7	82.8	3.9	2.4	0.6	0.5	0.1	59.7	148.9	58.2
1990	64.0	57.2	6.8	4.9	0.5	−2.9	0.0	42.9	104.9	61.0
1991	125.1	118.2	6.9	4.9	0.5	−0.5	0.0	16.7	144.1	86.8
1992	153.2	144.6	8.6	−0.5	1.6	0.3	0.3	161.0	171.0	89.6
1993	348.83	348.63	0.2	1.9	4.2	0.1	−0.4	17.9	372.52	93.6
1994	274.87	289.76	−14.89	5.7	1.0	128.59	−1.9	112.31	520.57	52.8
1995	266.1	253.69	12.4	3.2	6.2	1.7	−0.4	19.01	295.81	90.0
1998	559.7	585.3	14.4	9.1	2.0	2.2	−0.1	119.0	731.9	76.5
1999	467.7	449.0	18.7	3.8	−0.5	2.9	0.1	169.3	643.3	72.7
2000	437.9	423.4	14.5	31.8	4.7	3.7	−16.7	71.9	533.3	82.1
2001	412.5	383.2	29.3	20.0	0.0	1.0	12.2	22.1	467.8	88.2
2002	295.3	241.1	54.2	36.4	7.4	17.9	9.5	7.2	393.7	75.0
2003	536.6	403.3	133.3	0.3	15.0	2.9	19.7	40.0	614.5	87.3
2004	256.3	191.2	65.1	0.8	6.7	5.4	14.4	43.7	327.3	78.3
2005	613.9	404.4	209.5	1.2	0.7	2.7	81.4	41.7	741.6	82.8
2006	740.5	459.5	281.0	0.5	7.8	21.2	155.3	80.2	1,005.5	73.6
2007	704.9	400.6	304.3	0.5	19.8	32.8	171.2	71.5	1,000.7	70.4
2008	1,055.5	683.5	372.0	3.8	28.7	22.6	102.4	59.5	1,272.5	82.9
Average 1989–2008										77.9

Source: Balance of Payment Yearbook of Trinidad and Tobago (various years).

A: Petroleum industries; B: Mining exploration and production, refineries, petrochemical; C: Service contractors, marketing and distribution; D: Food processors and drink including tobacco; E: Distribution; F: Chemicals and non-metallic minerals; G: Assembly type and related industries; H: All other sectors.

Table 9.5a: Net foreign direct investment inflows to CARICOM member states, 1990–2008 (US$mn)

Country	1990	1991	1992	1993	1994	1995	1996	1997	1998	1999	2000	2001	2002	2003	2004	2005	2006	2007	2008
Antigua and Barbuda	61	55	20	15	25	31	19	23	27	27	33	39	48	179	106	129	207	391	255
Bahamas	-17	0	0	27	24	107	88	210	146	149	250	101	200	147	206	360	706	1131	700
Barbados	10	6	14	7	12	8	10	14	15	17	19	19	17	58	50	159	36	51	133
Belize	17	14	16	9	15	21	11	8	13	56	28	40	25	58	170	107	73	112	179
Dominica	13	15	20	13	23	54	18	21	7	18	11	12	14	20	19	27	34	48	60
Grenada	13	15	23	20	19	20	17	34	49	46	36	49	58	85	42	28	119	140	68
Guyana	8	13	146	70	107	74	92	52	47	48	67	56	44	26	48	77	102	152	178
Jamaica	138	133	142	78	77	81	90	147	287	524	471	614	479	721	650	601	850	779	789
St Kitts and Nevis	49	21	13	14	15	20	35	20	32	42	96	88	82	67	62	50	203	143	94
St Lucia	45	58	41	34	33	33	18	50	83	94	49	22	31	102	111	112	119	261	110
St Vincent and the Grenadines	8	9	15	31	47	31	18	42	28	46	28	21	32	55	56	34	85	92	96

Table 9.5b: Net inflows of foreign direct investment (as a % of gross capital formation), 1990–2008

	1990	1991	1992	1993	1994	1995	1996	1997	1998	1999	2000	2001	2002	2003	2004	2005	2006	2007	2008
Antigua and Barbuda	48.0	35.7	13.6	10.3	15.4	17.0	10.0	12.1	13.4	12.4	10.4	21.8	17.9	22.3	24.1	29.9	45.7	70.0	28.4
Bahamas	n.a.	n.a.	n.a.	n.a.	n.a.	n.a.	n.a.	n.a.	n.a.	23.5	38.9	15.7	31.2	22.6	10.5	20.3	38.2	57.5	29.7
Barbados	3.5	2.6	9.6	4.5	5.6	4.2	4.7	4.1	3.6	3.6	4.1	4.0	3.4	24.0	9.7	31.7	5.6	6.4	18.4
Belize	14.9	10.9	11.1	5.7	11.2	17.7	13.7	7.5	10.3	27.5	7.7	16.2	11.8	18.0	81.7	54.4	27.5	45.5	83.1
Dominica	19.2	26.3	37.1	24.2	39.0	74.6	27.4	28.4	9.4	24.3	12.9	15.6	25.3	23.6	24.9	37.4	45.1	54.6	51.3
Grenada	15.4	16.4	31.1	25.7	20.5	22.6	16.4	29.5	38.5	27.5	22.3	38.4	38.7	40.1	20.0	13.4	65.4	60.0	88.2
Guyana	0.0	0.0	94.0	36.8	72.5	37.7	44.0	23.3	22.7	29.0	41.6	36.7	27.4	16.5	26.5	39.5	36.4	31.5	63.6
Jamaica	11.7	13.3	13.6	5.6	9.8	10.2	13.0	9.3	18.7	27.8	22.1	26.4	17.7	21.8	24.0	20.8	24.1	22.9	18.5
St Kitts and Nevis	55.6	29.7	18.3	15.6	17.8	18.7	31.1	16.5	25.9	53.1	63.3	44.9	52.4	30.7	31.4	26.1	94.3	59.3	41.6
St Lucia	43.9	53.1	35.6	28.0	26.3	31.5	14.9	35.0	55.8	44.8	31.2	13.5	20.4	19.0	65.1	67.3	62.7	66.2	41.1
St Vincent and the Grenadines	13.6	14.4	26.5	50.6	68.5	38.4	54.6	105.6	88.4	52.4	33.1	20.5	30.0	37.3	38.7	21.5	47.1	57.3	42.2

Source: World Investment Report (various years).

economic development in the CARICOM region has been its role in financing domestic investment. In general, CARICOM economies have often times depended on FDI flows to reduce their two main financing gaps: the foreign-exchange and savings/investment gaps. FDI as a percentage of gross capital formation in the various member countries for which data is available is also shown in table 9.5b. In 1990, only St Kitts and Nevis had a net FDI inflow that as a percentage of gross capital formation exceeded 50 per cent. By 2007, the percentage representation of net FDI in gross capital formation increased for all of the listed CARICOM countries.

For CARICOM as a whole, the average share of FDI in gross capital formation increased by 23 per cent between 1990 and 2000 (from 22.6 per cent in 1990 to 46 per cent in 2008). Additionally, the ratio of FDI to gross capital formation was almost three times the international average for all developing countries. Part of the reason for this has to do with the fact that foreign investment projects in CARICOM tend to be expensive and capital intensive. In contrast, most projects in which domestic capital is involved are labour intensive.

9.6 Does FDI Lead to Economic Growth?

Figure 9.2 shows the scatter plot of the relationship between real economic growth and the inflows of FDI into the Trinidad and Tobago economy. As indicated in the scatter plot, there is a strong positive relationship between these two variables. This is reflected in a correlation score between these two variables of 70 per cent. This is not surprising, since FDI helps build up the stock of capital, which in turn enhances labour productivity, exports and economic growth.

9.7 FDI and Wage Inequality in Developing Countries

An important feature of the globalization process is that it enhances the free flow of factors of production to those parts of the world where they can attract the highest returns. The wave of globalization characterizing the world economy has had something of a paradoxical result in that it has placed increasing pressure on developing economies to

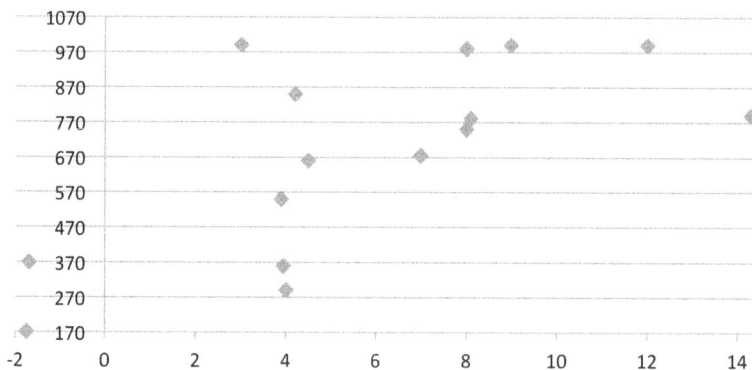

Figure 9.2: Scatter plot of the relationship between FDI and real economic growth, 1990–2006

drift towards production functions that deploy a greater level of capital and skills-biased technology, which tend to reduce the relative demand for unskilled labour; the consequence has been growing unemployment in the informal sector.

Skills-biased technological change (SBTC) as induced by modern technologies refers to change that leads not only to an increase in productivity but also to an increase in the employment of skilled workers. Consequently, employers will increase their demand for relatively greater amounts of skilled workers. At the same time, there will be a relative decline in the demand for unskilled workers.

FDI tends to promote SBTC and hence widens the gap between the remuneration of the skilled and unskilled workers in an economy. To explain the differences in remuneration between skilled and unskilled workers in the context of SBTC, we can draw reference to figure 9.3. In this diagram, the RD curve represents the national relative demand for skilled labour. The RS curve is the supply of skilled labour relative to unskilled labour. Initial equilibrium in this scenario occurs at the point where $RD_0 = RS_0$, indicated by e_0 in the diagram.

In figure 9.3, the relative wage of skilled workers to unskilled workers, W_0^r, is given by W^s/W^u where W^s is the wage of skilled workers and W^u is the wage of unskilled workers. Q^r is calculated in the same way and represents the relative employment of skilled workers to unskilled workers. In this setting, a skills premium occurs when rs shifts leftwards and/or rD shifts rightwards.[8] The RS curve can be influenced to shift by a number of factors, including investment in tertiary-level education, international trade and migration. Investment in tertiary-level education can help shift the RS curve rightwards by providing a greater flow of skilled students at every relative wage rate.

Given that factors of production are embodied in trade of goods and services, international trade can influence relative wages in an economy. Trinidad and Tobago exports ammonia, methanol, urea, liquefied natural gas, and iron and steel products, which are

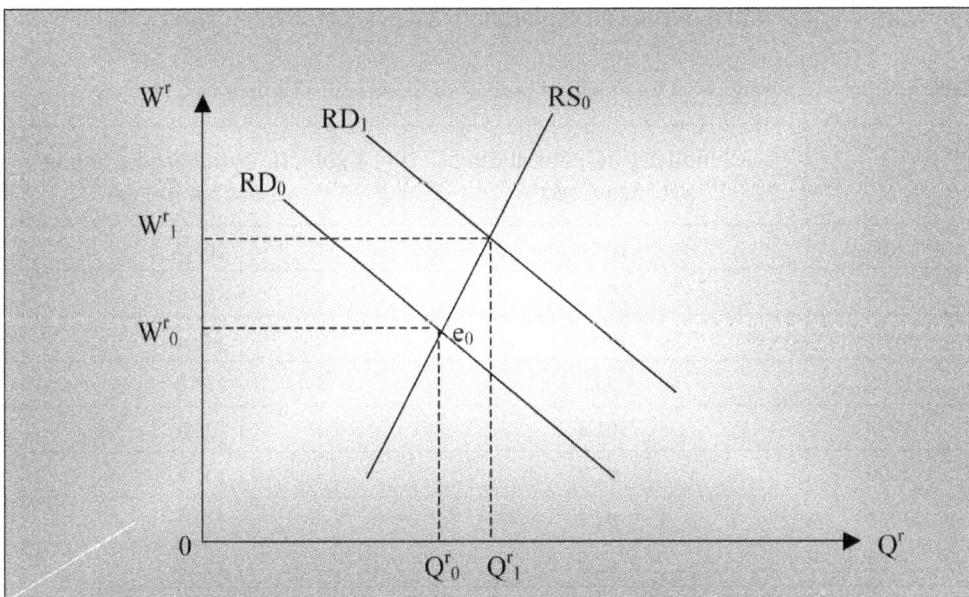

Figure 9.3: Relative wage determination in the labour market

much more skilled-labour intensive than unskilled-labour intensive. Trade in goods implies trade in factor services. In fact, if input-output tables are used, trade flows can be "converted" into "embodied factor services". The RS curve shifts leftward if the export of skilled labour relative to unskilled labour is greater than imports of the same.

Immigration increases the stock of skilled workers, while emigration reduces the stock. This "brain drain", by reducing the number of skilled workers in an economy, can therefore extend the size of the relative wage gap between skilled and unskilled workers.

The RD curve can shift to the right if there is SBTC in the economy. Thus if FDI has led to widespread SBTC, then this would lead to an increase in the wage of skilled workers relative to unskilled workers.

9.8 Wage Inequality in Trinidad and Tobago[9]

To reflect on the influence of FDI on wage inequality, it is necessary to investigate the trends in the wages of production workers (typically more skilled workers) to non-production workers (typically unskilled workers). Since the labour and employment database provided by the Central Statistical Office does not offer data on non-production workers, for Trinidad and Tobago data on all employees (which is provided) is used as a proxy.

Table 9.6 shows the average relative weekly wages of production workers to all employees in (a) all industries excluding the petroleum sector and (b) the exploration and production of crude oil and natural gas sector. What emerges is that in all industries excluding the petroleum sector, the average relative weekly earnings of production workers to all employees actually fell by 13 per cent; there was a lower degree of wage inequality. In the exploration and production of crude oil and natural gas sector, however, skilled workers realized a 54 per cent comparative increase in average relative weekly earnings in the time interval 1995–2002. The correlation between the relative average weekly earnings of production workers in the crude oil exploration and production sector and FDI/GDP was

Table 9.6: Ratio of average weekly earnings of production workers to all employees, 1995–2002

	All industry index excluding petroleum sector	Exploration and production of oil and natural gas
1995	100.0	100.0
1996	102.7	119.2
1997	100.3	140.6
1998	93.8	143.9
1999	101.3	125.8
2000	97.7	137.7
2001	94.3	144.5
2002	87.0	154.0

Source: Central Bank of Trinidad and Tobago, own computations.

70 per cent. This evidence supports the argument that a greater degree of globalization as measured by the ratio of FDI to GDP has facilitated the increase in the relative wages of skilled workers.

9.9 Conclusion

This chapter introduced and discussed some of the relevant economics associated with FDI flows. In particular, the chapter assessed the economic welfare gains associated with FDI flows and also outlined and discussed various determinants of FDI flows. The chapter also provided a sketch of FDI-related economic activity in the Caribbean and closed off by discussing the effect of FDI on wage inequality.

Summary of Key Points

- Foreign direct investment (FDI) refers to investment of long-term duration from a foreign country into a domestic (host) country that may take the form of a "composite bundle of capital stocks, know-how and technology".
- Corporations invest abroad to exploit technological, managerial, financial or marketing strengths; exploit natural resources and take advantage of low wages.
- Skills-biased technological change (SBTC) refers to change that leads not only to an increase in productivity but also to an increase in the employment of skilled workers.

Multiple Choice

1. Advocates of FDI as a source of economic growth base their arguments on which of the following areas:
   a) innovation and technological progress
   b) political corruption
   c) the environment
   d) income distribution

2. Which of the following are benefits of FDI to a developing country:
   a) an increase in the capital to labour ratio
   b) an increase in the productivity of labour
   c) an increase in the level of domestic income
   d) all of the above

3. All are reasons for private foreign direct investment except
   a) the horizontal and vertical integration of production processes
   b) to maximize profitability and to diversify risks
   c) to stimulate development
   d) to avoid paying taxes

4. A government policy with regards to FDI flows is dependent on several factors, including
    a) political ideology
    b) macroeconomic stability
    c) legal ideology
    d) all of the above

5. Which of the following is not a benefit of FDI inflows to a developing country:
    a) the resource transfer effect
    b) the employment effect
    c) potential for environmental destruction
    d) the balance of payments effect

Short Essay

1. Evaluate the factors that influence FDI inflows into any developing economy.
2. Discuss in detail the trends in FDI flows internationally.
3. Which has benefited the most from FDI flows over the last decade: Trinidad and Tobago or Barbados? Use statistical data to support your analysis.

Key Trade Terms

- International factor flows
- Foreign direct investment (FDI)
- Inward FDI
- Marginal product of capital
- Domestic investment
- Market access
- Industrialization by invitation
- Financial crises
- Poverty reduction
- Remittances
- Gross capital formation
- Wage inequality
- Skills Biased Technological Change (SBTC)

International Flows of Factors of Production

Labour

Learning Objectives

a. Identify the trends in migration flows.
b. Outline the migratory flow of nurses in a two-country setting from a theoretical perspective.
c. List the main push/pull factors affecting the migration of nurses in CARICOM economies.
d. Describe the trends in world remittance flows.
e. Identify the factors conditioning remittance flows.
f. Outline the economic impact of remittance flows.

10.0 Introduction

According to the International Organization for Migration (IOM 2003), at the beginning of the twenty-first century, one out of every thirty-five people in the entire world was an international migrant. Furthermore, 175 million people were classified as international migrants: 2.9 per cent of the world population. Overall, migration levels have more than doubled over the last thirty-five years, with 48 per cent of international migrants being women.

Figure 10.1 reflects a consistent increase in world population from 5.9 billion people in 1998 to 6.2 billion in 2002, whereas the population growth rate in percentage terms has experienced a fall from 0.0129 per cent in 1998 to 0.0118 per cent in 2002.

According to the IOM, among the Organization for Economic Co-operation and Development (OECD) countries in 1999, the United States had the largest number of foreign workers (16.7 million) followed by Germany (3.6 million) and then Australia (2.4 million), France (1.6 million) and the United Kingdom (1.1 million).

10.1 Labour Movement between Countries

In order to illustrate some of the mechanics associated with the migration of workers, let us focus our discussion on the international migration of nurses. First, it shall be assumed that there are no imperfections in the market for nurses' labour in the global economy. In figure 10.2, let MPP_{dg} represent the demand for nurses in the developing economies, while MPP_{dd} is the demand for nurses in developed economies. The combined stock of

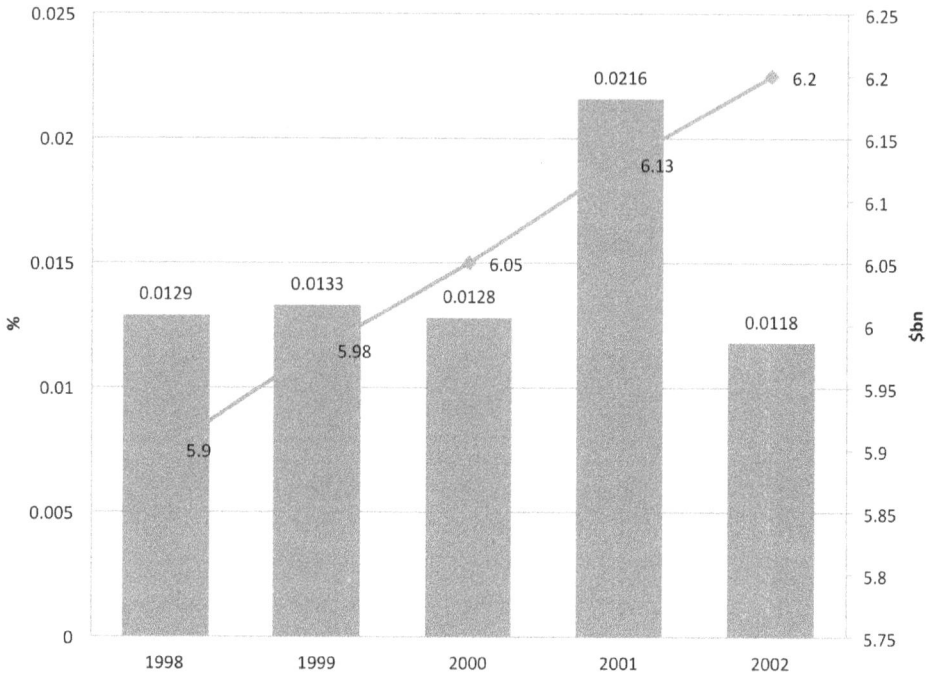

Figure 10.1: World population level and growth
Source: Clive, Hosein and Yan (2005).

nurses is shown on the horizontal axis, and the wage rates in either group of countries on the vertical axis. If we assume that nurses' labour is homogenous and nurses are perfectly mobile, then nurses will move out of the developing economy into the developed economy, where this type of labour is in short supply. The consequence of this migratory trend is that the wage rate in the developing country will eventually fall, while the wage rate in the developed economy will eventually rise. In equilibrium, the wage rate will settle at W_{eq} with L_1 nurses being employed in developing economies and $L_1 L_{tot}$ in developed economies.

In the real world, however, numerous labour market imperfections exist. To reflect this, let the starting point in figure 10.2 be adjusted to reflect that the labour market for nurses' skills does not clear internationally but rather clears in individual domestic markets. The consequence of this is that L_1 nurses will be employed in the developing countries at a wage rate of W_{eq} with the corresponding number of nurses employed in the developed economies being L_2 at a wage rate of W_2. The gap in the wages earned between nurses employed in the developed and developing world is therefore $W_2 - W_{eq}$.[1] This gap will be a significant pull factor for migration.

If there is an increase in nurses migrating to the developed world from the developing world, then the salaries of nurses in the developed world should fall while the salaries of nurses in the developing world should increase.

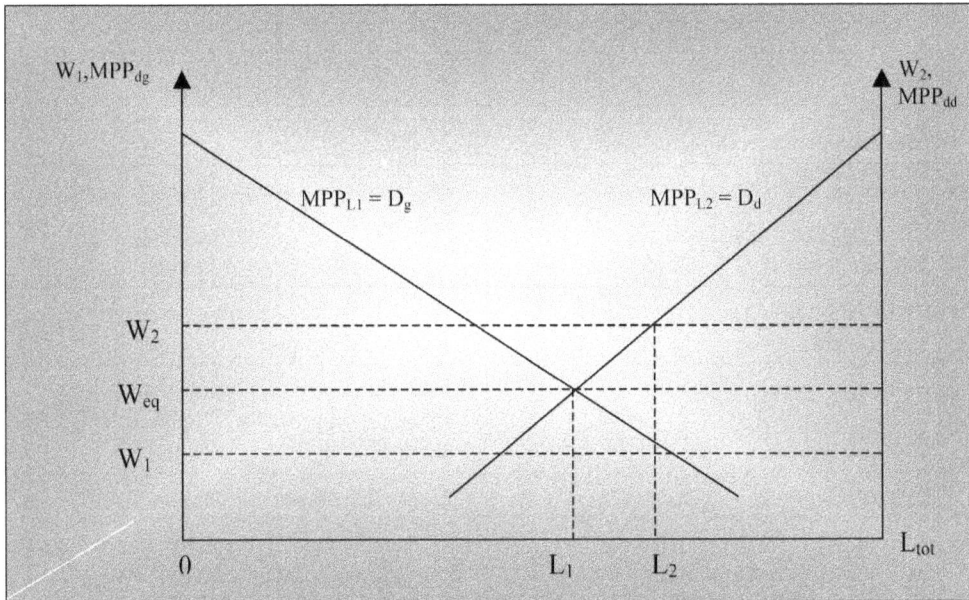

Figure 10.2: Determining the migratory flow of nurses in a two-country setting

10.2 Motives for International Labour Migration: Reflections on the Migration of Nurses from CARICOM

Labour is generally less mobile than capital. However, there have been great flows of labour from South-South countries to developed countries. This section outlines some of the general push/pull factors associated with the migration of nurses from the CARICOM. (The arguments made can be applied to other categories of migrant workers.)

Push/Pull Factors

The main push/pull factors identified by studies on the migration of nurses across international borders over the last fifty years are shown in table 10.1.

The push/pull factors from this table that are of relevance to CARICOM economies are discussed in the next section.

Low Wages in CARICOM Economies vs. High Wages in Destination Economies

One of the significant factors motivating the migration of nurses from CARICOM economies is the availability of relatively higher nursing-sector wages in the developed world. Nurses generally do not leave their home economy because they are unemployed but because they seek a higher standard of living. For example, with the formation of the North American Free Trade Area (NAFTA), many nurses crossed the border to work in the United States in pursuit of a higher salary. It is estimated that 80 per cent of these nurses migrated although they had jobs in Mexico. The reality is that economic agents

Table 10.1: Summary of push/pull factors affecting the migration of nurses

Push factors	Pull factors
• Inadequate remuneration and benefits	• Attractive payments and benefits
• Unfavourable working conditions	• Modern human resource management systems
• Lack of management and leadership	• Professional work environments
• Insufficient training and professional development	• Possibility of permanent residency in receiving economy
• Insufficient career perspectives	• Financial support for registration and immigration procedures provided by foreign employers
• Underutilization of acquired skills	• Supportive network of family and friends
• Burnout due to increased workload as a consequence of resignations	• Opportunities for professional development and career advancement
• Lack of recognition of profession	• Professional advancement
	• Improved quality of life for self and family

Source: UNECLAC (2003).

will not move from their home country to a foreign economy to benefit from a meagre increase in income, and as such, the difference in salaries must be sufficiently large so as to swamp the strong natural inclination of economic agents to remain at home.

Average salaries in Washington, DC, range from $38,000 to $62,000 with annual bonuses ranging from $2,000 to $6,000 and additional retention bonuses being offered by some hospitals. A comparative study conducted in Barbados revealed that the average nursing personnel salary range was between $15,000 and $21,000 (Buchan 2004). In the United Kingdom, a nurse can earn a variety of wages depending on his or her area of expertise. A staff nurse can earn a per annum salary of $32,354 to $35,711; an oncology nurse specialist salary (depending on experience) is $45,250 to $58,744 and a full-time lead nurse earns $38,347 to $47,886 (www.jobsearch.co.uk).

In addition to salary, non-cash benefits also influence migration decisions. Some of these non-cash benefits include insurance, housing, education grants and travel allowances. As it stands, the wage gap between health-care workers from developed and developing countries is so wide, incremental improvements will be insufficient to reverse the current migratory trends.

Poor Working Conditions in CARICOM vs. Better Working Conditions Abroad

Many of the nurses that leave CARICOM economies do so because of poor working conditions. This is predominantly manifested in the unavailability of basic complementary medicine and equipment. When nurses migrate, there is an increased workload for those who remain. This in turn can result in increased stress levels for the remaining nurses, higher levels of absenteeism as well as a movement of nurses from public- to private-sector health institutions.

An indication of working conditions in the health sector can be gleaned from considering per capita health sector expenditure. In 2000, Barbados and Bahamas spent $606 and $880 on health services per capita, respectively (these are the two highest levels of per capita health-sector expenditures for CARICOM economies), as compared to $1,747 and $4,499 spent by the United Kingdom and United States, respectively, in the same year. Along the same line of reasoning, note that in 2000 the Bahamas had 1.52 physicians per 1,000 people, higher than in any other CARICOM economy. In the United Kingdom and United States, the corresponding figures were 1.81 (2000) and 2.82 (2001), respectively. Again, if we assume that developed economies carry more optimal ratios of physicians to nurses, then the workload of nurses in the CARICOM sphere appears substantially higher than that of their developed-country counterparts.

Distinct Economic Disparity between Developed and CARICOM Economies

Differential economic conditions are perhaps the most important factors influencing migration decisions. Most of the developing economies from which nurses migrate are characterized by weak economic conditions, typified by high and rising levels of unemployment, low rates of real economic growth, high costs of living and little opportunity for economic advancement under existing circumstances.[2]

A reflection on figure 10.3 indicates that in the selected CARICOM economies, the per capita gross domestic product (GDP) was less than 45 per cent of that in the United Kingdom or United States for both the decade of the 1990s and the average of the period 2000–2001.

Another view of the very different economic conditions in the CARICOM sphere and the developed world to which CARICOM nurses migrate is reflected in table 10.2. In the first instance, the level of GDP in the United States, Canada and the United Kingdom is substantially greater than that of the two largest CARICOM economies, and at the same time the average annual growth rate of GDP was stronger in these same developed economies as compared to CARICOM economies for the time interval 1975–2005. From

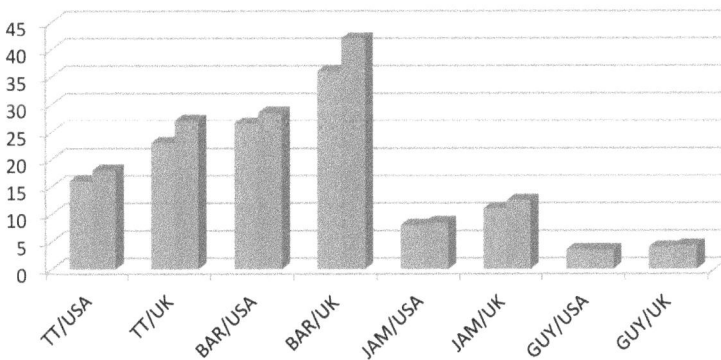

Figure 10.3: Ratio of GDP per capita in Trinidad and Tobago, Barbados, Jamaica, and Guyana to GDP per capita in the United States and United Kingdom, 1990s average

Table 10.2: Some indicators of economic performance in the economies

Country	GDP $ billions, 2005	GDP per capita growth rate, 1975–2005	Growth competitiveness ranking, 2005	Business competitiveness ranking, 2005
Jamaica	11.15	0.32	70	53
Trinidad and Tobago	15.98	2.06	60	65
United States	12,579.7	2.07	2	1
Canada	1,133.8	1.78	14	13
United Kingdom	2,280.1	2.15	13	6

Source: Global Competitiveness Report (World Economic Forum 2006).

another dimension, the Trinidad and Tobago economy is ranked sixtieth in growth competitiveness[3] and sixty-fifth in business competitiveness[4] in the world, as compared to seventieth and fifty-third for Jamaica, respectively. In contrast, observe the associated ranks of the growth competitiveness and business competitiveness variables for the predominant destination economies to which CARICOM nurses migrate.

There is some indication that in CARICOM economies, real GDP growth rates move in the opposite direction to nursing vacancy rates. This is reflected in the scatter plot in figure 10.4.

Differences in Standards of Living between Developed and CARICOM Economies

The Human Development Index (HDI) developed by the United Nations provides a summary measure of human development. It does so by means of measuring the average achievements of three broad dimensions of human development: life expectancy, literacy and economic growth.

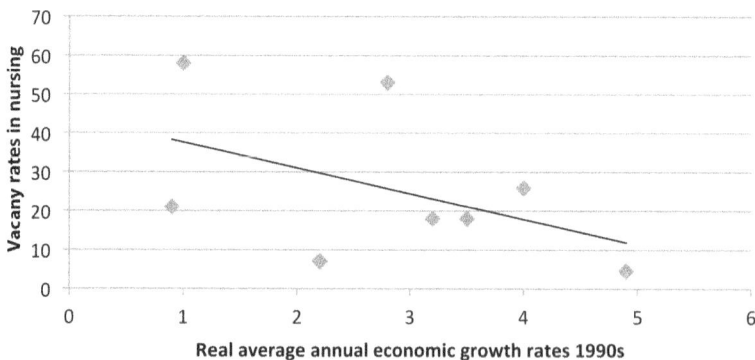

Figure 10.4: Scatter plot between real annual growth of some CARICOM economies in the 1990s and nursing vacancy rates, 2004

In table 10.3, observe that Canada has the highest HDI among the three listed developed countries, with a score of 0.966. The United States and United Kingdom follow closely with HDI scores of 0.956 and 0.947, respectively. In terms of the CARICOM countries, the region as a whole enjoys a similar level of human development with the noted exceptions of Barbados and Haiti, which have HDI scores of 0.903 and 0.532, respectively. All the other CARICOM countries have HDI scores ranging from 0.729 to 0.868. These differences in the standard of living among CARICOM economies and the United States, United Kingdom and Canada will have no doubt been instrumental in encouraging the migration of nurses out of CARICOM economies into the developed world.

Cost of Living Differential between Developed and CARICOM Economies

A significant push/pull factor influencing the movement of labour from the CARICOM to the developed world is the relative cost of living differential between both sets of economies. For CARICOM, figure 10.5 shows the relative price levels in Trinidad and

Table 10.3: HDI scores in CARICOM economies, the United States, the United Kingdom and Canada, 2007

Country	HDI
Antigua and Barbuda	0.868
The Bahamas	0.856
Barbados	0.903
Belize	0.772
Dominica	0.814
Grenada	0.813
Guyana	0.729
Haiti	0.532
Jamaica	0.766
Montserrat	n.a.
St Lucia	0.821
St Kitts and Nevis	0.838
St Vincent and the Grenadines	0.772
Suriname	0.769
Trinidad and Tobago	0.837
United States	0.956
United Kingdom	0.947
Canada	0.966

Source: Human Development Report (2009).

Tobago, Barbados, and Jamaica as a percentage of the price levels in the United Kingdom and United States. In the case of Barbados, the cost of living was similar to that in United Kingdom and United States for the 1990s and the period 2000–2001. However, the cost of living in Jamaica had skyrocketed since the 1990s. Trinidad and Tobago and Guyana, while relatively better off than Jamaica, both carried a higher cost of living in the period 2000–2001 relative to the United Kingdom and United States as compared to their situation in the 1990s.

Other things constant, relatively higher inflation rates in the CARICOM imply that one US dollar in the time periods considered will fetch a relatively greater amount of goods in the United States, United Kingdom and Canada as compared to CARICOM economies. The search for an improvement in their economic well-being will no doubt have encouraged some nurses pursuant of a lower cost of living and greater purchasing power to migrate to the developed world.

Relatively Superior Training Opportunities for Nurses in Developed Economies as Compared to CARICOM Economies

Another significant push/pull factor that necessitates attention is the training and post-basic education available in the developed countries as compared to the developing countries. In most developing economies, including those of the CARICOM, there is a deficiency in training opportunities beyond initial nursing training and this contributes to a general element of demotivation among nurses. In this regard, the greater degree of training, retraining and education in developed economies is a significant pull factor for migration of nurses from CARICOM. In some cases, the migrants are of the opinion that migration is the only way to further their careers.

In support of this point, Kingma (2001), commenting on the findings of a survey conducted by the International Council of Nurses that focused on the incentives and disincentives for nurses to migrate from developing to developed economies, highlighted that the greatest incentive indicated by the respondents was the availability of learning opportunities.

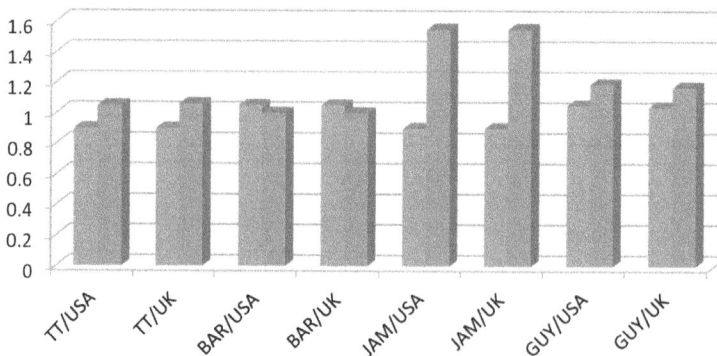

Figure 10.5: Ratio of retail price indices in Trinidad and Tobago, Barbados, Jamaica, and Guyana to those of the United States and United Kingdom, 1990s and 2000–2001 averages

Opportunity for Remittances

Migration facilitates increased financial security and hence provides an opportunity for remittances.[5] Remittances have the potential to directly improve the standard of living of relatives in the migrant's home country. Within the region, the amount of remittances has improved considerably with a current average of about 7–10 per cent of GDP per year. Moreover, remittances account for 14 per cent of GDP in Guyana, 21 per cent of GDP in Haiti and 14 per cent of GDP in Jamaica (see table 10.4). Notwithstanding that remittances more directly influence consumption rather than investment, the multiplier effect generated can potentially stimulate aggregate demand. It also provides capital for the start-up of small informal business enterprises.

The ability to remit some fraction of their discretionary income would have no doubt influenced the choice of some CARICOM nurses to migrate.

10.3 Persistence of Push/Pull Factors into the Medium and Long Term

There are also some pull factors that continue to motivate the migration of nurses, including the ageing nursing population in developed economies (Buerhaus et al. 2000). In 2001, 16.1 per cent of the population in the United Kingdom was age sixty-five or older, with the corresponding ratio for the United States being 12.6 per cent. In both countries, these shares are increasing. In terms of actual numbers, in 1960 the population over sixty-five in the United Kingdom was 6.1 million, but by 2001 this was estimated to be 9.4 million: a 54.2 per cent increase. In the United States, the population age sixty-five and above increased 116 per cent from 16.6 million to 35.9 million in the time period 1960–2001. Generally speaking, elderly people require more health-care services than other people, and as table 10.5 shows, the elderly population in destination countries will continue to increase well into the future even up until 2050.

Table 10.4: Remittances to the Caribbean, 2008

Country	Remittances ($ millions)	GDP ($ millions)	% of GDP
Barbados	55	3,670	1.51
Cuba	n.a.	62,705	n.a.
Dominican Republic	3,222	45,805	7.03
Guyana	274	1,939	14.13
Haiti	1,370	6,408	`21.38
Jamaica	2,021	14,245	14.19
Trinidad and Tobago	95	25,925	0.37
Total	7,036	160,696	4.38

Source: World Development Indicators (2008).

Table 10.5: Forecasted population in various age groups for Canada, the United Kingdom and the United States

Age	65–69	70–74	75–79	80+	65+
Canada					
2025	2,433,224	1,967,969	1,526,696	1,964,641	7,892,530
2050	2,400,497	2,130,481	1,854,306	3,950,340	10,335,624
United Kingdom					
2025	3,675,037	2,999,994	2,764,704	3,556,467	12,996,202
2050	3,749,052	3,246,723	3,047,456	6,376,572	16,419,803
United States					
2025	19,646,750	16,040,825	12,267,624	15,568,533	63,523,732
2050	20,443,823	17,498,614	15,066,841	33,696,559	86,705,837

Source: Pan American Health Organization (2002).

Table 10.6: Summary information on some studies forecasting the nursing shortages in selected developed economies

Study	Predicted shortfall
United States	
US Department of Health and Human Services (2002)	Shortfall of 800,000 registered nurses by 2020. This is based on a 40 per cent increase in demand but only a 6 per cent increase in the supply of registered nurses.
The Centre for Health Workforce Studies at the University of Albany (2002)	Growth of one million nursing jobs in the period 2000–2010, of which 561,000 will be new jobs and 449,000 because of retirement and other factors.
Canada	
Canadian Nurses Association (CNA) (1997)	Shortfall of nursing professionals ranging between 59,000 and 113,000 by 2011.
Ryerson, Centennial, George Brown, Collaborative Nursing Degree Program (2002)	Shortfall of 113,000 nurses by 2016.
United Kingdom	
United Kingdom, the British Medical Association (BMA) (2002)	Mainland Europe will require 300,000 more NHS staff by 2022. This includes 62,000 doctors and 108,000 nurses.

Source: Pan American Health Organization (2002).

Another strong pull factor for nurses to migrate in the future will remain the high level of nursing shortages in the developed world. Although there are contrasting forecasts by various researchers, these forecasts all indicate that the shortages will be substantive (see table 10.6).

10.4 Foreign Population Characteristics in Developed Countries

In table 10.7a, the foreign population composition of various OECD countries is shown. In the 1980s, for the listed countries the data ranges from 0.8 per cent in Japan to 16.1 per cent in Canada. During the 1990s, however, the foreign population for every one of the

Table 10.7a: Foreign population composition in the OECD countries (%)

	Late 1980s	Late 1990s
Belgium	8.8	8.7
France	6.8	6.3
Germany	7.3	8.9
Italy	1.1	2.1
United Kingdom	3.2	3.8
United States	7.9	9.8
Canada	16.1	17.4
Japan	0.8	1.2

Source: Faini (2001).

Table 10.7b: Migration rates by educational attainments (% of the host country's educational group)

Origin country	To the United States		To the OECD	
	Secondary education	Tertiary education	Secondary education	Tertiary education
Korea	1.2	5.7	3.3	14.9
Philippines	4.4	6.6	6.0	9.0
Ghana	0.3	15.1	0.7	25.7
Uganda	0.6	15.4	0.6	15.5
Dominican Rep.	29.7	14.2	30.5	14.7
Guatemala	29.1	13.5	29.1	13.5
Colombia	3.6	5.6	3.8	5.6
Mexico	20.9	10.3	20.9	10.3

Source: Carrington and Detragiache (1998).

listed countries except Belgium and France increased. Clearly then, there has been an increasing tendency for people to migrate to the OECD member states. Furthermore, Carrington and Detragiache (1998) showed that the general tendency has been for people with tertiary-level education to be more mobile than those with only secondary school education. Note that for some countries, migratory patterns to the United States (as compared to all OECD countries) have been higher for secondary school graduates than tertiary-level graduates (these countries are the Dominican Republic, Guatemala and Mexico, although in each case migratory patterns of tertiary-level graduates to the United States also topped 10 per cent; see table 10.7b).

10.5 World Remittance Flows

Table 10.8 shows that world remittance flows tallied $14,406.4 million in 1985 and rose to $230,853.3 million in 2008: an increase of 1,502.4 per cent. The distribution of these remittance flows has changed substantially during the period 1985–2008. In particular, while 83 per cent of remittance flows went to developed countries in 1985, this fell to 41.3 per cent in 2008. At the same time, the flow of remittances to the developing world expanded from 17.4 per cent in 1985 to 62.3 per cent in 2008. As concerns CARICOM countries, remittance flows improved considerably from a paltry $221.1 million in 1985 to $4,043.3 million in 2008, of which the Organization of Eastern Caribbean States (OECS) bloc received 5.5 per cent in 1985 and 3.8 per cent in 2008.

Factors Conditioning Remittance Flows

First, the number of workers and the wage rate offered in the host country are important variables conditioning the amount of money migrant workers remit. Depending on the elasticity of supply of the total migrant labour force in the host country, the individual will determine the amount to be remitted. If there are many low-skilled migrants in the host country, then an individual migrant will have to settle for lower wages, which sometimes may not be adequate for him or her to remit even subsistence amounts of money for his or her family. Therefore, his or her earnings determine consumption, savings and thus the potential for remittances.

Another determinant of remittances is the level of economic activity in the home and host countries. If the home country is experiencing an economic recession, then the migrant worker may be inclined to remit more to supplement the decline or loss of income of family members. On the other hand, the labour-importing country will set a quota on the number of migrants it is willing to receive depending on its level of economic activity; if it is currently experiencing a boom or an increase in economic activity, the number of jobs available will increase, and this will create further opportunity for potentially greater migratory flows.

The level of domestic inflation is another determinant of the amount of money that a migrant worker may be willing to remit or put in the form of savings in the host country. If the inflation rate were high at home, the migrant would be inclined to send more money to maintain his or her family's consumption level at home. On the other hand, inflation may deter remittances if there is a high level of uncertainty and risk involved.

The political environment in both the home and the host country will also influence

Table 10.8: Remittances, 1988–2008 (US$mn)

Year	World	Developed	Developing	Developed/world (%)	Developing/world (%)	CARICOM	OECS	OECS/CARICOM (%)
1985	14,406.4	11,892.7	2,513.6	82.55	17.45	221.10	12.20	5.52
1986	14,447.4	11,539.0	2,908.4	79.87	20.13	234.20	57.80	24.68
1987	16,699.4	13,205.3	3,494.1	79.08	20.92	270.70	69.10	25.53
1988	16,408.2	12,419.3	3,988.9	75.69	24.31	307.90	69.50	22.57
1989	16,925.0	12,237.7	4,687.3	72.31	27.69	351.60	69.90	19.88
1990	29,422.3	14,853.1	14,569.2	50.48	49.52	252.20	73.30	29.06
1991	20,680.7	6,035.0	14,645.6	29.18	70.82	195.50	15.60	7.98
1992	25,343.3	17,229.8	8,113.5	67.99	32.01	212.00	0.00	0.00
1993	26,078.8	17,050.4	9,028.4	65.38	34.62	320.40	70.40	21.97
1994	30,879.2	19,885.4	10,993.8	64.40	35.60	616.20	82.30	13.36
1995	43,216.8	21,463.5	21,753.3	49.66	50.34	754.10	85.20	11.30
1996	45,356.3	23,277.3	22,079.0	51.32	48.68	841.00	101.30	12.05
1997	45,977.0	24,422.9	21,554.1	53.12	46.88	862.40	102.00	11.83
1998	36,194.4	13,293.3	22,901.1	36.73	63.27	1226.70	106.00	8.64
1999	39,557.7	14,930.5	24,627.2	37.74	62.26	1381.60	109.80	7.95
2000	53,806.4	26,597.3	27,208.6	49.43	50.57	1653.90	114.10	6.90
2001	57,241.7	19,001.5	38,240.3	33.20	66.80	1868.60	115.10	6.16
2002	80,537.2	33,227.7	47,309.5	41.26	58.74	2186.10	118.70	5.43
2003	98,225.6	40,001.5	58,224.0	40.72	59.28	2536.50	122.20	4.82
2004	109,132.5	38,633.7	70,498.8	35.40	64.60	2928.70	153.20	5.23
2005	139,793.8	43,881.1	95,912.7	31.39	68.61	3183.20	137.20	4.31
2006	168,271.6	54,666.4	113,605.2	32.49	67.51	3448.60	142.90	4.14
2007	203,617.8	68,896.0	134,721.8	33.84	66.16	4021.50	149.10	3.71
2008	230,853.3	86,984.5	143,868.8	37.68	62.32	4043.30	154.20	3.81
Total	1,563,072.8	645,625.6	917,447.2	41.30	58.70	33918.20	2231.00	6.58

Source: Computed using *World Development Indicators* data.

the level of remittances of a migrant worker. If the migrant perceives that there is political instability in the home country, he or she will reduce or even altogether stop any remittance flows because of the risk that his or her family may not receive the amount remitted. Similarly, if there is political instability in the host country, the migrant may be unable to remit because of the disruption of the distribution channel for these remittances.

Another determinant of the level of remittances is the exchange rate between the home country and the host country. Depending on the exchange rate differential, the migrant will determine the amount to be remitted and the channel of remittance. Generally, the higher the exchange rate between the two countries, the more the migrant is required to remit to the home country to meet his or her family's requirements. In some cases, black markets exist in the home country, and this makes it more profitable to exchange units of the foreign currency for the domestic currency outside of the formal system. In addition, if the avenues through which remittances flow from the developed to the developing world are undeveloped, then this will encourage a greater flow of unrecorded remittance flows to the labour-exporting country. This is a particularly significant problem and makes it difficult to estimate the actual amount of remittances that flow from developed to developing countries.

The tax rate in the labour-exporting country and the host country is another important macroeconomic determinant of the level and flow of remittances. If the tax rate is higher in the host economy than in the labour-exporting country, then the migrant would remit fewer funds to the labour-exporting country.

Decisions to remit are also influenced by the real interest rate differential between the host country and the labour-exporting economy. If the real domestic interest rate is lower in the domestic economy than in the foreign economy, then the migrant would probably keep more of his or her income in the host economy.

Some other influences that condition the level of remittances are the marital status of the migrant, his or her level of education and occupational, whether or not dependants accompany him or her, the number of years spent in the host country and the employment of other household members.[6]

Measuring Remittances

How do we measure remittances? In general, the flows of remittances are not very accurate, and usually the official figures are estimated. Very often, the covered items are much less than the actual amount of remittance flows, since a significant amount of remitted flows are through unofficial channels and as a consequence are not captured in official statistics. Customarily, remittances are measured in the balance of payments under private (unrequited) transfers and include migrant transfers, worker remittances and other private remittances.

Economic Impact of Remittances

One of the constraints on CARICOM economic development is a shortage of capital. In this regard, remittances represent an important source of foreign exchange. At the macroeconomic level, the flow of remittances can ease the strain on the balance of payments directly when remittance flows are in hard foreign currencies or indirectly by reducing the imports of capital goods when the inflows of remittances are of that nature. Typically, all CARICOM countries have at best fledgling capital sectors and as a consequence import most of their capital requirements. In this sense, the flow of remittances can play an important role in terms of the financing of the developmental process.

Many poor people are unable to acquire loans from traditional financial institutions, and hence remittances can provide the relevant financial capital for middle- and lower-middle-income households to start up their productive activities. Remittances can be in the form of cash, capital goods, raw materials and inventory. Such remittance flows can then be used for industrial development and small-business creation, which can increase the level of investment and by extension the capital stock of the country. Since not every household is interested in investing, remittances can provide a valuable source of savings (which can be channelled into productive investments through the operation of financial intermediaries) and hence funds for investment, capital formation and development.[7]

It may be argued that remittances can be treated as an injection into the circular flow of income. Net remittances (remittance inflows minus outflows) are what really matters; ceteris paribus, an increase in net real remittance expands economic activity working through the multiplier, while negative net real remittance has the opposite effect (working through the demultiplier).[8]

It is widely understood that a fraction of remittances are expended on consumption goods. For consumption to contribute to economic development, it must foster improvements in the productivity of the participating households. Some positive externalities can be derived from private consumption – for example, improved healthcare and education of siblings.[9] Education, in turn, creates new employment opportunities and at the same time increases the stock of productive workers within any country.[10] More specifically, if remitted funds are expended on education, it can help improve the ratio of human capital to labour in the labour-receiving country, which in turn can create externality spillovers for the non-human capital component of the workforce. More so, if human capital is associated with greater absorption of foreign technology and higher quality products and new export opportunities, then the overall effect of using remittance in education can be profound.

Migration can also encourage the export of goods from the home country to diaspora markets in host countries. The migrant can be used to promote the exports of the labour-exporting country in the host country (for example, in cities such as Cambridge and Oxford in the United Kingdom, the main supermarkets have an abundance of overseas products that cater especially to overseas residents). For Caribbean countries, this is best done by the introduction and rooting of Caribbean culture in the host country, which in turn creates a demand for Caribbean exports. A positive externality from this promotion is increased tourist arrivals in the labour-exporting countries, especially as concerns the return of second- and third-generation migrant offspring.

However, there are also some negative impacts of remittances. For example, remittances can trigger a demonstration effect, which can induce increased consumption among non-migrant households. Furthermore, remittances can worsen social disparities and encourage even further migration, particularly (and as mentioned previously) when they are invested in education.

In some instances, remittances can lead to real-estate speculation, which raises the price of property. More specifically, if workers migrate and improve their purchasing capability, then their demand for real estate in their home country increases. As Rubenstein

(1982, 250) notes in relation to St Vincent, "Many of the lots are being held for investment purposes or in case their owners want to use them as building sites on their return to the island. In both cases the lands acquired in this way are not being cultivated".[11]

While the costs of education are carried by the home country, the returns to this investment accumulate to the host economy. If remittances are large enough, their inflows can offset these (training cost) losses. For example, Faini (2001) identified that Jamaica had to train a total of five doctors in order to keep one.[12] Carrington and Detragiache (1998) have shown that overall the current tendency is that individuals with little or no formal education have limited access to international opportunities for migration, and migrants in general are much more educated than the rest of the people in both their host and home countries.[13]

It is possible for the combination of remittances and non-farm labour demands to attract such a high proportion of young people that there is a shortfall in the supply of agricultural labour. In some countries (e.g., St Vincent), a dependence on remittance to finance education and obtain highly valued foreign imports only increased the desire of households to migrate. As Rubenstein (1982, 248) again notes, the strong desire to leave

Table 10.9: A summary of some of the costs and benefits associated with remittances

Benefits	Costs
1. Ease foreign exchange constraints and improve balance of payments	1. Foreign exchange flows are unpredictable
2. Permit imports of capital goods and raw material for industrial development	2. Spent on consumer goods, which increases imports
3. Provide a potential source of savings and capital formation for development	3. Result in little or no investment in capital-generating activities
4. Provide a net addition to household income	4. Replace other sources of income, thereby increasing dependency, eroding good work habits and heightening potential negative effects of return migration
5. Raise the immediate standard of living of recipients	5. Spent on unproductive or personal investment
6. Improve income distribution (if poorer/less-skilled migrate)	6. Create envy and resentment and induce consumption spending among non-migrants
7. May increase the per capita capital stock	7. May reduce foreign direct investment; the loss of skilled labour may be deleterious for long-term growth

Source: Russell (1986) and author's additions.

creates "a kind of 'migration mentality' in which migration from the island is viewed as the only means of achieving anything in life".[14]

Some forms of worker remittances, especially "barrels of foreign goods", may promote "demonstration effects" and encourage the emergence of alien taste patterns in the labour-exporting country, which in turn can have adverse implications for the balance of payments.

For some authors, these negative effects are considered to be so significant that it has been argued that "(remittances) are rarely the spark that creates enough economic activity to make migration unnecessary" (Martin 1990, 657).

In the final analysis, the influence of remittances on the economic development process has to rely on case studies, as the theoretical literature is still unclear. The literature is replete with these case studies. One such study conducted by UNECLAC (1991) highlighted that in El Salvador remittance flows benefited 55 per cent of the population and consisted of 72 per cent of the household income. Although remittances may have improved the standard of living of El Salvadorians, a number of researchers concur that remittances have modified the culture, taste patterns and attitudes towards work and widened the composition of the elite in El Salvador.

10.6 Conclusion

Building on the concepts discussed in the previous chapter and placing emphasis on the economic effect of the international flows of labour, this chapter discussed with empirical evidence the push/pull factors associated with the migration of nurses and remittance flows.

Summary of Key Points

- Labour is generally less mobile than capital. However, there have been great flows of labour from South-South countries to developed countries.
- Some of the general push/pull factors associated with the migration of nurses from the CARICOM include low wages in CARICOM vs. high wages in destination economies, poor working conditions in CARICOM vs. better working conditions abroad, distinct economic disparity between developed and CARICOM economies, differences in standards of living between developed and CARICOM economies, cost of living differential between developed and CARICOM economies, relatively superior training opportunities for nurses in developed economies as compared to CARICOM economies, and the opportunity for remittances.
- Remittances represent an important source of foreign exchange and play an important role in terms of the financing of the developmental process.

Multiple Choice

1. Which of the following are push factors of migration?

    a) poor remuneration
    b) high crime levels
    c) heavy workload
    d) all of the above

2. In addition to the push/pull factors, what are the other factors that contribute to migration?

    a) state incentives
    b) private recruitment agencies
    c) non-profit organizations
    d) a and b only

3. All of the following are pull factors for migration except

    a) poor remuneration and benefit package
    b) professional and career advancement
    c) institutional support and representation
    d) higher income levels

4. What are the main motivations for remittances?

    a) to assist family members remaining in the home country financially
    b) to assist with health expenditures for family members
    c) to assist in the accumulation of assets in the home country
    d) all of the above

5. Remittances are recorded in which of the following accounts:

    a) the current account
    b) the official reserves account
    c) the transfers account
    d) the capital account

Short Essay

1. What are the push and pull factors of migration in the Caribbean?
2. Evaluate the international migration trends over the last decade.
3. What are some of the policies that can be implemented to reduce migration?

Key Trade Terms

- International migration
- Push/pull factors
- Destination economies
- GDP per capita
- Human Development Index (HDI)
- Retail Price Index

Tariffs

Learning Objectives

a. Distinguish between an ad valorem and specific tariff.
b. Illustrate the economic effects of a tax in a small economy.
c. Briefly describe the general equilibrium effects of a tariff in a small economy.
d. Outline the Prisoner's Dilemma.
e. Briefly describe the arguments for a tariff within its theoretical validity.
f. Define an effective tariff.
g. Illustrate the economic effects of a tariff in a large-country case.
h. Define tariff retaliation.
i. Describe the impact of a tariff on the offer curve and terms of trade of the home country.
j. Describe an optimal tariff.

In this chapter, the discussion focuses on a variety of instruments that are deployed by governments from both developed and developing countries for intervention in the trade sector. The analytical tools used in this chapter include demand and supply curves as well as offer curves. The analysis is typically partial equilibrium, but where relevant, general equilibrium theory is used to complement the discussion.

11.0 Some Introductory Definitions

The international trade environment carries a wide range of interventionary trade tools used by practitioners under varied circumstances. This chapter focuses on some of the economics associated with tariffs, while the next chapter deals with other non-tariff barriers to international trade. Tariffs can be either specific or ad valorem. A specific tariff is one in which a specific amount is charged per unit of the good imported. For example, for every tyre brought into Jamaica, a specific tariff of J$1,500 would apply. An ad valorem tariff is a tariff that is charged per unit of the commodity. For example, for every tyre imported into Jamaica, a 15 per cent ad valorem tariff on the value of the commodity would apply. A tariff can also be applied in a combined form. For example, for every tyre brought into Jamaica, a combined duty consisting of a specific amount of J$1,500 and an ad valorem tariff of 15 per cent would apply.

11.1 Economic Effects of a Tariff

In figure 11.1, the export supply and import demand schedules for a commodity are illustrated. Free trade equilibrium would take place with an equilibrium price P_{m0} and equilibrium quantity traded Q_{m0}. A specific tariff shifts the supply curve upwards parallel to itself from S_m to $S`_m$, the consequence of which is a rise in the price level from P_{m0} to P_{m1} and a fall in the equilibrium quantity traded from Q_{m0} to Q_{m1}. The differential $P_{m1} - P_{m2}$ is the amount of tariff revenue per unit of the commodity imported. Since the amount imported is now Q_{m1}, then the amount of revenues collected by the government is $P_{m1}P_{m2}cb$.

11.2 The Specific Tariff in the Small-Country Case

In the small-country case, the supply curve of the commodity is horizontal, indicating that it is too small to influence the international price of the good. Given a demand schedule D_m, initial equilibrium price and quantity would be at P_{m0} and Q_{m0}, respectively. The imposition of a specific tariff would lead to a rise in the price level from P_{m0} to P_{m1} and a fall in the amount of the commodity exchanged. With the tariff, foreign firms continue to receive P_{m0}, but the government in the tariff-imposing economy would now collect $P_{m1}bcP_{m0}$ in revenues (see figure 11.2).

11.3 The Welfare Effects of Tariffs

To illustrate the welfare effects of a tariff, we can proceed as follows. Let the world price of the commodity be W^p (see figure 11.3). With a tariff, the domestic price is now the

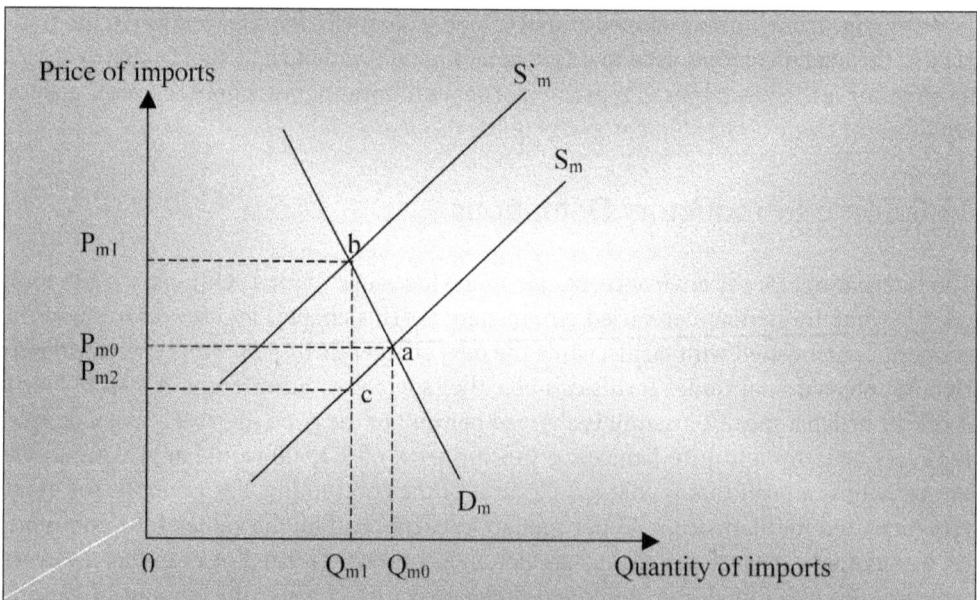

Figure 11.1: The economic effects of a specific tariff

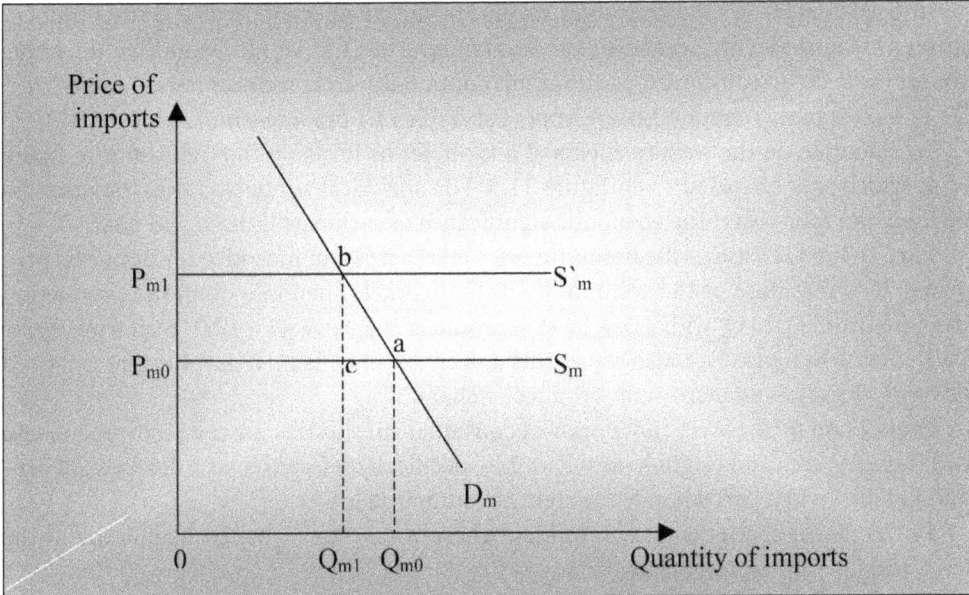

Figure 11.2: Economic effect of a specific tariff with a perfectly elastic supply curve

original world price plus the tariff. Specifically, if w^p is the world price and we impose an ad valorem tariff, t, the domestic price level becomes $p^d = w^p (1 + t)$. The imposition of a tariff, by virtue of providing a hike in the price of the foreign commodity on the domestic market, benefits domestic producers of this commodity, whose output would now be competing against a higher-priced substitute. Note that higher price level reduces consumer surplus.

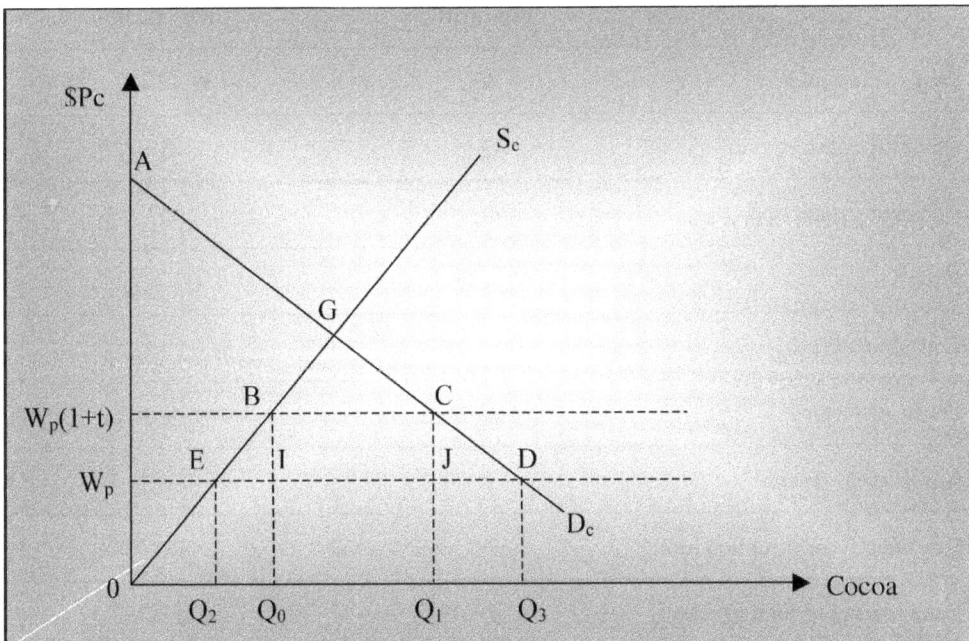

Figure 11.3: Economic effect of a tax in a small economy

In particular, at W^p the consumer surplus of the small economy is ADW^p. Producer surplus associated with a domestic production level of Q_2 is $W_p E0$. Given that the home country will like to consume Q_3 units of this commodity and produces only Q_2 units, then $Q_3 - Q_2$ units of this commodity are imported. Table 11.1 provides summary information.

To elaborate on the welfare effects of a tariff, let us focus on the trapezium in figure 11.4, which was extracted from figure 11.3. For analytical simplicity, this trapezium is divided into four parts. The economic significance of each part is discussed next.

Part 1: The increase in the domestic price level acts as an incentive for domestic producers to bring more of the commodity to the market. Therefore domestic production increases from Q_2 to Q_0 with a new level of producer surplus $w_p(1 + t)b0$ (read from figure 11.3). Part 1 in figure 11.4 also represents a decrease in consumer surplus that is passed on to producers as an increase in producer welfare.

Parts 2 and 4: These are those parts of consumer surplus that are not recovered. These two triangles are deadweight losses. Part 2 is specifically referred to as a deadweight production loss, while part 4 is a deadweight consumption loss.

Part 3: This represents tariff revenues, where $w_p(1 + t) - _{wp}$ is the magnitude of the tariff and $Q_1 - Q_0$ represents imports.

Thus, in implementing a tariff, consumer welfare falls and society carries a deadweight cost. The reader should observe that the slope of the demand and supply curves conditions the size of these deadweight losses.

Table 11.1: Economic effects of the tariff in figure 11.3

	Pre-tariff	Post-tariff
Price to consumer	W_p	$W_p(1 + t)$
Domestic consumption	Q_3	Q_1
Domestic production	Q_2	Q_0
Imports	$Q_3 - Q_2$	$Q_1 - Q_0$
Consumer surplus	$W_p A D$	$W_p(1 + t) AC$
Producer surplus	$0 W_p E$	$0 W_p(1 + t) B$
Government revenue	0	IBCJ
Deadweight consumption loss	0	JCD
Deadweight production efficiency loss	0	EBI

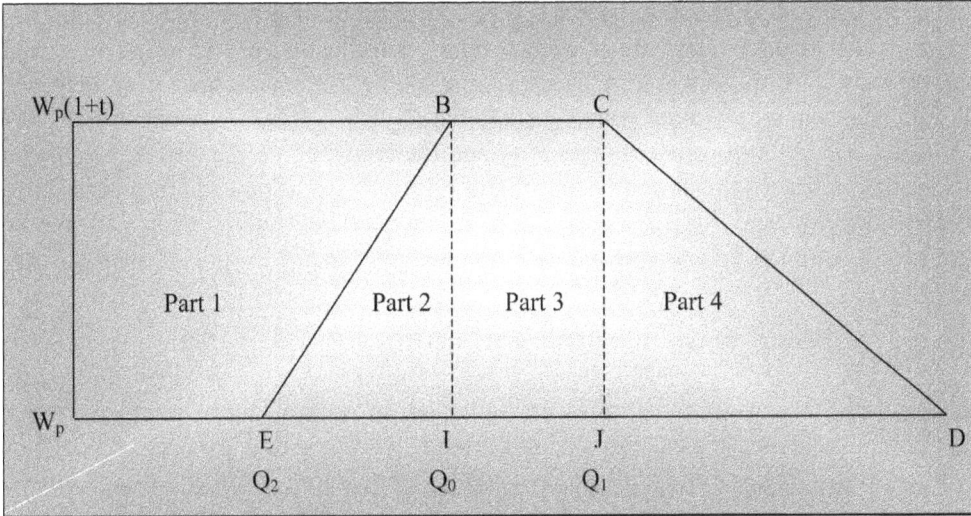

Figure 11.4: Decomposition of the fall in consumer surplus associated with a tariff

11.4 General Equilibrium Effects of a Tariff in a Small Economy

In figure 11.5, the initial terms of trade is given by $(P_x/P_y)^w$. When the small country implements a tariff, there is a shift in its relevant terms of trade to $(P_x/P_y)^w_{1+t}$. Domestic producers responding to the new terms of trade will produce at point P_1 instead of point P_0. The domestic production loss associated with the move from P_0 to P_1 on account of

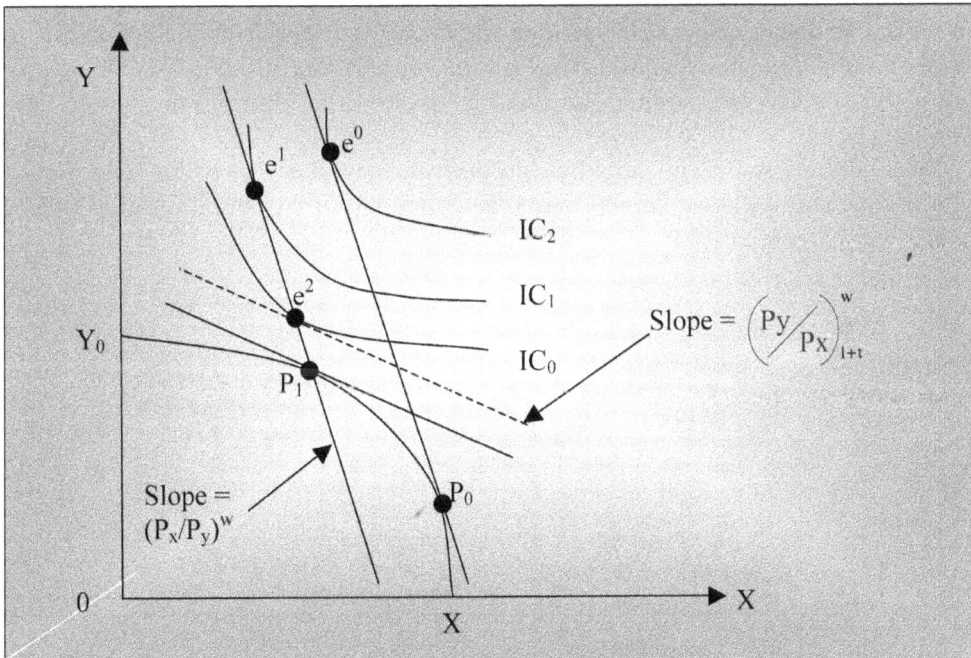

Figure 11.5: General equilibrium of a tariff in a small country

the tariff results in a welfare loss from e_0 on IC_2 to e_1 on IC_1. Furthermore, since domestic consumers have to consume at the new terms of trade, they are forced to operate at a level of welfare such as point e_2 as compared with e_1. (e_1 would have been obtained if domestic consumers could have consumed at $(P_x/P_y)^w$.) Consumption occurs at the tariff-distorted price relative of $(P_x/P_y)^w_{1+t}$, and the reduction in the welfare level from IC_1 to IC_0 represents the domestic consumption loss. (Note welfare still improves above the autarky level, and this occurs because of the increase in economic rents of domestic producers as well as the increase in tariff revenues collected by the government.)

11.5 The Prisoner's Dilemma and International Trade

The decision to engage in free trade or implement protection can be treated in terms of the familiar Prisoner's Dilemma from game theory. To further the discussion, let us assume we have two countries, a home country (HC) and a foreign country (FC). The permutations of the trading relationships between these two economies are

- the HC and FC engage free trade,
- the HC engages free trade but the FC protects its economy,
- the HC protects its economy but the FC engages free trade, and
- both countries protect their economies.

The gains from trade are greatest if both the HC and FC engage in free trade, but with protection as an option and not knowing how the other country might respond both the HC and FC may opt for protection.

To illustrate further, consider table 11.2. If both the HC and FC implement free trade, then they both benefit by $1,000 million each. If the HC implements free trade but the FC protects, then the FC gains $1,000 million and the HC gets only $100 million. In the reverse case of the HC protecting and the FC going with free trade, the HC get $1,000 million and the FC gets $100 million. However, if both the FC and HC implement protection, they only benefit by $200 million each.

Since neither country can judge how the other will respond, they both opt for protection and gain only $200 million. If this is the option taken, then both countries lose by opting out of free trade.

Table 11.2: Prisoner's Dilemma in trade theory

		FC	
		Cooperation free trade	Defection (protection)
HC	Cooperation free trade	1 $1,000mn, 1,000mn	2 100mn, 1,000mn
	Defection (protection)	3 1,000mn, 100mn	4 200mn, 200mn

11.6 Arguments for Tariffs and Their Theoretical Validity

The literature carries a number of arguments favouring the implementation of a tariff. Some of these arguments are theoretically valid, while others are not. This section reviews some of these arguments and their theoretical validity.

Labour Market Protection: A tariff can help to protect domestic labour against cheap foreign labour. This argument is invalid in the sense that the wages of labour alone does not condition the employment of labour: employment is also dependent on the productivity of labour. As such, if productivity levels in any Caribbean economy are sufficiently higher than in, say, China, then that Caribbean economy would need no protection from cheap Chinese labour.

Scientific Tariff: If an economy were to impose a tariff of such a magnitude that the cost of purchasing the foreign good is equated to the cost of producing the good domestically (a scientific tariff), then this would allow domestic producers of the protected commodity to compete with foreign producers. However, if all nations were to impose the scientific tariff, then this would remove differential costs as a basis for trade and hence eliminate all opportunities for trade along with the attendant gains from trade.

Unemployment: Apart from protecting domestic labour, the imposition of a tariff and hence the facilitation of some domestic production of a commodity can help increase domestic employment levels. While it is possible for a nation to implement a tariff to protect domestic labour, if all nations were to do the same (tariff retaliation), then all nations would lose in the end. The implementation of a tariff to protect domestic employment levels is an example of a beggar-thy-neighbour type of strategy.[1]

Current Account: If a nation has a current account deficit, then by imposing a tariff it can reduce imports relative to exports and help improve its balance of payments. However, this action may prompt retaliation. The country should seek to improve its balance of payments by economic policies such as an expenditure switching policy in the form of currency devaluation or by improving its productivity, and so on.

Terms of Trade: A large country can influence its terms of trade favourably by imposing a small tariff. However, while this may be true, again, it can prompt retaliation strategies by partners.

Dumping: The literature refers to a number of different forms dumping may adopt. *Predatory dumping* is sometimes practised by some firms in foreign markets to drive other producers out of the market. Once a near monopoly position is attained, the price is then increased to ensure the firm makes profits (any initial losses may be treated as part of fixed costs). In the presence of predatory dumping, an import tariff is justifiable, but it is not easy to prove the existence of predatory dumping. Additionally, it is sometimes difficult to impose a tariff on a foreign firm's dumped commodities as domestic consumers benefit from the lower prices.

Sporadic dumping refers to the occasional sale by a foreign firm in the HC at a price below that sold in the HC market.

Persistent dumping refers to the continuous sale of a commodity at a price in the HC above that in the FC.[2]

Infant Industry Argument: The infant industry argument was introduced in 1971 by Sir Alexander Hamilton in his *Report on Manufactures*. Friedrich List, a German economist, applied it in the early nineteenth century as the basis of an argument for shielding German industries from British industries. A country may sometimes implement a tariff to allow its infant industries the opportunity to mature under protected market conditions until firms can effectively participate in international trade. However, some economists have argued that the successful maturity of an infant does not provide sufficient proof that the industry would not have emerged on its own.

Tariff Revenues: Many of the small developing countries in the CARICOM sphere have low income levels and a small fraction of their workforce employed in the formal sector, indicating that overall these economies have low taxable bases. In light of this, it is generally easy to manage the inflows of goods through international ports in these economies. Local authorities have therefore found it worthwhile to impose tariffs to collect significant amounts of fiscal revenues at these points of entry. However, as we have seen before, although governments stand to gain from the collection of tariff revenues, overall economic welfare in these economies will decrease.

To provide an idea of the evolving fiscal dependence of CARICOM countries on international trade taxes, consider the data in table 11.3. The fiscal dependence (import taxes as a percentage of fiscal revenues) of all the listed CARICOM member countries shows a declining trend between the snapshot years 1992 and 2006.

11.7 Effective Tariffs

For commodities that carry tariffs, it is necessary to consider the effective tariff rate. The effective tariff rate illustrates the overall level of protection given to a commodity when nominal tariffs are attached both to the commodity itself and the factor inputs used in producing it.

Specifically, the effective tariff rate (ETR) may be represented as

$$\text{(Value added in HC with protection-value added in free trade) / value added in free trade}$$

We can evaluate the ETR in the following manner: Let p be the fixed international price of the final commodity. If we are making a pen with n parts, for example, then we can represent

$$a_i p + \ldots + a_n p = \Sigma \, a_i \, p$$

as the cost of the imported n items, where $a_i \, p$ is the cost of the imported input i into pen production.

Domestic value (DV) can be represented as

$$DV = p - \Sigma a_i \, p$$

$$DV = p - p \, \Sigma a_i$$

If we assume that a tariff is imposed at every stage (i.e., for each imported input) and on the final product, then

Table 11.3: Import taxes as a percentage of fiscal revenues, 1992–2006

Country	1992	1993	1994	1995	1996	1997	1998	1999	2000	2001	2002	2003	2004	2005	2006
Antigua and Barbuda	21.15	20.73	19.95	19.36	20.28	20.19	19.54	18.92	19.98	17.61	15.69	14.87	14.16	15.65	14.40
Anguilla	67.84	48.33	54.93	53.37	58.24	57.12	65.64	62.09	61.53	51.60	46.64	45.83	39.94	47.36	40.69
Bahamas	55.62	54.97	67.83	66.15	67.01	66.59	63.14	64.70	62.86	63.89	64.93	62.44	58.12	61.14	60.67
Barbados	8.08	8.08	8.63	8.61	8.61	8.08	9.26	9.35	8.86	7.56	9.08	9.88	10.93	10.60	8.84
Belize	47.82	49.20	58.01	60.70	40.22	37.27	37.91	42.61	38.57	41.77	45.71	43.99	n.a.	n.a.	n.a.
Dominica	17.44	17.61	14.67	14.28	13.99	14.97	13.53	14.59	13.94	13.08	15.87	11.75	12.20	12.12	11.46
Guyana	9.50	12.60	12.80	11.60	11.70	11.80	12.10	n.a.	n.a.	n.a.	n.a.	n.a.	n.a.	n.a.	n.a.
Jamaica	13.70	13.60	10.90	11.90	10.80	11.30	10.60	10.40	n.a.	n.a.	n.a.	n.a.	n.a.	n.a.	n.a.
St Kitts/ Nevis	25.79	26.21	25.28	23.97	24.19	21.56	20.29	21.25	20.96	16.03	15.89	15.61	14.43	14.26	13.21
St Lucia	n.a.	n.a.	18.29	18.18	20.24	19.43	17.27	17.98	15.21	13.51	13.09	16.19	14.67	15.53	15.71
St Vincent	n.a.	n.a.	12.34	13.95	12.12	11.88	10.96	11.10	10.37	11.01	9.38	10.72	10.14	10.64	9.40
Trinidad and Tobago	9.40	9.59	8.13	6.23	5.56	6.65	7.17	7.76	6.44	6.06	6.35	6.17	6.16	5.15	4.64

Source: UNELAC database.

$$DV^* = p(1 + t) - p \Sigma a_i (1 + t_i)$$

where

t = nominal ad valorem tariff on pens,
t_i = nominal ad valorem tariff on input i.

To determine the growth in protection (or the rate of protection), we can form

$$\text{Effective Tariff Rate} = \frac{DV^* - DV}{DV}$$

$$= \frac{p(1+t) - p\sum a_i(1+t_i) - p(1 - \sum a_i)}{p(1 - \sum a_i)}$$

$$= \frac{(1+t) - \left(\sum a_i + \sum a_i t_i\right) - \left(1 + \sum a_i\right)}{1 - \sum a_i}$$

$$= \frac{t - \sum a_i t_i}{1 - \sum a_i}$$

If we have only one imported input, the expression reduces to

$$ETR = \frac{t - a_1 t_1}{1 - a_1}$$

Let us consider an example. Assume that the world price of a pen is $100, but the HC implements a nominal tariff of 10 per cent on each pen so that the price paid by domestic consumers is $110. Assume that the factor inputs to produce pens are imported and cost $80. Thus far we have

Domestic price = $110
of which domestic value added = $20

We can calculate the effective tariff rate as

$$\text{Effective Tariff Rate} = \frac{t - a_1 t_1}{1 - a_1} = \frac{10\% - (80/100)(0)}{1.0 - 0.8} = 0.1/0.2 = 50\%$$

This illustrates that the effective tariff rate is 50 per cent greater than the nominal tariff rate of 10 per cent.

Observe that the value of the effective tariff rate is conditioned by the values of t, a and t_1. Even more, the number of permutable values the effective tariff rate can adopt is very large, and if $a_1 t_1 > t$, the effective tariff rate can even be negative. Thus, in the example above, if the government imposed a 20 per cent nominal tariff rate on the imported input, then

$$\text{Effective Tariff Rate} = \frac{0.1 - (0.8)(0.2)}{0.2} = -0.3 \text{ or } -30\%$$

In general, observe that the effective rate of protection increases as the tariff rate on the finished good increases or as the nominal tariff rate on the imported input falls.

11.8 A Large Country and Tariffs That Improve Its Terms of Trade

A large country as defined here is a country that can influence the price level it pays for imports and exports. When a large country implements a tariff, it is possible that the large country can improve its welfare. In figure 11.6, we represent the domestic supply curve by S^d. S^w represents the domestic plus rest-of-the-world supply curve – that is, it represents world supply. In initial conditions with a domestic demand curve D and world supply curve S^w, the unrestricted trade price level is P_f with domestic demand of Q_1 and domestic supply of Q_0 so that $Q_1 - Q_0$ units are imported.

The imposition of a tariff (we use a specific tariff for simplicity) shifts the world supply curve to $S^w + t$. With the tariff distortion, the new price level is $\overline{P}$, and the large country demands Q_3 units of the commodity but supplies only Q_2 units so that $Q_3 - Q_2$ units are imported.

As in the small-country case, areas 1 and 4 remain as traditional deadweight production and consumption losses, respectively. Total tariff revenue garnered by the large country is represented by the area $(\overline{P} - P_w)(Q_3 - Q_2)$, indicated in the figure as the sum of areas 2 and 3. Area 2 represents a transfer from consumer to government and area 3 represents a transfer from foreign producers ($P_f - P_w$ per unit of imports) to government. Area 3 is therefore a gain.

The imposition of a tariff (in a large country) causes two changes for that large economy's welfare. These changes occur through

1. a volume of trade effect and
2. a terms of trade effect.

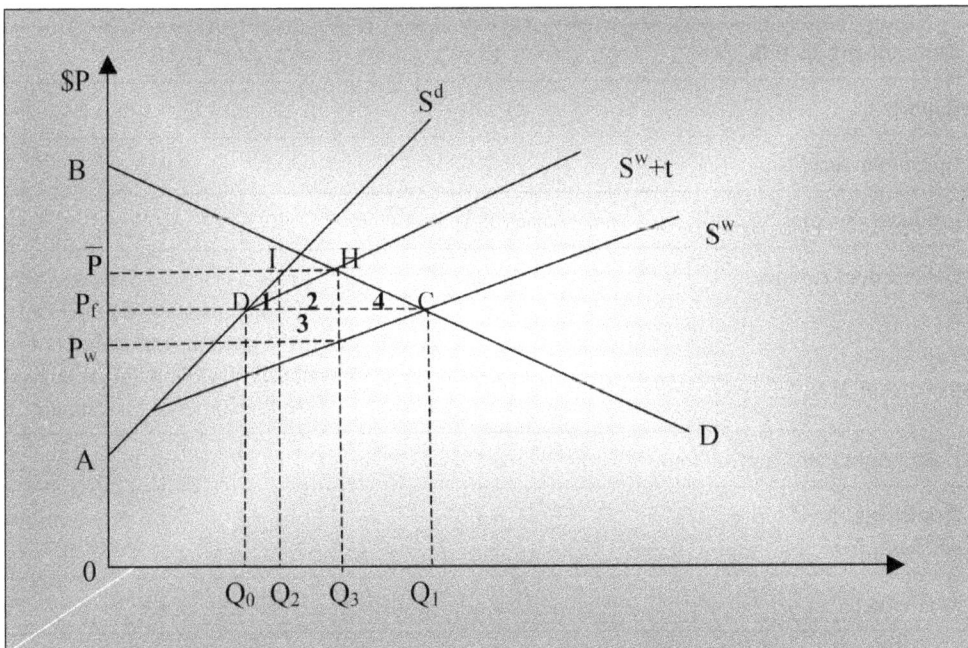

Figure 11.6: Economic effects of a tariff in a large country

The volume of trade effect occurs because the tariff lowers welfare by reducing trade. It occurs because of the simultaneous increase in domestic production and decrease in domestic consumption. The tariff also lowers the price received by foreign producers, and so this has a favourable effect on the HC's terms of trade.[3]

In notational form,

Net Economic Welfare (NEW) =
Volume of Trade Effect (VOTE) + Terms of Trade Effect (TOTE)

Table 11.4 outlines the economic effect of a tariff in a large country.

The terms of trade effect makes it much more difficult to predict the welfare impact of a tariff in a large country. Specifically, the large country gains accrue at the expense of the trading partner, which will now have to work with a lower price for its exports of good Y. Thus, regardless of the size of the trading partners, a tariff adversely impacts on world welfare. Tariffs induce a domestic production loss and a domestic consumption loss and result in a permanent loss of part of the gains from trade. A tariff can also limit the extent to which a firm can benefit from economies of scale and specialization.

A summary of the various permutations on welfare a tariff can have in a large country is provided in table 11.5.

Table 11.4: Economic effects of the tariff in a large economy

	Pre-tariff	Post-tariff
Price to consumer	P_f	$\overline{P}$
Domestic consumption	Q_1	Q_3
Domestic production	Q_0	Q_2
Imports	$Q_1 - Q_0$	$Q_3 - Q_2$
Consumer surplus	P_f B C	$\overline{P}$ B H
Producers surplus	A P_f D	A$\overline{P}$ I
Government revenue	n.a.	Areas 2 + 3. Area 2 is a transfer from domestic consumers to the government. Area 3 is a transfer from foreign producers to the domestic government.
Deadweight consumption loss	n.a.	4
Deadweight production efficiency loss	n.a.	1
VOT effect	n.a.	1 + 4
TOT effect	n.a.	3

Table 11.5: Possible net welfare effects of a tariff by a large country

If:	Then:
1 + 4 = 3	No net effect on domestic welfare Negative net effect on world welfare
1 + 4 < 3	Positive net effect on domestic welfare Negative net effect on world welfare
1 + 4 > 3	Negative net effect on domestic welfare Negative net effect on world welfare

11.9 Tariffs That Reduce Welfare

If the TOTE of a tariff is less than the VOTE, then a large economy that imposes a tariff can become worse off by it. Let initial conditions be such that the HC produces at A and consumes at B, at the terms of trade tot_w (see figure 11.7). With a tariff, the internal terms of trade of the HC changes to tot_t. The change in the relative prices of good Y and good X results in an international terms of trade of tot^*_w. In this case, the welfare effect of imposing a tariff pushes the tariff-imposing large country onto an indifference curve such as IC_1 as compared to IC_0. The large country operates on an overall lower level of welfare because the volume of trade effect is greater than the terms of trade effect (see figure 11.7). Table 11.6 provides a summary of the welfare-reducing effects of a tariff in a large country case.

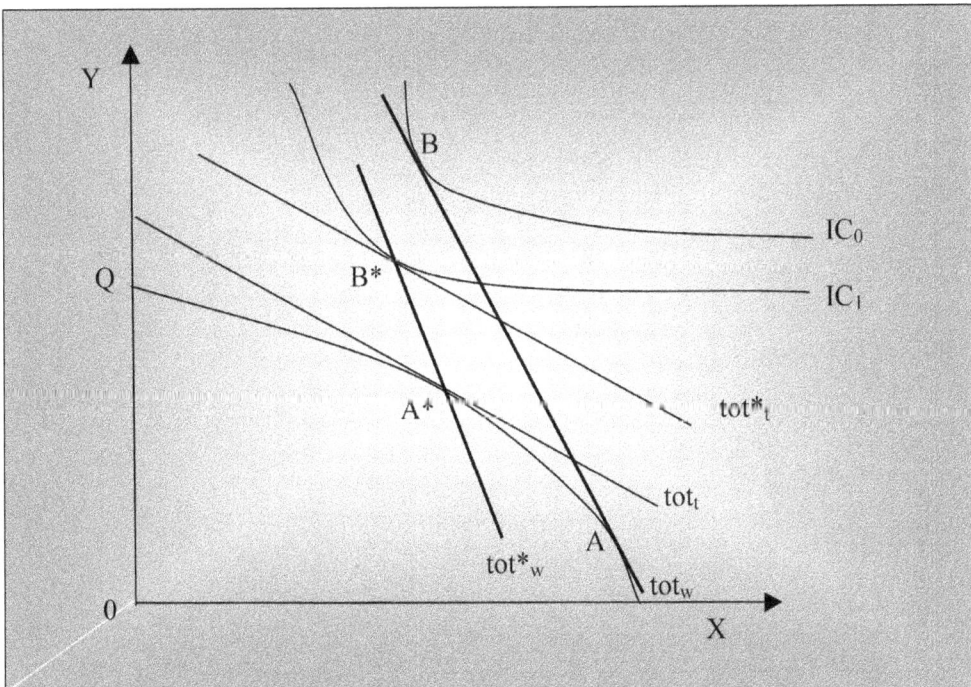

Figure 11.7: A tariff that reduces welfare in a large country

Table 11.6: Summary of the welfare effects of a tariff in a large country

	Pre-tariff	Post-tariff
Terms of trade in HC	tot_w	Improves domestic terms of trade to tot^*_t but decreases world price ratio to tot^*w
Domestic production	A	A*
Consumption	B	B*

Note that in figure 11.7, with the imposition of a tariff and the move from A to A*, the import competing industry Y expands at the expense of the export good X. In this case, the terms of trade effect is swamped by the volume of trade effect.

11.10 Tariffs That Improve Welfare

Figure 11.8 illustrates the case of a tariff that improves welfare in a large country. If the tariff is imposed on good Y, then as the price of good Y increases, the terms of trade will progress to tot_t. With a tariff on good Y, its consumption decreases in the HC. Since the HC is a large economy, it means that the international price of good Y will fall. At the same time, the reduction in the production of X will result in an eventual increase in

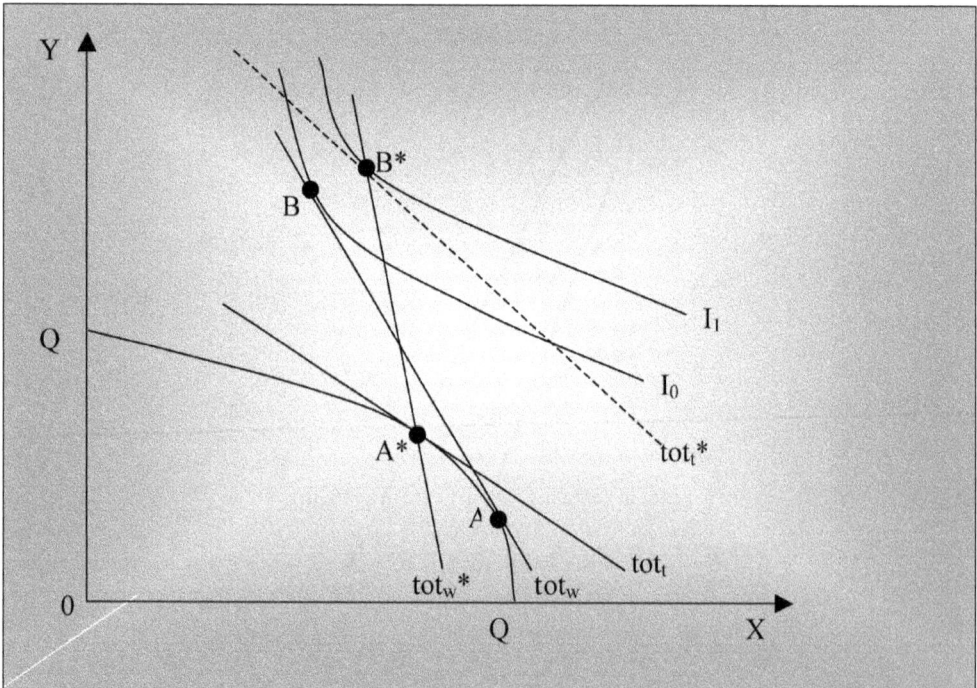

Figure 11.8: A tariff that increases welfare in a large country

Table 11.7: Summary of the welfare effects of a tariff that improves welfare in a large country

	Pre-tariff	Post-tariff
Terms of trade	tot_w	tot^*_t
Domestic production	A	A*
Domestic consumption	B	B*

its price level, so that overall the terms of trade of the large economy will improve from tot_w to $totw_.$. Note that at the new point of production A* on the production possibility frontier, the tariff-implementing large economy produces more of good Y than before (see figure 11.8).

In this large-country case, the tariff increases the welfare of the economy as the TOTE swamps the VOTE.

11.11 Tariffs and Tariff Retaliation

Tariff retaliation is one form of trade war, whereby countries set tariffs that alter the terms of trade to their own advantage. One country sets a tariff that compels their trade

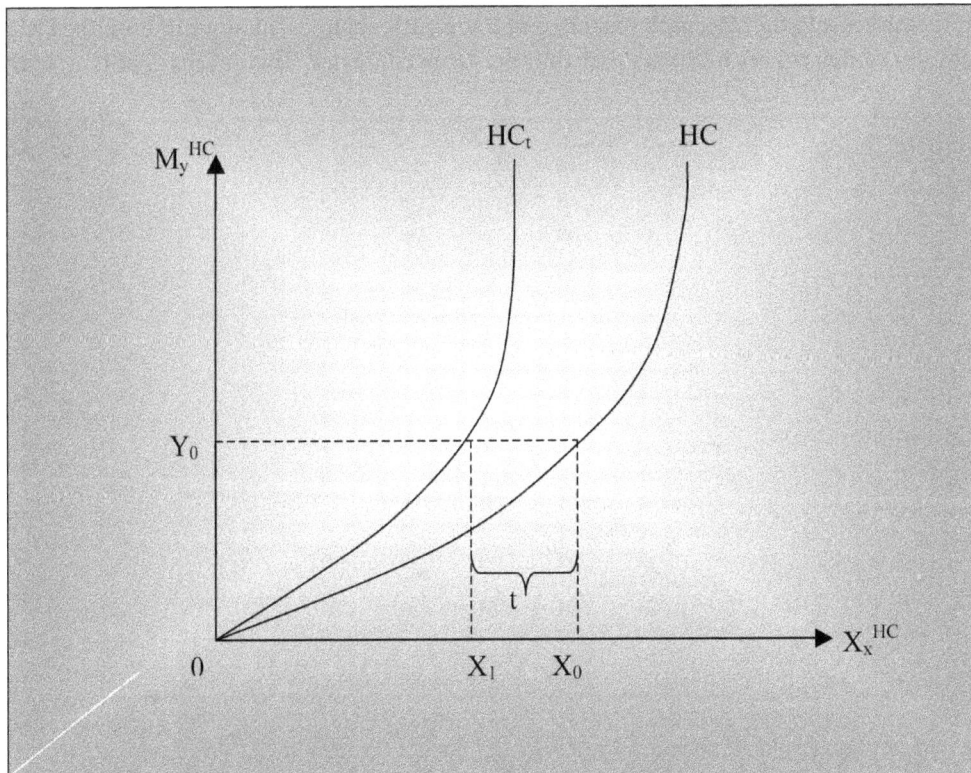

Figure 11.9: Impact of a tariff on the HC's offer curve

partner to reciprocate by altering its own tariff rates. This section utilizes offer curves to help provide some theoretical insights regarding tariff retaliation.

In figure 11.9, let

M_y^{HC} = import of good Y by country HC,
X_x^{HC} = export of good X by country HC.

A tariff will shift the HC's offer curve from HC to HC_t. This shift indicates that the HC is only willing to give up X_1 units of its export good X to obtain Y_0 units of the import good as compared to the X_0 units it was willing to part with previously.

X_{FC}^y = export of Y by country FC,
M_{HC}^y = import of Y by country HC,
X_{HC}^x = export of X by country HC,
M_{FC}^x = import of X by country FC.

When the HC is a relatively small country, regardless of the tariff rate it establishes, there will be no impact on the international terms of trade; for a small country, the FC's offer curve coincides with the international terms of trade. As figure 11.10 illustrates, if the small HC imposes a tariff of magnitude t, then this will result in a decrease in the willingness of the HC to trade (from X_0 for Y_0 to X_2 for Y_2). However, the change in willingness to trade does not impact on the terms of trade.

In the large-country case, the initial offer curves for the HC and FC are HC_0 and FC_0, respectively, and the international terms of trade settles at tot_0. The slope of both the HC's and FC's offer curves indicates that they are large countries. This means that they both

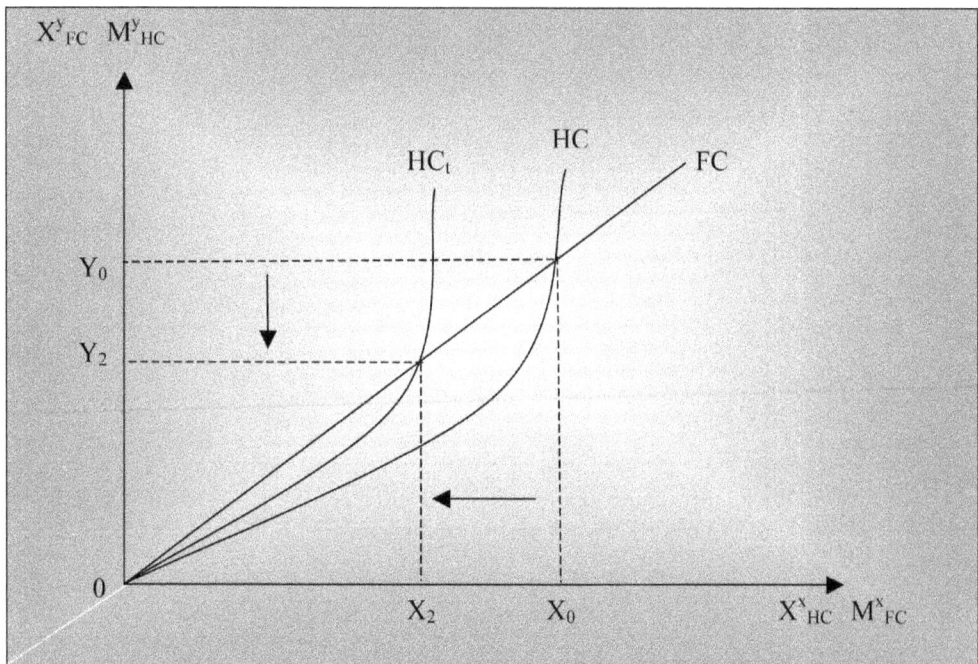

Figure 11.10: The impact of a tariff on the terms of trade in the small-country case

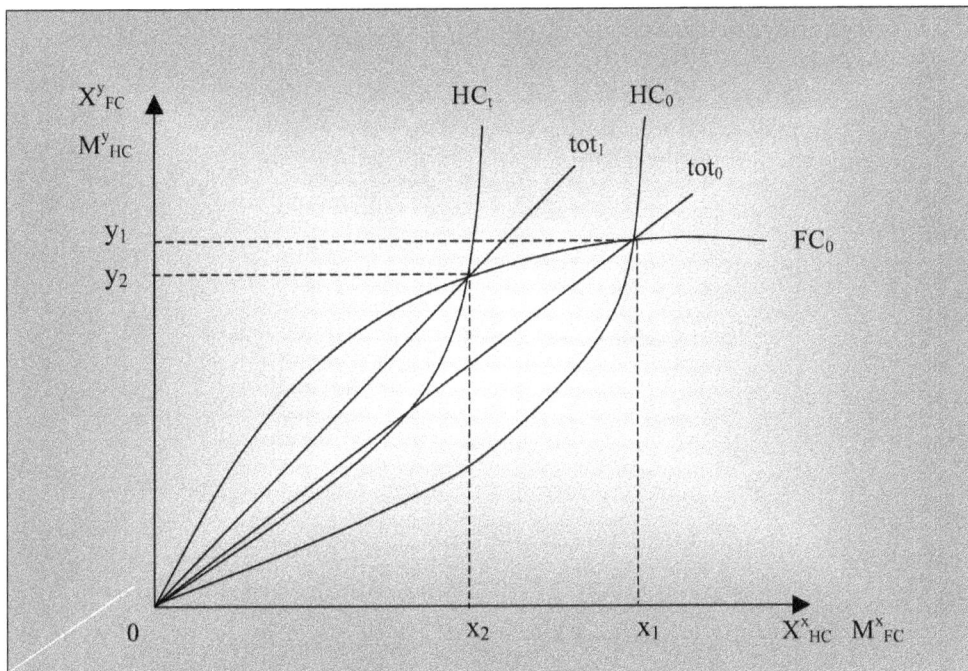

Figure 11.11: A tariff to improve the terms of trade

have some degree of market power, so that the imposition of a tariff by either country has, as before, a VOTE and a TOTE. The welfare impact of the tariff depends on the relative size of the VOTE and TOTE. If the HC now imposes a tariff so that its offer curve moves to HC_t, then the new international terms of trade will move to tot_1. At tot_0, the HC exchanged x_1 units of X for y_1 units of Y. With the implementation of the tariff, the volume of trade falls to x_2 and y_2 units of exports and imports, respectively (see figure 11.11).

All this assumes no retaliation by the FC. However, the implementation of a tariff by the HC can (and often does) prompt retaliation by the FC. If the FC retaliates and implements a tariff of its own that moves its offer curve to FC_t, as in figure 11.12, then this will further compromise the level of international trade exercised by the HC to y_3 units of imports and x_3 units of exports as the terms of trade changes to tot_{post} (post-tariff) as compared to tot_{pre} (pre-tariff in the HC).

The eventual effect on the terms of trade depends on the size of the HC's tariff in relation to the FC's tariff. It also depends on the shapes of the offer curves of these trading partners.

11.12 The Optimal Tariff

It is possible that a large economy's welfare can improve with the implementation of a small tariff but alternatively worsen with the implementation of a large tariff. This then implies that somewhere in between there is an optimal tariff. An optimal tariff maximizes the difference between the terms of trade gains and the losses from the volume of trade effect.

As illustrated in figure 11.10, for a small country a tariff has no impact on the international price level (and hence terms of trade for the small country), and so there will be

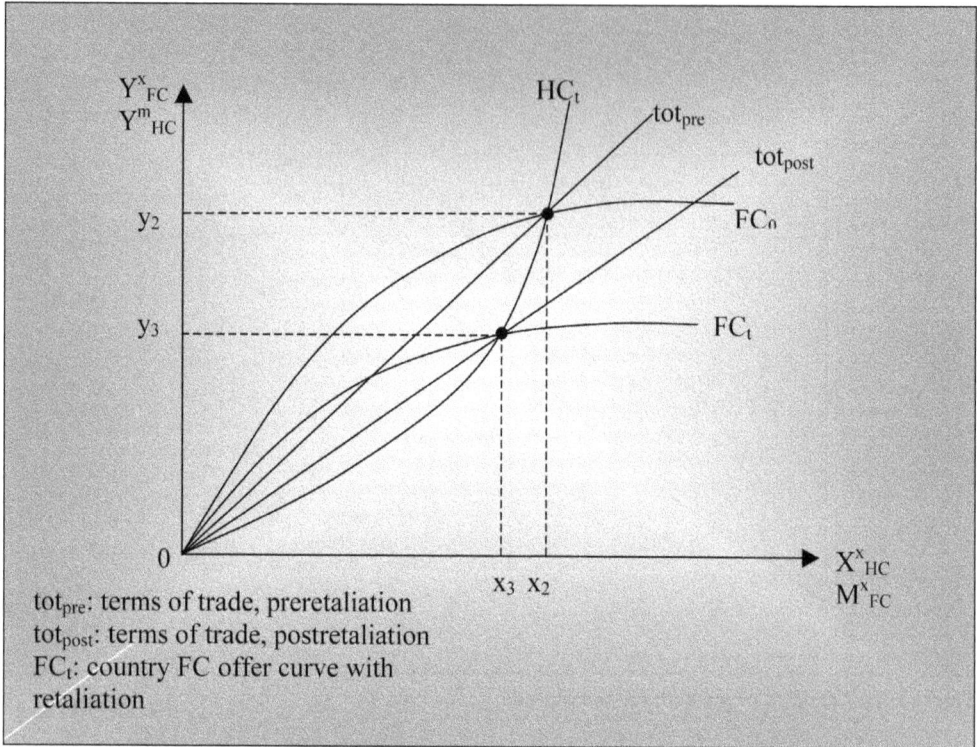

Figure 11.12: Foreign country tariff retaliation

tot_{pre}: terms of trade, preretaliation
tot_{post}: terms of trade, postretaliation
FC_t: country FC offer curve with
retaliation

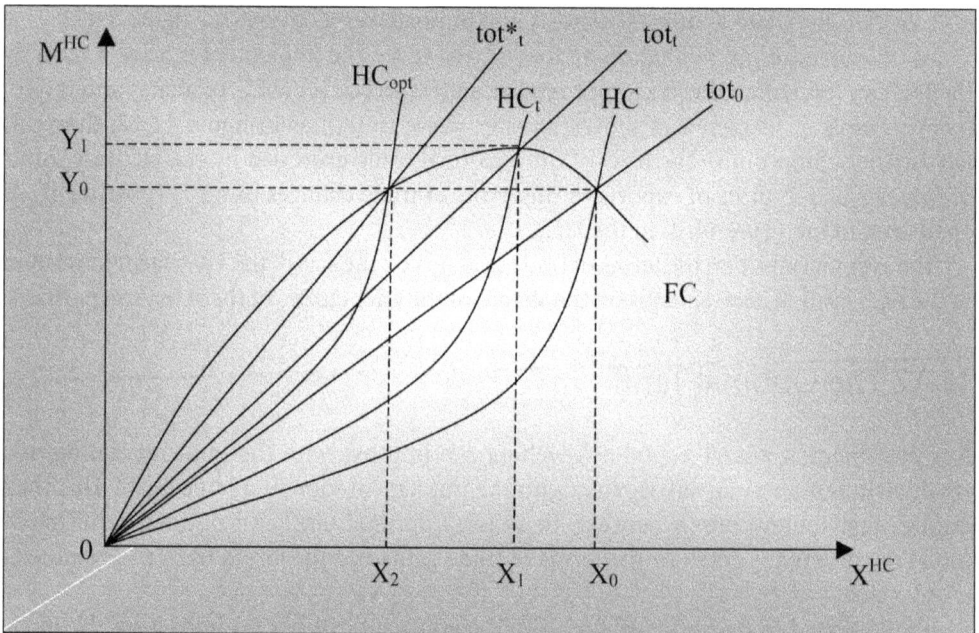

Figure 11.13: The case of the optimum tariff in the large country, general equilibrium setting

an overall loss in welfare because of the volume of trade effect. For a small country, the optimal tariff is a zero tariff.

To illustrate the notion of an optimum tariff in the large-country general equilibrium setting, consider figure 11.13. In initial conditions, the international terms of trade is tot_0, with the large HC trading X_0 units of X for Y_0 units of Y. If the HC alone imposes a tariff, its offer curve shifts to HC_t and the international terms of trade to tot_t. Observe that at tot_t, the HC retains more of X for its own consumption and at the same time receives more units of imports. In fact, any tariff up to tot^*_t will raise the welfare of the tariff-imposing economy, as it will represent an increased amount of imports for less exports when compared to the initial point tot_0. The tariff that moves the HC to an offer curve such as HC_{opt} is the optimal tariff, in the absence of retaliation by the FC.

The Welfare Effect of an Optimal Tariff in a Large Country, an Algebraic Illustration

The national welfare level at each tariff rate can be defined as the sum of consumer surplus, producer surplus and tariff revenue. In what came to be known as the *Terms of Trade Argument for Protection*, Robert Torrens (1844) was first to note the possibility that a tariff could improve national welfare for a large country in international markets. When a large country implements a tariff rate at the optimal level, the country can realize the highest level of national welfare – even one that is higher than if it engages in free trade.

$\bar{P}$, P_w and P_f are illustrated in figure 11.14.

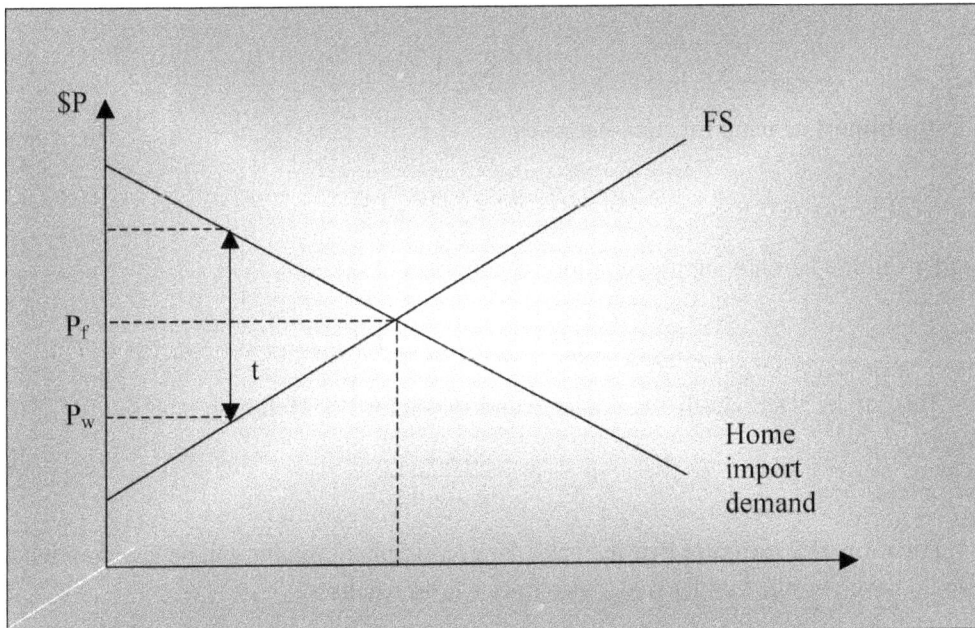

Figure 11.14: $\bar{P}$, P_w and P_f

Let us represent domestic demand by

$$D = \theta - \lambda \overline{P} \qquad \text{(Domestic Demand function)}$$

and domestic supply by

$$S = \alpha + \beta \overline{P} \qquad \text{(Domestic Supply function)}$$

Domestic demand less domestic supply gives import demand as

$$D - S = (\theta - \alpha) - \overline{P}(\lambda + \beta) \qquad \text{(Import Demand function)}$$

Let us represent the foreign supply of exports as

$$(S^* - D^*) = g + h \, P_w \qquad \text{(Foreign Supply function)}$$

Let P_F be the free trade price level.

In free trade equilibrium, domestic demand is equal to world supply, and so we can form

$$(\theta - \alpha) - (\lambda + \beta) \, P_F = g + h \, P_F$$

from which we can derive the free trade price level as

$$P_F = \frac{\theta - \alpha - g}{\lambda + \beta + h} \qquad (11.1)$$

With a tariff, however,

$$\overline{P} = P_w + t$$

The import demand function becomes

$$(\theta - \alpha) - (\lambda + \beta)(P_w + t)$$

and given the Foreign Supply function we can form

$$(\theta - \alpha) - (\lambda + \beta)(P_w + t) = g + h \, P_w$$

This can be algebraically manipulated and solved for P_w as follows:

$$P_w = P_f - \frac{t(\lambda + \beta)}{h + \lambda + \beta} \qquad (11.2)$$

Equation 11.2 indicates that the price foreign suppliers receive will be less than what would have prevailed under free trade. Since a tariff results in

$$\overline{P} = P_w + t \qquad (11.3)$$

then using equation 11.3 we can manipulate equation 11.2 to get

$$\overline{P} = P_f + \frac{th}{h + \beta + \lambda} \qquad (11.4)$$

where $\overline{P}$ is the tariff-induced price.

As indicated earlier, a tariff in a large country results in a deadweight production loss (D^P_L), a deadweight consumption loss (D^C_L) but a gain of area 4 that represents a transfer from foreign producers to the government of the large country imposing the tariff (see figure 11.15).

It is in fact possible to quantify the actual magnitude of the various gains and losses and so doing establish the criteria for the net welfare effects of a tariff in a large country (see figure 11.15). To do this, observe that from the domestic supply curve at the price P_f and $\overline{P}$, respectively, we can form

$$S_1 = \alpha + \beta P_f$$

$$S_2 = \alpha + \beta \overline{P}$$

and so $S_2 - S_1 = \beta \left(\overline{P} - P_f \right)$

which, using equation 11.4, can be simplified to give an expression that relates S_2 to S_1:

$$S_2 = S_1 + (\beta th / \lambda + \beta + h) \qquad (11.5)$$

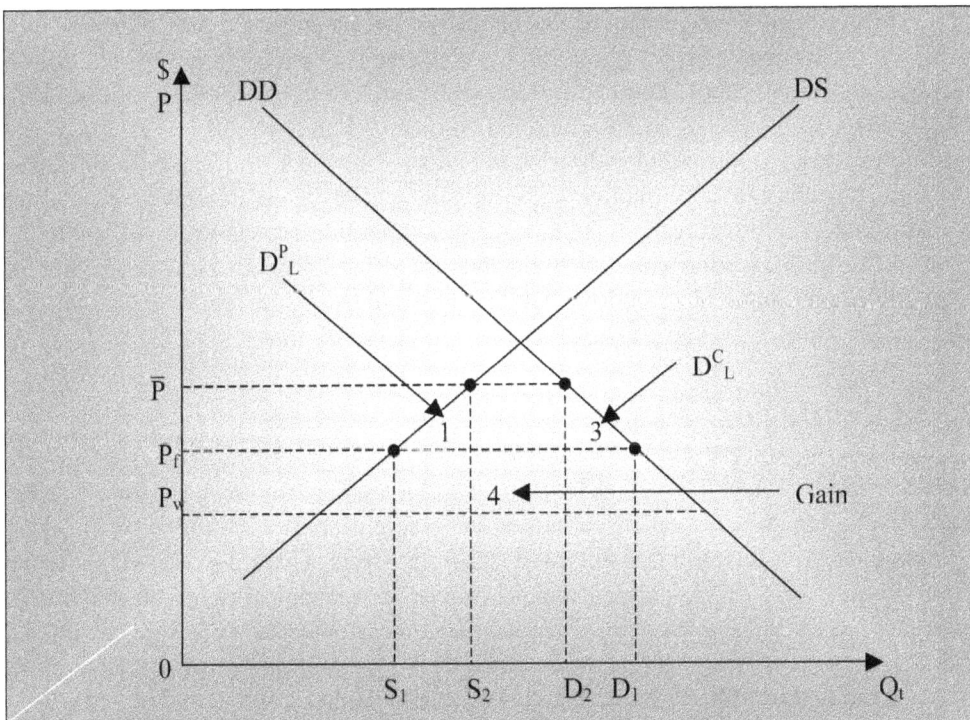

Figure 11.15: Partial equilibrium of the gains and losses from a tariff in a large country

Similarly,

$$D_2 = D_1 - (t\lambda h/\lambda + \beta + h)$$

From figure 11.15, we can represent the gain to the HC as

$$Gain = (D_2 - S_2)(P_f - P_w)$$

$$Loss = \tfrac{1}{2}(S_2 - S_1)(\overline{P} - P_f) + \tfrac{1}{2}(D_1 - D_2)(\overline{P} - P_f)$$

It is possible to express the gain and loss as

$$Gain = t\,U$$

$$Loss = t^2\,V$$

where both U and V are functions of D and S, respectively.

$$Net\ welfare\ gain = tU - (t)^2 v$$

Observe that as the tariff gets smaller, the net effect will eventually become positive. The use of an optimal tariff, as with many other policies which offer monopoly power, is a beggar-thy-neighbour type of policy that comes only at the expense of others. The gains to the monopolist are smaller than the losses imposed on others.

Most islands in the Caribbean have begun to dismantle trade barriers that were in place since independence. Many of the islands had implemented a post-independence protectionist strategy of strict quotas and a "negative list", particularly for light manufactured consumer goods. Departure from such restrictive trade policies in the 1980s and 1990s was motivated by International Monetary Fund stipulations and a global push towards free trade and globalization as endorsed by the World Trade Organization (WTO). In reaction to this, many islands implemented higher tariff rates to afford their local producers some protection. De Rosa (2002) noted that the average tariff rate in the Eastern Caribbean is approximately 20 per cent for all traded goods and even higher for agricultural products. He also noted that for some islands such as Antigua, Barbados, St Kitts and St Lucia, these rates are appreciable.

11.13 Conclusion

This chapter discussed the various instruments that are deployed by governments from both developing and developed economies for intervention in the trade sector. The discussion included a focus on the general equilibrium effects of a tariff as well as the partial equilibrium effects. The various arguments proposed in favour of the erection of tariffs were also raised and the strengths and weaknesses of these arguments were elaborated. Additionally, the chapter examined the economic welfare and losses from the imposition of such trading instruments on both large and small countries.

Appendix 11.1: CARICOM and the Common External Tariff

The Caribbean Community (CARICOM) came into existence in 1973, after the Caribbean Free Trade Area (CARIFTA) had failed to fully integrate the region. CARIFTA failed to fully develop partly because members relied heavily on tariff revenue and were therefore reluctant to reduce tariffs. As a result, trade between the members was limited. In short, national interests of member states were allowed to dominate. Although CARIFTA failed, it provided the basis for the formation of CARICOM. CARICOM matured into a single market and economy by the year 2006.

CARICOM existed in the range between a customs union and a common market. This arrangement allows for the free movement of capital and some categories of skilled persons. Also, a common external tariff (CET) has been implemented by all member states of CARICOM.

The Caribbean Single Market and Economy (CSME) entails the integration of all CARICOM states into a singular economic unit and the subsequent removal of the tariff barriers within the region. This attempt at unification serves to address challenges that small developing CARICOM economies face in light of increasing globalization. It is anticipated that the CSME will stimulate growth and enhance the international competitiveness of the CARICOM member states.

The main objectives of the CSME include the following:

- Freer intra-regional movement of capital: This entails the movement of capital from one CARICOM state to another. The freer intra-regional movement of capital is to be facilitated through the elimination of foreign exchange controls, the convertibility of currencies and, with time, a regional stock exchange.
- Free intra-regional movement of labour: This involves the uninhibited movement of labour, particularly university graduates, within the region.
- Establishment of a common external tariff on goods originating from non-member states.
- Harmonization of economic policy, especially monetary and fiscal policies: This entails the coordination of exchange rate and interest rate policy within the region as well as agreed targets for budgetary deficits.
- Formation of a common currency: In time, it is hoped a common currency can be formed that can facilitate easier comparison of key prices among the member states. This would also facilitate a reduction in intra-regional transaction costs.

The CSME promises a number of benefits for CARICOM economies:

- Access to a larger regional market of more than fifteen million people if Haiti is included, thus providing more opportunities for production and trade for CARICOM members. The CSME will help diversify the range of markets in which CARICOM goods and services will be traded.
- Creation of more opportunities for investment, both by CARICOM residents and in attracting FDI flows.
- Opportunity for improved services at the regional level.
- Opportunities for artistes to display and advertise their talents in all member states.

- Opportunities for CARICOM nationals to gain employment in any CARICOM member state they wish.
- More opportunities for nationals to study in the CARICOM countries of their choice.
- Pooling of talents to improve the participation in international debates and negotiations with one voice.

Table 11.8 reveals that both intra-CARICOM exports and imports have been increasing steadily for the period 2001–10, although the latter has been marginally higher. In general, total intra-CARICOM trade has grown almost threefold in 2010 as compared to its 2001 value.

CARICOM's trade in services has accounted for the largest percentage of gross domestic product (GDP) for most of the listed countries. Although this statistic has been on the decline since 2001, it still remains significant and a major source of revenue for the majority of the Caribbean islands.

The main intra-regional trade instrument is the CET. It was the annex to the Treaty of Chaguaramas that established the Caribbean Common Market and Article 4 of the treaty that advocated the implementation of the CET. In the CARICOM context, the common external tariff is a regime of customs tariffs that are placed on goods that are imported, either from third countries or from member states in the CARICOM market, that do not meet the qualifying conditions within the Common Market Rules of Origin. Article 31 of the annex discusses the establishment of the CET, while Articles 32 and 33 provide for its workings. Article 34 demonstrates the commitment of member states to seek progressive coordination and expansion of their trade relations with extra-regional parties.

Initially, the treaty had set August 1981 as the deadline for member states to fully adjust to the implementation of the CET with respect to the importation of commodities into CARICOM from extra-regional sources. However, this deadline was never attained

Table 11.8: Intra-CARICOM trade, 2001–2010 (US$mn)

	Intra-CARICOM exports	Intra-CARICOM imports	Total intra-CARICOM trade
2001	1,344.58	1,230.2	2,574.78
2002	1,129.22	1,150.41	2,279.63
2003	1,329.09	1,433.03	2,762.12
2004	1,583.72	1,704.01	3,287.73
2005	2,090.72	2,251.5	4,342.22
2006	2,239.77	2,408.6	4,648.36
2007	2,827.14	3,035.95	5,863.09
2008	3,540.36	3,810.62	7,350.98
2009	2,438.73	2,610.99	5,049.72
2010	3,039.83	3,234.42	6,274.25

Source: IMF Direction of Trade Statistics (2012).

Table 11.9: CARICOM trade in services as a percentage of GDP

	2001	2005	2006	2007	2008	2009	2010
Antigua and Barbuda	71.8	67.4	63.3	61.4	60.7	60.0	60.5
Bahamas	49.1	58.3	58.9	57.8	53.9	48.9	47.6
Barbados	58.5	70.2	71.9	69.4	69.7	61.6	57.7
Belize	32.9	41.3	42.5	44.3	40.9	37.5	36.8
Dominica	37.7	37.1	38.6	40.7	40.6	39.0	38.8
Grenada	41.8	30.4	33.6	33.8	31.6	31.3	30.9
Guyana	52.3	42.3	27.0	25.6	27.8	21.9	26.6
Haiti	11.4	16.5	16.1	15.7	17.1	17.7	22.5
Jamaica	37.5	36.3	38.9	38.7	36.2	36.0	31.3
St Lucia	59.2	69.6	53.7	52.8	51.3	49.1	49.2
St Vincent and the Grenadines	44.2	42.9	42.4	40.2	36.3	33.3	32.5
Suriname	30.6	31.0	23.5	23.2	22.3	17.6	—
Trinidad and Tobago	10.7	9.0	6.4	6.0	4.7	5.8	—

Source: World Development Indicators (2012).

by most of the members (only Guyana, Jamaica, and Trinidad and Tobago had implemented the CET by 1976, with Barbados joining in 1981). By 1990, the CET was still not in place, although plans were agreed on to have the CET implemented by 1 January 1991.

However, by 1991 all member countries still had not implemented the CET, and as a consequence the CARICOM Heads of Government ordered a full revision of the CET in 1992.[4] The decision by the CARICOM Heads of Government to review the CET was intended to facilitate greater attention being paid to the international trends in trade liberalization, regional trade blocs and a general phasing out of preferential trading agreements. The new rate structure of the CARICOM CET was influenced by several factors, including the competitiveness of CARICOM products, revenue collection by member states fiscally dependent on international trade taxes, the cost of living and the economic conditions in the Organization of Eastern Caribbean States (OECS) and Belize. This review resulted in the following sequential process for the implementation and lowering of the tariff schedule over a five-year period between 1993 and 1998.[5]

As mentioned previously, CARICOM members agreed on a relatively simple rate structure, as well as a programme that would allow for the gradual reduction of the rate over a five-year period, sub-divided into four phases. This was to commence on 1 January 1993 and conclude on 30 June 1998. The targeted outcome was that, by the date of completion,

Table 11.10: Proposed implementation and reduction of the CARICOM common external tariff (CET)

Period of application	Period allowed to effect implementation	Rate structure	
		MDC%	LDC%
1 January 1993 to 31 December 1994	1 January 1993 to 30 June 1993	5 to 30/35	0–5 to 30/35
1 January 1995 to 31 December 1996	1 January 1995 to 30 June 1995	5 to 25/30	0–5 to 25/30
1 January 1997 to 31 December 1997	1 January 1997 to 30 June 1997	5 to 20/25	0–5 to 20/25
1 January 1998 onwards	1 January 1998 to 30 June 1998	5 to 20	0–5 to 20

a maximum tariff of 40 per cent and 20 per cent would be applied to "agricultural products" and "all other products", respectively. Even though there were significant delays in the implementation process, most countries were able to implement the first three phases as at the end of 1997. However, not all economies in CARICOM were able to implement the four phases of the reduction in the five-year period. By June 1998, only two countries had implemented the four phases, although by December 2008, eleven countries had.[6] As it stands, CARICOM member states are implementing the revised CET structure based on the 2002 Harmonized System. Several countries have already implemented this revised structure; these are Barbados, Guyana, Jamaica, Montserrat, and Trinidad and Tobago.

One of the most cogent arguments in favour of a rapid dismantling of the CARICOM CET comes from no less a place than the nineteenth Meeting of the Conference of Heads of Government of the Caribbean Community. At this meeting, one of the discussion papers noted,

> The idea of keeping some defensible margin of preference for local producers in the form of a tariff is no longer tenable for a small CARICOM market seeking to link trade and production with the rest of the hemisphere and region. While such a policy can still bring creation gains for large schemes such as Mercosur and even reconcile regional trade protection with universal liberalization, if it bears a low tariff, it is counterproductive for CARICOM. (Gonzales 1998, 6)

CARICOM's external tariff rate structure is illustrated in table 11.9. The structure is divided into inputs and finished goods. These goods are then subdivided into competing and non-competing.[7] Within the CET legislation are a range of tariff exemptions, and these are contained in four lists (A, B, C and D). The CET legislation also contains a list of conditional duty exemptions as well as a list of ineligible for duty exemptions. This list includes those items for which CARICOM produces 75 per cent of the total output.

Table 11.11: Structure and evolution of the CET

Inputs	Groups				Range		
	A	B	C	D Non-basic	MDCs	LDCs	Period of application
Primary	0–5	30/10			5 to 30/35	5 to 30/35	01/93 to 12/94
					5 to 25/30	5 to 25/30	01/95 to 12/96
					5 to 20/25	5 to 20/25	01/97 to 12/97
					5 to 20	5 to 20	01/98
Intermediate	10/0–5	30/15			5 to 30/35	5 to 30/35	01/93 to 12/94
					5 to 25/30	5 to 25/30	01/95 to 12/96
					5 to 20/25	5 to 20/25	01/97 to 12/97
					5 to 20	5 to 20	01/98
Capital	10/0–5	20/10			5 to 30/35	5 to 30/35	01/93 to 12/94
					5 to 25/30	5 to 25/30	01/95 to 12/96
					5 to 20/25	5 to 20/25	01/97 to 12/97
					5 to 20	5 to 20	01/98
Final goods	20	30/20	45/20	30/20	5 to 30/35	5 to 30/35	01/93 to 12/94
					5 to 25/30	5 to 25/30	01/95 to 12/96
					5 to 20/25	5 to 20/25	01/97 to 12/97
					5 to 20	5 to 20	01/98

The implementation of the CARICOM CET in the member states of CARICOM has led to an overall reduction in the region's unweighted tariff from an average of 20 per cent in the 1990s to around 10 per cent to date (see table 11.10).

As it stands, CARICOM does not have a common trade policy in relation to its extra-regional trading partners. In this regard, the World Bank (2000, 29) notes, "The challenge for the coming years is for CARICOM countries to design a common trade policy, which

Table 11.12: CARICOM: CET and national applied tariffs in selected countries, 2003

HC sec	Simple average (%) description	CET	Barbados	Guyana	Jamaica	St Kitts and Nevis	Trinidad and Tobago
01	Live animals products	24.9	53.3	27.1	25.3	11.5	24.5
02	Vegetable products	18.2	28.0	18.4	16.4	13.2	16.2
03	Animal vegetable fats	26.7	32.1	25.8	23.9	21.9	24.0
04	Processed foods/tobacco	19.7	34.2	25.0	15.5	16.1	16.2
05	Mineral products	4.8	6.9	6.2	2.6	2.4	3.0
06	Chemical industrial products	5.4	6.6	6.1	2.0	5.6	2.3
07	Plastic rubber	7.4	9.1	8.7	5.6	6.7	6.3
08	Animal hides/skin	8.2	9.6	9.2	5.6	7.6	5.8
09	Wood/wood articles	9.6	10.6	9.5	6.8	9.7	6.9
10	Paper cellulose material	7.3	5.9	8.0	4.8	8.1	5.2
11	Textiles	10.4	10.8	10.8	7.6	11.1	7.9
12	Footwear misc. articles	16.6	16.2	16.0	15.4	18.5	15.2
13	Stone/glassware	8.8	9.6	8.8	6.2	9.8	8.4
14	Precious/semi-precious metals	20.1	29.7	28.6	16.8	14.4	14.7
15	Base metals	5.6	6.8	6.7	2.7	6.2	4.6
16	Machinery electrical equipment	6.5	7.8	7.5	3.5	7.7	4.9
17	Motor vehicles/vessels	9.6	10.0	9.4	6.4	9.7	7.2
18	Precision instruments	11.5	14.4	14.2	8.9	10.8	9.9
19	Arms/ammunition	38.1	47.7	44.7	22.7	46.8	22.9
20	Misc. manufacturing articles	16.2	16.2	15.8	15.2	19.3	15.7
21	Art/antiques	20.5	20.0	20.0	20.0	25.0	20.0
	Average tariff (%)	10.1	13.1	11.0	7.2	9.4	7.9
	Standard deviation	14.7	26.4	12.9	12.4	12.1	12.3

Source: World Bank (2000).

is the backbone of a full and well-functioning single market. Ultimately the success of the CSME will depend largely on the effective implementation of a common trade policy".

As it stands, these are some issues with CET that remain unresolved. The World Bank (2000, 28) identifies four areas:

> First, many countries (mainly the OECS), which rely heavily on trade taxes as a source of government revenue, have introduced revenue compensation measures to mitigate the revenue losses stemming from the introduction of the CET. These include, among others: import-related levies such as stamp duties, import surcharges, and discriminatory rates of the consumption tax. Second, the CET offers broad scope for tariff suspensions and reductions, as well as for national derogations from the common tariff. This complicates the region's joint negotiating efforts with third countries, creates additional transaction costs and reduces transparency of market access for exporters targeting the CARICOM market. Third, the level of tariff dispersion in the CET remains high, resulting in additional efficiency costs and further complicating the group's market access negotiations with other countries and regions. Fourth, although CARICOM's tariffs are lower than a decade ago, they are still relatively high, particularly in the food and manufacturing sectors, where products remain highly protected from external competition.

Appendix 11.2: CARIFORUM–EC Economic Partnership Agreement

The Economic Partnership Agreement (EPA) between CARIFORUM[8] and the European Community (EC) was concluded in December 2007 and replaced the previous Lomé IV Convention and Cotonou (2000) Agreement. These multilateral arrangements offered non-reciprocating preferences from the African, Caribbean and Pacific (ACP) bloc of economies to the European Union. The Cotonou Agreement in particular was granted a waiver by the WTO to extend the European Union's preferential trading practices with the ACP countries until December 2007. This action incited severe criticism, especially by other developing economies that would ultimately be disadvantaged by the arrangement. The signing of the EPA prevented EU-CARICOM trade relations from observing the Generalized System of Preferences regime that would have effected increased competition for all developing economies, and as such nations were viewed as equal trading partners. EPA negotiations were conducted in four phases beginning April–September 2004 and addressed the following topics: market access, services and investment, trade-related issues, and legal and institutional issues. Furthermore, cooperation priorities of this EPA comprise technical assistance, capacity and institution building, support for private sector and enterprise development, diversification, technology and research capabilities, as well as infrastructural support (Trinidad and Tobago 2008). For Trinidad and Tobago in particular, areas of benefit from the signing of this EPA include trade in goods, services and investment and development cooperation (Trinidad and Tobago n.d.).

Trinidad and Tobago, Jamaica, Dominican Republic, and Guyana have been the largest exporters to the European Union from the CARIFORUM bloc for the period 2002–10. In terms of imports from the European Union, Barbados features in the previous sub-group. Further, CARIFORUM's total exports to the European Union appear to have outweighed total imports, but only marginally.

Table 11.13: CARIFORUM merchandise trade with the European Union, 2002–2010 (US$mn)

CARIFORUM exports to EU, 2002–2010 (US$mn)									
	BHS	BRD	BLZ	DMA	DMAR	GUY	JAM	VCT	TTO	CARIFORUM
2002	67.57	37.64	51.79	12.27	270.93	112.19	337.05	15.59	433.18	1,736.66
2003	78.77	37.2	57.45	9.81	276.68	159.82	360.45	4.11	411.16	2,030.76
2004	71.75	38.84	61.4	11.37	308.75	186.8	433.35	12.67	355.61	1,782.29
2005	79.99	44.4	56.11	11.6	411.11	203.16	348.8	10.83	605.05	2,073.74
2006	107.63	45.77	84.6	11.1	425.09	199.12	482.88	9.89	1,495.02	3,524.22
2007	102.08	38.7	84.75	8.79	865.19	232.65	582.76	9.61	1,652.34	3,963.28
2008	89.02	52.45	79.11	10.84	765.97	244.9	676.78	5.0	2,598.85	5,082.29
2009	93.79	42.54	92.02	9.13	477.49	216.13	225.69	3.92	1,257.7	2,954.77
2010	59.5	63.16	88.15	5.72	600.03	231.29	178.19	5.15	—	3,957.33

CARIFORUM imports from EU, 2002–2010 (US$mn)									
	BHS	BRD	BLZ	DMA	DMAR	GUY	JAM	VCT	TTO	CARIFORUM
2002	35.07	173.19	30.63	16.48	648.83	75.23	411.54	27.28	608.34	2,537.54
2003	68.76	199.35	26.15	17.16	565.96	65.99	386.17	25.99	708.38	2,585.53
2004	42.89	174.96	25.61	21.51	553.75	54.59	314.22	36.5	1,089.14	2,807.45
2005	50.02	219.56	30.73	22.18	696.01	64.66	342.38	36.14	660.44	2,692.33
2006	48.16	221.41	42.47	21.07	859.14	87.38	464.91	36.76	672.19	3,393.63
2007	59.85	220.85	38.8	22.32	1,197.98	115.06	435.8	46.43	835.75	3,632.77
2008	39.5	230.71	44.64	22.27	1,456.61	108.48	499.15	53.62	1,184.42	4,509.49
2009	31.69	172.22	38.86	27.39	1,188.90	127.17	387.33	41.4	784.35	3,576.06
2010	52.56	175.61	33.01	17.84	1,386.97	114.34	350.74	36.02	—	3,605.74

Source: Trade Map (2012).

Appendix 11.3: Economic Effects of Dumping

Dumping occurs when markets can be segmented by virtue of different price elasticities of demand so that price discrimination can be practised.

Not surprisingly, as figure 11.16 illustrates, the market with the more inelastic demand schedule charges a higher price for the same units of a commodity as compared to a more elastic market.

Figure 11.17 and table 11.14 can be used to help explore some of the economic effects of dumping for the HC.

Dumping occurs when the FC sells below P_w in the HC. Observe that consumers gain from dumping while producers lose. Specifically, at the price P_w, the consumer surplus

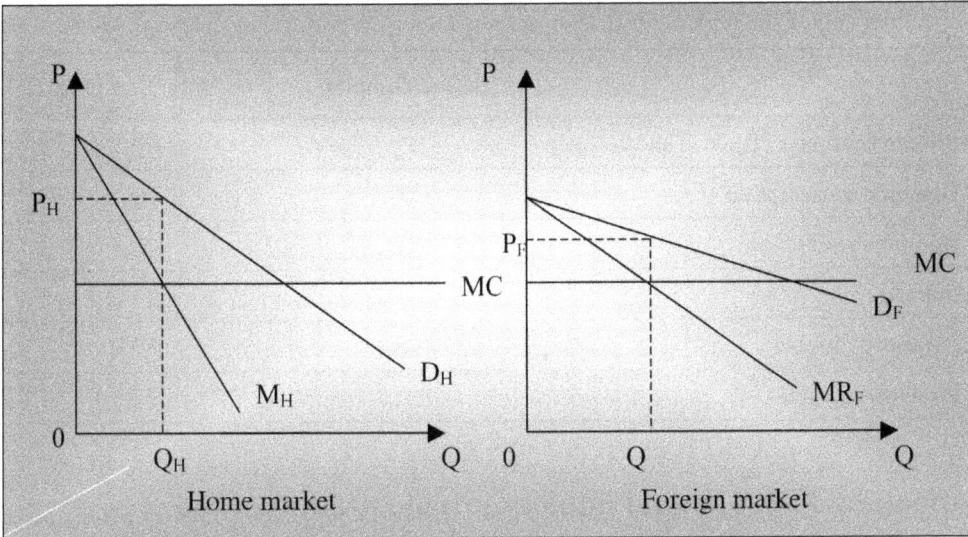

Figure 11.16: International price discrimination

in the HC is $P_w AB$. If the price level at which dumping occurs in the HC is P_1, then consumer surplus increases to $P_1 AH$.

But why intervene if consumer welfare improves? Two simple reasons are

1. the HC government will want to maintain the profits of HC producers and
2. dumping may be predatory. Specifically, if a price such as P_2 was charged in the HC instead of P_1, then all domestic producers would be forced out of production and the foreign firm could gain monopoly presence in the HC.

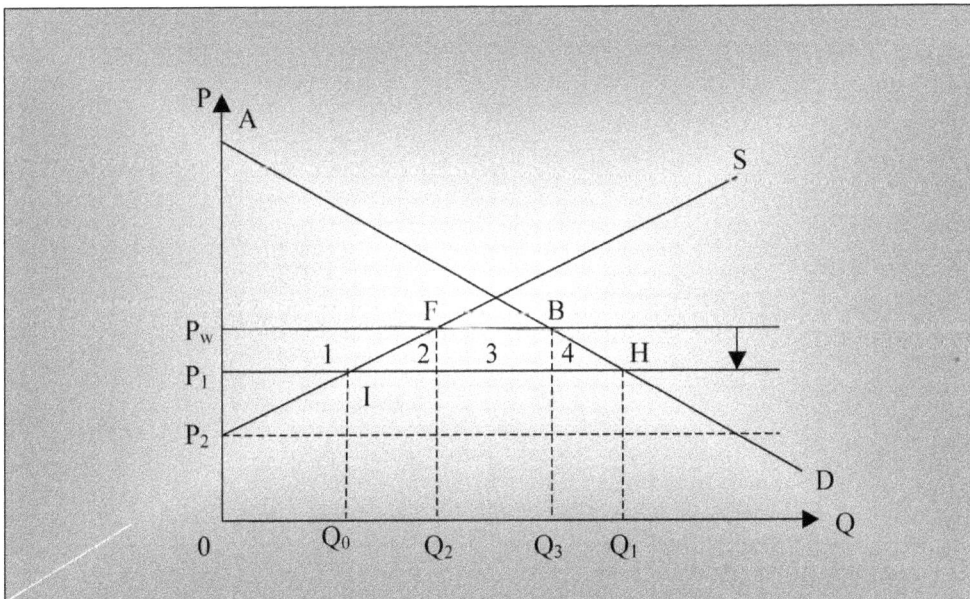

Figure 11.17: Economic effects of dumping

Table 11.14: Economic effects of dumping

	Before dumping	After dumping
Price to consumer (Trinidad and Tobago)	P_w	P_1
Domestic consumption	Q_3	Q_1
Domestic production	Q_2	Q_0
Imports	$Q_3 - Q_2$	$Q_1 - Q_0$
Consumer surplus	$P_w AB$	$P_1 AH$
Producers surplus	$P_2 P_w F$	$P_2 P_1 I$

Appendix 11.4: General Equilibrium Illustration of the Infant Industry Argument

To illustrate the economic thinking underlying the infant industry argument, consider figure 11.18. Here we show that the per unit cost of production of the infant firm (d^c) is higher than the world price (p^w) of the commodity at low levels of output, which is realized by the most efficient international suppliers. The infant industry argument purports that if the infant is allowed protection and the opportunity to mature then beyond some level of output, say Q_0, the per unit cost of production of the maturing domestic firm will be lower than the world price level. It is perceived that this now mature firm can recover the initial protectionary outlay expended on it to make it viable in the first place.

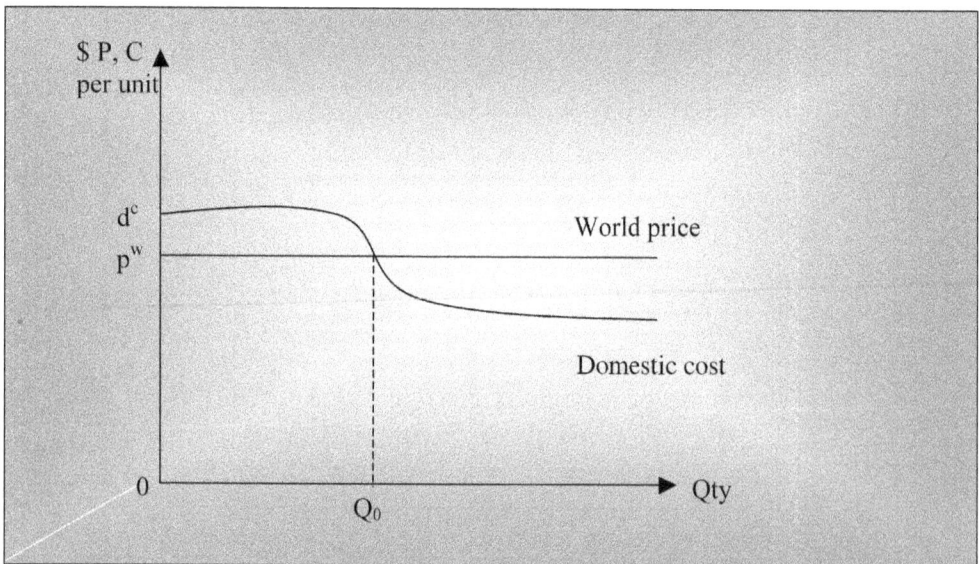

Figure 11.18: Reduction in the production costs of an infant industry as output increases

Summary of Key Points

- A specific tariff is one in which a specific amount is charged per unit of the good imported, while an ad valorem tariff is a tariff that is charged per unit of the commodity.
- In terms of the economic effect of a tariff, a fall in consumer surplus is associated with the imposition of a tariff.
- Issues associated with the imposition of a tariff include labour market protection, scientific tariff options, unemployment, current account and terms of trade implications, dumping, the impact on infant industries, and tariff revenues.
- The effective tariff rate illustrates the overall level of protection given to a commodity when nominal tariffs are attached both to the commodity itself and the factor inputs used in producing it.
- The imposition of a tariff in a large country makes two changes to that large economy's welfare. These changes occur through a volume of trade effect and a terms of trade effect.
- Tariff retaliation is one form of trade war, whereby countries set tariffs that alter the terms of trade to their own advantage. One country sets a tariff that compels its trade partner to reciprocate by altering its own tariff rates.
- An optimal tariff maximizes the difference between the terms of trade gains and the losses from the volume of trade effect.

Multiple Choice

1. A tax per unit on imports is called
   a) an ad valorem tariff
   b) a specific tariff
   c) a positive tariff
   d) a negative tariff

2. To manufacture an aeroplane worth $1,000,000, $200,000 worth of raw materials must be imported. The nominal tariff rate on the raw materials is 10 per cent, while the nominal tariff rate on the aeroplane is 20 per cent. What is the effective tariff production rate?
   a) 22.5 per cent
   b) 25 per cent
   c) 27 per cent
   d) 97.5 per cent

3. The welfare effects of the imposition of a tariff can be summarized as follows:
   a) an increase in government revenue
   b) an increase in producer surplus
   c) a decrease in consumer surplus
   d) all of the above

Short Essay

1. Why do countries impose tariffs?
2. Discuss the various forms of protection.
3. Discuss the reasons for and against protection.

Key Trade Terms

- Tariff
- Specific tariff
- Ad valorem tariff
- Welfare effects
- Economic effect
- Consumer surplus
- Producer surplus
- Prisoner's Dilemma
- Scientific tariff
- Tariff retaliation
- Dumping
- Infant industry
- Tariff revenues
- Effective tariff
- Net economic welfare
- Volume of trade effect
- Terms of trade effect
- Optimal tariff
- Common external tariff
- Price discrimination

12.

Other Non-Tariff Instruments of Trade Policy

Learning Objectives

a. Define non-tariff instruments and provide examples.
b. Differentiate between an import subsidy and an export subsidy.
c. Define quota.
d. Understand the Lerner Symmetry theorem.

12.0 Introduction

Non-tariff instruments refer to the composite set of trading restrictions excluding tariffs. They are commonly used to evade free trade rules set by the World Trade Organization (WTO) and other major trading agreements that restrict tariffs. Non-tariff instruments became increasingly popular after the WTO introduced rules to significantly reduce the use of tariffs.

Non-tariff barriers to trade typically include

- import and export subsidies;
- export taxes;
- quotas;
- national regulations on health, safety and employment;
- product classification;
- voluntary export restraint (VER);
- foreign exchange controls;
- overelaborate or inadequate infrastructure;
- "buy national" policies;
- Intellectual property laws (*patents and copyrights*);
- bribery and corruption; and
- unfair customs procedures.

This chapter provides some of the theoretical details associated with non-tariff barriers, especially import subsidies, export subsidies, quotas and voluntary export restraints.

12.1 Import Subsidies

Import subsidies refer to those subsidies that become payable per unit of a commodity that is imported.

In this section, we investigate the impact on a small economy of imposing an import subsidy. As figure 12.1 illustrates, the free trade price of the commodity that will benefit from the import subsidy is P_w. However, with the implementation of an import subsidy, there will be a fall in the import price level from P_w to $P_w(1 - s)$.

At the price of P_w, the domestic consumption level is Q_4 and the domestic level of production is Q_3. With free trade, the home country's (HC's) import level is $Q_4 - Q_3$. Also at P_w, the consumer has a consumer surplus of P_wAB, and producers have a producer surplus of $0P_wD$. With the implementation of an import subsidy, the relevant price to domestic consumers falls to $P_w(1 - s)$, and as a consequence domestic consumption extends to Q_1. At this lower price of $P_w(1 - s)$, domestic supply falls to Q_0 so that imports increase to $Q_0 - Q_1$. The fall in price triggers a rise in the size of the consumer surplus by areas $1 + 2 + 3 + 4 + 5$, but producer surplus falls by $1 + 2$. Given government expenditure of $2 + 3 + 4 + 5 + 6$, it means that the economy carries a net welfare loss equivalent to areas $2 + 6$.

The information from figure 12.1 is summarized in table 12.1.

The best policy for a small country remains free trade. The market distortion of an import subsidy in this case reduces economic welfare in the import-subsidy-imposing economy.

12.2 Export Subsidies

An export subsidy consists of those subsidies that are payable when an export good leaves the country where it is produced and is delivered to non-resident users.

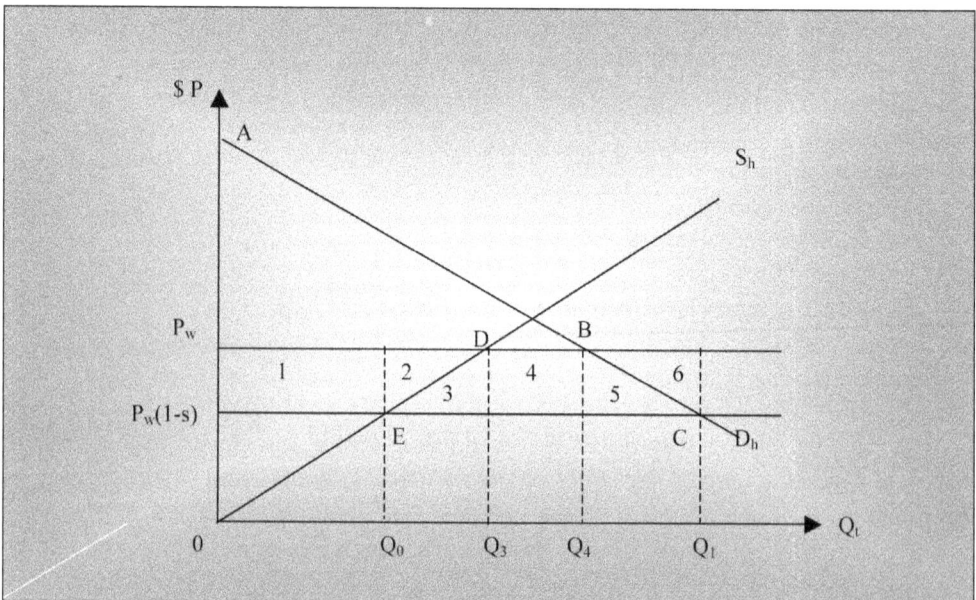

Figure 12.1: Economic effects of import subsidies in a small country

Table 12.1: Economic effects of an import subsidy in a small country

	Free trade	After subsidy
Price to consumer	P_w	$P_w(1-s)$
Domestic consumption	Q_4	Q_1
Domestic production	Q_3	Q_0
Imports	$Q_4 - Q_3$	$Q_1 - Q_0$
Consumer surplus	$P_w AB$	$P_w(1-s)AC$ i.e., increases by $1 + 2 + 3 + 4 + 5$
Producer surplus	$OP_w D$	$OP_{w(1-s)}E$, i.e., decreases by $1 + 2$
Government expenditure	Not applicable	$2 + 3 + 4 + 5 + 6$
Net welfare loss		Net loss to the economy is $2 + 6$ (CS – PS – government expenditure)

To consider some of the dynamics associated with the implementation of an export subsidy, we refer to figure 12.2. In initial conditions, with demand curve D^h and supply curve S^h and a prevailing world price of P_w, the HC demands Q_0 units of X and supplies Q_1 units, implying an export level of $Q_1 - Q_0$. If the HC implements an ad valorem export subsidy, then domestic prices will increase to $P_w(1 + s)$, at which $Q_4 - Q_3$ will be exported, as domestic production increases to Q_4 and domestic consumption falls to Q_3.

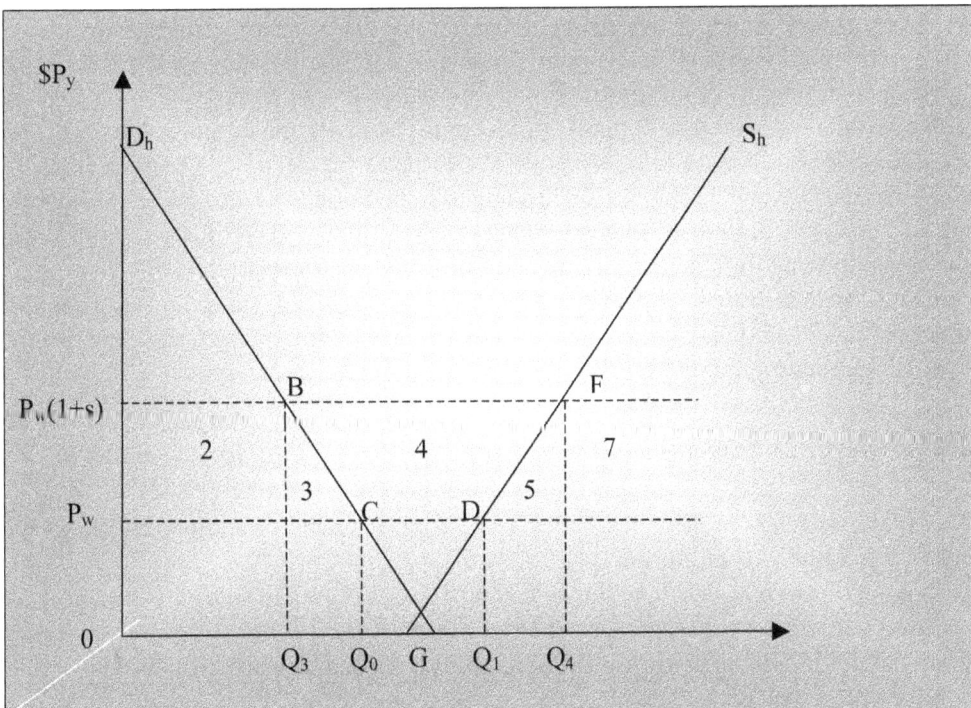

Figure 12.2: Export subsidies in a small country

Table 12.2: Economic effects of an export subsidy in a small country

	Free trade	Post export subsidy
Price to consumer	P_w	$P_w(1 + s)$
Domestic consumption	Q_0	Q_3
Domestic production	Q_1	Q_4
Exports	$Q_1 - Q_0$	$Q_4 - Q_3$
Consumer surplus	$P_w D^h$ C	it decreases by area 2 + 3
Producer surplus	0 P_w D G	it increases by 2 + 3 + 4
Tax payer cost	n.a.	Export subsidy costs tax payers 3 + 4 + 5
Deadweight consumption loss	n.a.	3
Deadweight production efficiency loss	n.a.	5
Net welfare loss	n.a.	3 + 5

With the subsidy, consumer surplus decreases by areas 2 and 3, but producer surplus expands by the areas 2 + 3 + 4. To provide this subsidy, tax payers need to put out $(Q_4 - Q_3) \times (sP_w)$, or 3 + 4 + 5.

Export subsidies induce two distinct types of trade distortions in the domestic market and foreign market. When an economy implements an export subsidy, it results in an increase in the supply of the commodity on the international market and leads to a fall in the world price level. The domestic producer in the exporting economy benefits from a higher price level. With a higher price in the exporting economy's market place, its consumption falls and its output rises, leading to an increase in its exports. In the importing economy, the lower price level encourages consumption and discourages production, thereby increasing the demand for imports. The lower price level in the import economy results in open unemployment, as some producers are crowded out of the market. It also threatens the livelihoods of those who remain and subsist at the lower price level. In the importing economy, infant firms may be chased out of the marketplace.

12.3 Export Tax in a Small Country

An export tax refers to those taxes that become payable when a commodity leaves the country in which it is produced.

A government may decide to implement an export tax for the following reasons:

Food Security: A tax on the export of food items will serve as a disincentive for producers in the HC to sell their produce abroad. As a result, more produce would be available for sale in the HC.

Tax Revenues: Since taxes are the main source of revenue for governments of developing economies, an increase in export taxes would directly imply an increase in government's revenue. As the proportion of exports increase, tax revenues also increase.

Downstream Production: An increase in export taxes on commodities creates the opportunities to reduce exports and divert production to downstream industries.

The export tax will bring the domestic price below the level of the world price, so that if t is the ad valorem tax rate, then $P_w / (1 + t)$ is the domestic export-tax-induced price level.

To elaborate on the welfare effect of an export tax, let us consider figure 12.3.

With an export tax, exports contract from $Q_1 - Q_0$ to $Q_3 - Q_2$ as domestic supply contracts from Q_1 to Q_3 and domestic demand expands from Q_0 to Q_2. With the export tax, consumer surplus expands by areas 2 and 3, but producer surplus contracts by areas 2, 3, 4, 5 and 6. The export tax will generate a revenue of magnitude $(Q_3 - Q_2) \times (P_w - (P_w/(1+t)))$, or area 5. The net welfare loss is thus areas 4 and 6.

Table 12.3 provides summary information on the effect of an export tax on economic welfare.

Barbados and Jamaica do not apply any export taxes, levies or charges on exports. Guyana applies a general 1.5 per cent export tax to almost all commodities, except manufacturing. Shrimp carries a 10 per cent export tax. However, exports to CARICOM are not subjected to taxes. Antigua and Barbuda applies export taxes on lobsters and fish. St Kitts taxes the exports of live animals, cotton and other products.

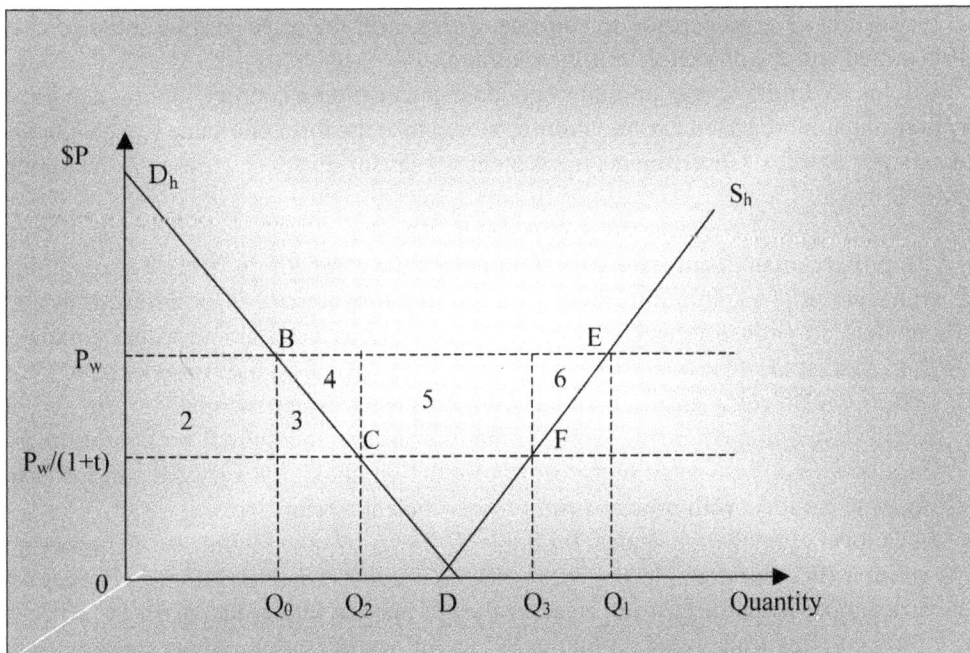

Figure 12.3: Export tax in a small country

Table 12.3: Economic effects of an export tax in a small country

	Pre-export tax	Post-export tax
Price to consumer	P_w	$P_w/(1 + t)$
Domestic consumption	Q_0	Q_2
Domestic production	Q_1	Q_3
Export	$Q_1 - Q_0$	$Q_3 - Q_2$
Consumer surplus	$P_w D^h B$	$P_w/(1 + t) D^h C$ or expands by area 2 and 3
Producers surplus	$0 P_w E D$	$0 P_w / (1 + t) F D$ or contracts by areas 2, 3, 4, 5, 6
Government revenue	n/a	Area 5
Net welfare loss	n/a	4 + 6

12.4 Economic Effect of a Quota

A tariff directly influences the price level of a commodity. An import quota, however, influences the price level on the market indirectly by affecting the quantity of imports that can enter a country. An import quota specifies the amount of the commodity that can be brought into the country for a particular period of time (e.g., 50,000 cars per annum). Thus with a quota the trading authorities determine the volume of imports and let the market determine price. In contrast, with a tariff the price level on the market is determined and the market determines volume.

Quotas are limits on the amount of goods that can enter a country. Quotas can be of a physical nature (e.g., ten cars per month) or can take the form of a value (e.g., $500,000 in cars per month). Governments implement quotas for a variety of reasons, including the following:

- To protect small infant industries from large scale competition. Since a quota limits the amount of a commodity entering a country, the interests of local industries and small infant industries will be protected. Quotas act as a measure to reduce competition against local products. Quotas in some cases give local industries some level of monopoly power to ensure their survival. This is necessary especially in the case of small developing countries, which sometimes utilize suboptimal production techniques with an associated high cost of production, making it very difficult for local firms to compete with products from more efficient foreign firms.
- As a form of retaliation against trading policies set by other countries. If the foreign country (FC), for example, imposes tariffs on products from the HC, the HC may restrict goods from the FC from entering the HC market, thus reducing the FC exports.
- To evade free trade rules set by the WTO and restrict commodities entering their country.

To illustrate the welfare effects of tariffs, consider figure 12.4. At initial conditions, the price of commodity X is P_w and the HC imports $Q_1 - Q_0$ units of the commodity. Let us assume that the government now implements a quota restriction of $Q_3 - Q_2$ units. As a consequence, the domestic price level increases to P_1. At P_1, domestic consumption decreases to Q_3, and domestic supply increases to Q_2. With the quota, consumer surplus falls from $P_w AC$ to $P_1 AF$, and producer surplus increases from $DP_w E$ to $DP_1 G$.

The HC's market will now clear at a price of P_1 and imports will be equal to $Q_3 - Q_2$. Similar to the effects of a tariff, the quota will result in fall in economic welfare. According to figure 12.4, producer surplus will increase by area 1. The higher price, however, will lead to a fall in consumer surplus by all of areas 1, 2, 3, 4. As it stands, a tariff that increases the domestic price level to P_1 would have the same effects on producers and consumers in the HC.

At this point, let us look at area 3 a bit closer. If the HC had implemented a tariff, area 3 would have accrued to the government in the form of tariff revenues. With the quota, however, area 3 will now accrue to those economic agents with the licence to import the restricted goods. In the event that licences are issued without charge, then domestic importers accrue all of area 3 for themselves. In the other extreme, if the government were to sell the licence for the maximum price possible, then it would extract all of area 3 for itself. Note though that regardless of how area 3 is allocated, the net loss from the quota will be areas 2 and 4.

Economists have cited two reasons why a tariff is superior to a quota. In the first instance, if the FC firm benefits from a successful innovation, it is questionable how much

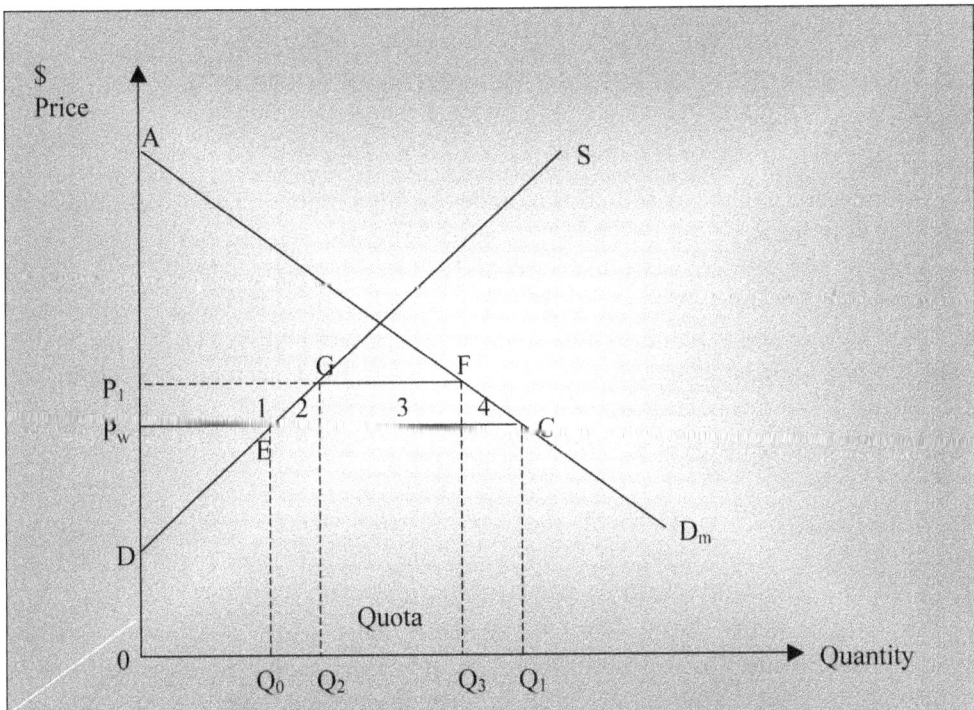

Figure 12.4: Welfare effects of a quota

Table 12.4: Welfare effects of a quota

	Before quota	After quota
Consumer price	P_w	P_1
Domestic consumption	Q_1	Q_3
Domestic production	Q_0	Q_2
Imports	$Q_1 - Q_0$	$Q_3 - Q_2$
Consumer surplus	P_w A C	P_1 A F or falls by 1, 2, 3, 4
Producer surplus	D P_w E	D P_1 G or increases by area 1
DPL		2
DCL		4
NWL		2 and 4

of that benefit will be passed onto the consumers in the HC if it implements a quota. Specifically, the foreign firm will not benefit from being able to sell more in the market of the HC and as a consequence loses this dimension (of an expanded target market) as an incentive to innovate.

Second, with a tariff an increase in economic growth will result in more goods traded in the HC but at a higher price. With a quota, economic growth results in a higher price only.

12.5 The Effect of a Quota on the Terms of Trade of a Large Country

The impact of a quota on the terms of trade of a large country can be illustrated using figure 12.5. In initial conditions, the offer curves of the HC and FC are OC_{HC} and OC_{FC}, respectively, with the terms of trade at tot_1 and x_1 units of good X offered by the HC for y_1 units of good Y from the FC. If the HC now imposes a quota that binds its imports of the good Y to y_2 units, then the home country's offer curve becomes OC'_{HC} (i.e., it corresponds to a horizontal line through y_2), and a new international terms of trade such as tot_2 results. The terms of trade tot_2 is superior to the terms of trade tot_1 for the large HC, and so an import quota improves the terms of trade.

12.6 Voluntary Export Restraint (VER) and the Terms of Trade

A VER is an agreement where an exporting country voluntarily limits the amount it exports to a particular country. A VER is implemented when an import-competing industry seeks protection from an increase in imports from an exporting country. The exporter sometimes agrees to a VER in order to appease the importing country and avoid the effects of possible trade restraints that the importer may threaten. It is usually

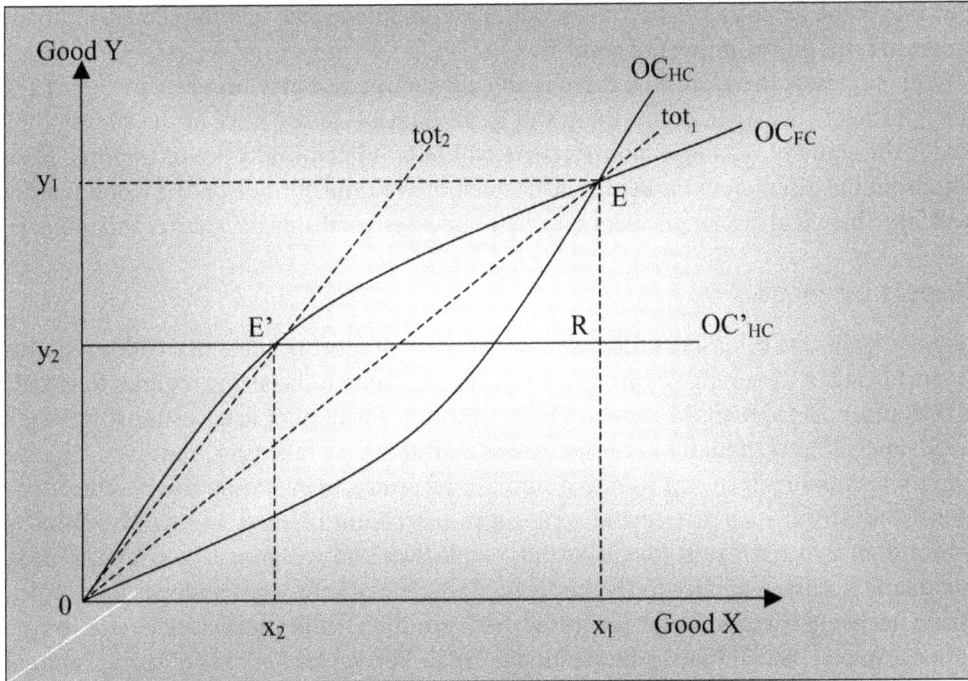

Figure 12.5: The impact of an import quota by the HC on the terms of trade

implemented at the request of the importing country's government. Therefore, a VER is rarely completely voluntary.

12.7 Lerner Symmetry Theorem

Lerner (1936) illustrated that in the long run an ad valorem export tax has the same effect as an ad valorem import tariff. To see this, note that if the HC imports Y and exports X and implements an export tax on good X so that the HC's price is lower than the FC's price, then

$$P^{HC}_X = P^w_x / (1 + t)$$

where

P^{HC}_x = price of X in the HC,
P^w_x = price of X in the world,
t = ad valorem export tax.

Given that the price of Y in the HC will remain P^{HC}_Y (which is equal to P^w_y), then the relevant domestic price ratio becomes

$$P^{HC}_x / P^w_y = [p^w_x / (1 + t)] / p^w_y$$

$$\frac{P^w_x}{1+t} \bigg/ \frac{1}{P^w_y} = \frac{P^w_x}{P^w_y (1+t)} \tag{1}$$

But this is the same expression we would have obtained if we had implemented an ad valorem tariff on the import of good Y.

This indicates therefore that there is an equivalent symmetry between an export tax and an import tax. Specifically, there will be an increase in the price of the commodity, and if the country is a large country, there will be a fall in world price of imports. Note also from the discussions earlier in the chapter, the volume of trade on the world market will fall. There is also an equivalent symmetry between a subsidy on exports and imports.

Import Licences

Some CARICOM economies also require the use of import licences. Barbados requires import licences for a range of products and applies different licensing regimes to CARICOM and non-CARICOM economies. Application for import licences must be made in advance of importation of relevant goods, and this may take up to ten days. Guyana applies an import licensing rule to a number of products including the output of national industries, such as rice and cane sugar, petroleum imports and its by products, wheat flour and fertilizers, medical drugs, explosives and weapons. For Grenada, non-automatic licensing applies to the imports of whole chickens, eggs and war toys. Automatic licensing is required for processed pork products, milk (bulk), sugar, rice (bulk), ground spices, oils and fats, jellies and jams, malt beverages, high proof spirits, animal and poultry feed, cigarettes, paints, varnishes and lacquers, wooden doors, toilet paper, corrugated galvanized sheets, aluminum windows and doors, mattresses and mattress supports and doors. A range of goods from Jamaica also require import licensing.

In the Organization of Eastern Caribbean States (OECS) bloc, outright prohibition is targeted at commodities that pose health and safety risks. In Dominica, import licences are required for the imports of potatoes and wheat flour. In St Kitts, import licences are required for agricultural goods for which local production is on the increase. Suriname has a negative list on which goods can be subjected to import restrictions, including import licensing. Trinidad and Tobago also carries a range of goods that require import licences.

Tariffs

Consistent with an open regionalism stance, the most-favoured nation (MFN) tariff in CARICOM member states declined in those member states where data was available. The tariffs on agricultural goods were everywhere higher than the tariffs on non-agricultural goods.

Import Prohibition

Import prohibitions are implemented by some Caribbean economies. Import prohibitions are defined by the WTO as a trade policy instrument designed to reduce imports. Import prohibitions are imposed for a variety of reasons but are particularly applied for sanitary, phyto-sanitary and national security reasons. In Trinidad and Tobago, the reasons cited for the outright prohibition of goods extend to moral issues (goods associated with obscene prints) and curbing of smuggling. Restrictions in other Caribbean economies are typically for sanitary, phyto-sanitary or moral reasons.

Table 12.5: MFN tariffs in various CARICOM member states, summary analysis

	# of tariff lines	Current average (%)	Previous average (%)	Agricultural goods (%)	Other goods (%)
Antigua and Barbuda	6,413 (2007)	10.7 (2007)	Unchanged since Phase IV of the CET was introduced in 2001		9.7
Barbados	6,890 (2007)	16.2 (2007)	16.5 (2001)	33.7	12.8
Belize	6,292 (2004)	11.3 (2004)		17.9	10.1
Dominica	6,479 (2007)	12.2 (2007)		25.8	9.5
Grenada	6,330 (2007)	11.2 (2007)		18.2	9.8
Guyana	6,397 (2009)	12.0 (2008)	12.1 (2003)	22.5	10.0
Jamaica	6,439 (2004)	8.6 (2004)	10.9 (1997)	18.1	6.7
St Kitts	6,340 (2007)	10.3 (2007)		14.2	9.6
St Lucia	6,352 (2007)	10.0 (2007)		16.7	8.6
St Vincent	6,274 (2007)	10.9 (2007)		18.0	9.6
Suriname	5,291 (2007)	11.1 (2007)	35.0 (1994)	18.6	9.5
Trinidad and Tobago	6,437 (2005)	9.1 (2005)	9.1 (1998)	17.1	7.6

Source: Compiled from various WTO reports.

Anti-dumping and Countervailing Measures (ADCM)

In some Caribbean economies, ADCM are in use. Between 1995 and 2004, the authorities in Trinidad and Tobago initiated eleven anti-dumping investigations with a final determination made on nine cases regarding "cheddar cheese from NZ, table salt from Venezuela, macaroni and spaghetti from Costa Rica, Portland grey cement from Thailand; Portland grey cement from Indonesia, woven polypropylene bags from China, three-strand polypropylene ropes from India, lead acid batteries from Thailand and air conditioning units from China" (WTO 2005, 21). The OECS countries did not initiate any investigations in the period 2000–2007. Barbados has not initiated any anti-dumping investigations, although in 1996 it introduced countervailing measures against the imports of milk from Trinidad and Tobago, though these were not notified. Guyana has not introduced any legislation regarding ADCM measures. In the period under review, Jamaica initiated four anti-dumping investigations regarding Portland grey cement and inorganic fertilizers. In all four cases, duties were imposed. Suriname has not applied any anti-dumping or countervailing measures.

Rules of Origin

A free trade area offers trading benefits and rules of origin that help to define the perimeters regarding the basis of preferences for commodities. Among CARICOM member states, Guyana has the most recently completed *Trade Policy Report* (July 2009). The rules of origin criteria as applied by Guyana, but which are also extendable to other CARICOM member states, are shown in table 12.6.

Table 12.6: Rules of origin maintained under CARICOM rules

Agreement/country	Rules
CARICOM	Article 84 of the Revised Treaty deals with rules of origin. Goods must have been wholly obtained or produced within CARICOM (intra-CARICOM cumulation applies). Goods produced within CARICOM from materials imported from third countries must have been substantially transformed: this may be specifically defined for each tariff heading as set out Schedule I of the Revised Treaty; otherwise it is achieved by a change of tariff heading. Guyana has incorporated CARICOM rules of origin into domestic law, in the Fourth Schedule to the Customs Act, Cap. 82:01.
CARICOM–Colombia	Rules of origin on imports into Guyana (as a CARICOM MDC) from Colombia only apply to a limited number of goods listed in the Agreement. Rules of origin on imports are set out in Article 9 of the Agreement. Substantial transformation is generally determined by a change in tariff classification. Cumulation among parties applies.
CARICOM–Costa Rica	Rules of origin are set out in Chapter IV to the Agreement. Goods must have been wholly obtained or produced within one or both of the parties (cumulation applies). Otherwise, non-originating materials used in the production of a good must have either undergone a change in tariff classification or confirm to specific requirements, both of which are set out in Annex IV: 3. Goods are considered as originating if the value of all non-originating materials does not exceed 7% of the transaction value of the good on an FOB basis. With respect to textiles and clothing, the deminimize threshold for non-originating yarns and fibres is 10% of the total weight of the material.
CARICOM–Cuba	Rules of origin on imports into Guyana (as a CARICOM MDC) from Cuba only apply to the specific goods listed in Annexes II–IV to the Agreement. Rules of origin are set out in Annex VI. Goods must be wholly obtained or produced in the territories of the parties (cumulation among parties applies). Otherwise, products which incorporate parts from third countries must undergo a change in tariff classification, and value of materials used from third countries must not exceed 50% of the FOB price of the goods.

Agreement/country	Rules
CARICOM– Dominican Republic	Rules of origin are set out in Appendix I to Annex I of the Agreement. Goods must be wholly obtained or produced in the territories of the parties (cumulation among parties applies). Otherwise, products that incorporate parts from third countries (which account for over 7% of the transaction value) must in most cases undergo a change in tariff classification. For chemicals, plastics, and some fertilizers, the criterion for substantial transformation is that a chemical reaction or purification must have taken place. Origin is determined in some specific cases by regional-value content as specified in an attachment to Appendix 1. There are also some instances where rules of origin criteria have yet to be developed.
CARIFORUM–EC	Rules of origin are set out in Article 10 to the Agreement and Protocol I. Products must have been wholly obtained within the parties or have undergone sufficient working/processing as set out in Annex II to Protocol I. Cumulation among the parties applies and, under certain conditions, may also include ACP states and the EC's overseas countries and territories (OCT's). At the request of the CARIFORUM states, and under certain conditions, CARIFORUM origin may also be conferred on goods incorporating materials from certain neighbouring countries without sufficient working/processing being required. These countries are Colombia, Costa Rica, Cuba, El Salvador, Guatemala, Honduras, Mexico, Nicaragua, Panama and Venezuela. Goods are considered as originating if the value of all non-originating materials does not exceed 15% of the ex-works price of the product.

Source: Guyana's Trade Policy Report (2009).

Sanitary and Phyto-Sanitary (SPS) Measures

Barbados has not notified any SPS measures to the WTO since 2002. However, Venezuela has raised concerns to the SPS committee that Barbados restrictions applied to its imports of citrus from Venezuela are unwarranted. Barbados in turn has stated that its actions are consistent with its Plant, Pest and Disease Control Act. The Food and Drug Act of Guyana (1971) generally prohibits the sale of unfit, harmful and adulterated or unsanitary food as well as adulterated drugs or cosmetics. The importation of livestock and other animals into Guyana requires a permit from the Animal Services Division and the Plant Quarantine Section.

The Jamaican authorities notified the WTO between 1998 and 2004 of SPS measures it imposed regarding products of animal and plant origin from its various trading partners. These measures were related to bovine spongiform encephalopathy in beef and beef products from the United States and European Union as well as foot and mouth disease in relation to the imports of liver, ruminants and pigs, and meat and meat products. Other SPS measures were linked to untreated milk, milk products, oil seeds and oleaginous fruits or medicinal plant straws from Argentina, France, Ireland, Netherlands, the United

Kingdom and Uruguay. The WTO was also notified of measures taken on the imports of wooden pallets from Trinidad and Tobago on account of their infestation with wood-boring beetles.

In the OECS bloc, Antigua and Barbuda is the only member state to have notified the WTO of any SPS measure. In general though, the imports of plants and unprocessed products into the OECS require an accompanying phyto-sanitary certificate issued by the exporting country.

Trinidad and Tobago has made four notifications to the WTO committee on SPS measures. These notifications involve a notification on the imports of fruits and vegetables from Grenada, an emergency measure on the impact of birds and bird products from the US states of California and Nevada, the imports of birds and bird products from Belgium and the Netherlands, and the temporary prohibition on the import of live cattle and all beef products from Canada.

12.8 Conclusion

This chapter examined the effects of non-tariff trade policies on both large and small countries. The chapter focused on export subsidies and export taxes in a small country and the economic effects of a quota. The chapter also discussed voluntary export restraint and the terms of trade. The chapter closed off with a discussion of the Lerner symmetry theorem.

Summary of Key Points

- Non-tariff instruments consist of the composite set of trading restrictions excluding tariffs.
- Import subsidies consist of those subsidies that become payable per unit of a commodity that is imported.
- Export subsidies consist of those subsidies that are payable when an export good leaves the country where it is produced and is delivered to non-resident users.
- Export taxes refers to those taxes that become payable when a commodity leaves the country in which it is produced.
- An import quota influences the price level on the market indirectly by affecting the quantity of imports that can enter a country. It specifies the amount of the commodity that can be brought into the country for a particular period of time.
- A VER is an agreement where an exporting country voluntarily limits the amount it exports to a particular country. It is implemented when an import-competing industry seeks protection from an increase in imports from an exporting country.
- According to the Lerner symmetry theorem, in the long run an ad valorem export tax has the same effect as an ad valorem import tariff.

Multiple Choice

1. All of the following are non-tariff barriers to trade except

   a) embargoes
   b) sectoral bilateral agreements
   c) anti-dumping rules
   d) import licences

2. Non-tariff barriers can include all of the following except

   a) government procurement laws with "buy domestic" requirements
   b) voluntary export restraint (VER)
   c) a 10 per cent duty on imported goods
   d) national standards for health and safety

3. What effect does an import quota have on consumers?

   a) Producer surplus falls.
   b) Consumer surplus falls.
   c) Domestic consumption increases.
   d) The domestic price of the imported commodity falls.

4. What are the economic effects of an import quota on domestic producers?

   a) Domestic production falls.
   b) Consumer surplus increases.
   c) Producer surplus falls.
   d) Producer surplus increases.

5. With the imposition of a voluntary export quota by exporting countries, foreign exporters

   a) raise their export prices
   b) lower their export price
   c) expand exports
   d) reduce exports

Short Essay

1. Evaluate the economic effects of a quota.
2. Evaluate the economic effects of a VER.

Key Trade Terms

- Non-tariff instruments
- Import subsidy
- Export subsidy
- Export tax
- Food security
- Quota
- Voluntary export restraint
- Lerner Symmetry theorem
- Import licences
- Import prohibition
- Anti-dumping and countervailing measures
- Rules of origin
- Sanitary and phyto-sanitary (SPS) measures

Notes

Chapter 1: International Trade

1. The analytical framework used to measure the growth of the Chinese economy is based on the changes to the production possibility frontier.
2. In China, because of the distortion of prices by government influence, purchasing power prices should be interpreted with caution.
3. The Caribbean Community (CARICOM) was established with the ratification of the Treaty of Chaguaramas in 1975. The arrangement has since progressed to a single market and economy. Currently CARICOM has fifteen full members: Antigua and Barbuda, Bahamas, Barbados, Belize, Dominica, Grenada Guyana, Haiti, Jamaica, Montserrat, St Kitts and Nevis, St Vincent and the Grenadines, St Lucia, Suriname, and Trinidad and Tobago.
4. It is interesting the plethora of advisories about China's demand for crude oil and other commodities that are made, almost as if the growth thrust by large developing economies is an undesirable effect.
5. Additionally, the *Asia Times* predicted in 2006 that by 2010 China's consumption of natural gas would reach 140 billion cubic metres. To address its growing demand for energy, China's three main oil giants, PetroChina, Sinopec and China National Offshore Oil Corporation (CNOOC), are currently expanding their operation into LNG, with CNOOC exploring new import market options.

Chapter 2: The Pure Theory of International Trade: Supply

1. Comparative advantage theory was first introduced by Robert Torrens in 1815 in an essay on the corn trade. However, a systematic explanation was developed by David Ricardo in 1817 in the book *The Principles of Political Economy and Taxation*.
2. Greenaway and Milner (1993, 81) noted that these indirect methods obviously needed to make assumptions about the relationship between observable and unobservable variables.
3. "The reason why RCA has gained wider acceptance among applied international trade economists than the measures based in net exports is that it is a more comprehensive indicator of the concept of specialization" (Brasili et al. 2000).

Chapter 4: Gains from Trade in Neoclassical Theory

1. Oil exports are approximated by the export of single international trade classification (sitc 3).
2. Exports of petrochemicals (approximated by the sum of exports on the sitc 5 and 6 accounts) increased from TT$481.87 million in 1972 to TT$3,954.3 million in 1998, or from 12.2 per cent of total exports to 88.04 per cent, at constant prices.

Chapter 5: Offer Curves

1. In short, the curve shows the willingness to trade at various possible terms of trade. You will note that the offer curve is really a combination of a demand curve (the demand for imports) and a supply curve (the supply of exports). The concept itself was introduced by John Stuart Mill (1806–73) and put into graphical form by Alfred Marshall (1842–1924) and F.Y. Edgeworth (1845–1926).
2. The HC in this case is assumed to be a large country; the same does not apply for a small country and will be discussed later in the chapter.

Chapter 6: A Basis for Trade: The Factor Proportion Hypothesis

1. When we say that commodities are expensively priced, we mean in relation to the FC where an alternative resource endowment bundle is so constituted that the price of the same commodity in the FC is much cheaper than in the HC. For example, Trinidad and Tobago has so much natural gas that the rents we would accrue from its use domestically would be small as compared to what we currently obtain.
2. Both Ohlin and Samuelson would go on to win Nobel prizes.
3. Ohlin backed the H/O theorem with real-world observation and appeals to intuition. Samuelson took the mathematical road, adding narrow assumptions that allowed a strict proof of the theory's main prediction. The H/O predictions follow logically in Samuelson's narrow case and seem broadly accurate in the real world.
4. Ethier (1974) brought together various parts of the H/O theorem.
5. Note that the specific factor model can be treated as illustrating a short-run phenomena, as over time all factors of production will be more mobile and less distinctive so that the predictions of the original SS model are reestablished.
6. As with many other outstanding pieces of work, the path-breaking research of Stolper and Samuelson did not find immediate academic acceptance and indeed was rejected by the *American Economic Review*, as it was considered "a narrow study in formal theory".
7. The Trinidad and Tobago Central Statistical Office records data on economic activity in two main formats: the Trinidad and Tobago Standard National Accounts (TTSNA) and the International Standard Industrial Classification (ISIC). The TTSNA format places petrochemicals and oil refining as part of the petroleum industry, while the ISIC approach places petrochemicals and oil refining under the umbrella of manufactured goods. In this chapter, we follow the ISIC methodology as far as the data allows.
8. Note the falloff in the number of primary school children graduating is in synchrony with the trend in the segment of the population aged four to twelve years, which has fallen in Trinidad and Tobago. Further, this variable as presented is a flow concept; its cumulative stock between 1966 and 2000 would be considerably larger than the value in 1966.
9. Since Leontief published his findings, enough evidence has accumulated to disprove Leontief's claim that American labour productivity is superior.

Chapter 7: Alternative Theories of Trade and Intra-Industry Trade

1. It may be argued that developed-country markets are characterized by Keynes's law (demand creates its own supply), while developing-country markets are characterized by Say's Law (supply creates its own demand).
2. Brecher and Choudhri (1984) illustrate how the existence of newly invented products can help explain away the Leontief paradox. These researchers argue that if producing new goods is a labour-intensive process, then US trade patterns in these goods would be labour intensive. For these newly invented goods, heavy investments in fixed capital formation are likely to be delayed until the producer is clear as to which of the particular features of the product are most desired by the consumer. When the good becomes standardized, it would be mass produced using capital-intensive techniques, so that, understandably, US imports at this stage of the production process (if it materialized) would be capital intensive.
3. In a recent study investigating the PCH, Gagnon and Rose (1995) found that net US exports in 1962 remained net US exports in 1988. A similar pattern was observed for Japan, and the authors concluded that these empirical findings were inconsistent with changing comparative advantage changing over time.
4. A community indifference curve denotes the various combinations of two commodities the yield the same level of satisfaction to a country as a whole.
5. See also Falvey (1981) and Falvey and Keizkowsky (1987).
6. The Balassa index still maintains some degree of appeal but has lost some of its popularity because pure IIT was scheduled by construction with a score of zero.
7. It is also this aspect of trade that connects factor markets and IIT.
8. Another measure of MIIT was developed by Thom and McDowell (1999).
9. For a statistical description of the G/L index, see Greenaway and Milner (1986).

Chapter 8: Economic Growth and International Trade

1. The zone 180° to 270° is quoted for completeness. Production cannot occur in this quadrant if the economy is growing.
2. Only the part of this quadrant labelled 4 makes intuitive sense if the economy is growing.
3. The real import variable was obtained by deflating nominal imports by the nonpetroleum GDP deflator, while the real exports variable was obtained by deflating nominal exports by the petroleum GDP deflator.
4. It should be noted that the Dutch Disease model has been consistently deployed in the literature to deal with countries that have experienced energy sector booms. This model, however, is equally well applicable to any economy that is experiencing a boom in a tradable-goods sector for which domestic absorption is limited.
5. For simplicity, it is assumed that factors of production are internationally immobile and factor prices are flexible. See Corden and Neary (1982) for other permutations.
6. The real effective exchange is a trade-weighted, inflation-moderated nominal exchange rate.
7. Differential labour-productivity growth in manufacturing and services provides a more empirically plausible explanation as to why the manufacturing share of employment has tended to contract as an economy matures. Faster relative productivity growth in manufacturing implies that the share of manufacturing in real value added can remain constant or even increase while the share of employment and nominal output is declining.
8. Economic rents can be calculated using the formula $ER_t = TO_t \times (XP_t - TC_t)$ where ER_t = economic rents, TO_t = total output of crude oil, XP_t = export price of crude oil and TC_t = lifting

and transporting cost of crude oil. It is assumed for ease of analysis that transport cost is zero, as data on this is difficult to compile (this will only affect the intercept and not the slope of ER). LC is treated as \$14.4, the lowest price of crude oil in the period 1990–2005.

9. In the Bhagwatian world where this case was considered, population was assumed to be constant so as to discount the possibility that the fall in per capita consumption could have been induced by a rise in population.

10. Note that apart from the assumptions underlying the Heckscher-Ohlin theorem, the Rybczynski theorem further assumes a constant terms of trade and a constant capital stock.

Chapter 9: International Factor Flows: Foreign Direct Investment

1. The debt crisis emerged in the early 1980s when many developing countries that had borrowed money found themselves unable to repay.

2. To see this, one has to subtract from the new international total product (OFEB + O`JEB) the old national product of OFGA + AJ`MA.

3. Note also that firms operate under the rationale for cost minimization and profit maximization. For more, see Jalilian (1996).

4. Another factor along this line is property rights legislation emphasizing the rights of foreign firms and limitations on their ownership portfolios, property taxes and profit taxes.

5. A favourable investment climate is important to facilitate technological spillover. Bhagwati (1978) has argued that an export-promoting regime tends to attract FDI to those industries where it has a comparative advantage.

6. From another angle, note that Bhagwati (1978) has pointed out that both the volume and efficiency of FDI are higher in export-oriented economies.

7. FDI exerts demonstration, competition and linkages effects on domestic producers, which coaxes them to invest in upgrading their technologies and practices. This requires, especially for new and potential entrepreneurs who lack internal funds, the presence of financial institutions than can provide access to external finance and better allocate and monitor these funds.

8. Slaughter's labour market perspective infers that wage inequality between skilled and unskilled workers is the result of the interaction of the demand and supply for skilled labour.

9. In general, wages and salaries usually constitute the largest component of the average household income in Trinidad and Tobago, so that an increase in wage inequality is usually indicative of an increase in income inequality.

Chapter 10: International Flows of Factors of Production: Labour

1. Significantly, the current equilibrium wage in developing economies may be a disequilibrium one.

2. Healthy workers are much more productive than unhealthy workers. Good health influences the savings and expenditure decisions of the household. Increased longevity can influence the savings decisions of a household as individuals postpone current consumption to cater for long-term old age health and other expenditures. So while the elderly use up savings, their savings also create an investment dynamic. Endemic diseases can restrict the access of certain types of natural resources to human usage. Healthier children also attend schools more frequently and can absorb, process and assimilate information at a faster pace as compared to less healthy children.

3. The growth competitiveness index is a composite index that measures the rate of technological innovation, the efficiency of public institutions and the stability of the macroeconomic

environment. Each one of the broad areas covered by this index includes other subindices, which are detailed as follows: The technology index is comprised of innovation, technology and information communications technology subindices. The public institutions index comprises two subindices: one on contracts and law and the other on corruption. The macroeconomic index includes the macroeconomic stability subindex, the institutional investor country rating and the government waste composite index (World Economic Forum 2005).

4. The business competitive index (BCI) is also a composite index, which measures the sophistication of business operations and strategies as well as the quality of the national business environment (World Economic Forum 2005).

5. There are three principle feedback benefits of skilled emigration. These are (a) workers returning with an improved stock of nursing sector skills and experience, (b) remittances and (c) the associated diasporic networks so developed which help to increase the pace of technology transfer.

6. More elaborate discussions on some of the determinants of remittances listed in this paragraph are provided in Russell (1986).

7. Remittances from overseas raise the standard of living of those left behind. In this regard, we can mention the work of Lewis (1954). Lewis detailed how a labour-surplus economy could use an abundant stock of labour to develop. Importantly, when workers leave the labour-surplus economy, it raises the ratio of capital per worker in the developing economy.

8. Given that in CARICOM member states the construction of housing characteristically involves a large domestic component, it means that the associated domestic multiplier of housing expenditure on growth and employment in these less-developed countries would be higher than if remittances were expanded on goods that facilitate a large import leakage.

9. An important aside here is the influence of the migrant worker on the host economy. In a recent paper, Jasso, Rosenzweig and Smith (1998) note that since the mid-1980s the average skill level of the immigrant to the US population was relatively higher than the overall average skill level of Americans. They argue that part of the reason for this is that US immigration laws have changed to admit people with human capital endowments that are in scarce supply in relation to the US population.

10. In this regard, we may reference the recent advances in endogenous growth theory by Lucas (1988) and Romer (1994), which clearly illustrate how an improvement in human capital contributes to the economic growth process.

11. In Yemen, the use of remittances to purchase land has caused the price of land especially in developed country areas to escalate very rapidly. Similarly, one researcher notes that in the Malabar district of Keralla, as soon as the migrant worker had covered any debt claims the process of his or her migration may have caused, the assets that were next-most preferred were land, buildings and jewellery. As a consequence, the price of real estate in this region increased substantially (Russell 1986).

12. In Grenada the ratio is much worse, with twenty-one out of twenty-two doctors from that country working abroad.

13. A recent scenario reflecting large-scale migrant behaviour is the flow of highly educated individuals from Russia to Israel. The net impact of the flood of migrants to Israel from the 1989 through 1996 was an increase in the population of Israel by 11 per cent and its labour force by 14 per cent. In addition, the data clearly shows that the share of the Russian population in Israel with a college education is considerably higher than the share of the Israelite population with college education. Given the characteristics of this migrant flow to Israel, the impact was a substantial improvement in the overall labour force of Israel and a substantive downgrading of the labour force in the Russian economy (Gandal, Hanson and Slaughter 2000).

14. The migration mentality that is partly promoted by remittance inflows can discourage FDI inflows, especially if the nature of the foreign direct investment project requires a stock of skilled domestic talent.

Chapter 11: Tariffs

1. Beggar-thy-neighbour type strategies try to boost one economy's performance at the expense of other economies.
2. Appendix 11.1 provides a discussion of some of the relevant economic issues that arise with dumping.
3. When the HC imposes a tariff on the import of good Y, the domestic production of this good will increase and domestic consumption will fall. For a large country that reduces demand, this will lead to a general decrease in the world price level of this commodity. At the same time, the associated reduction in the production and export of good X will increase its international price, so that on both counts the international terms of trade of the large country will improve.
4. In 1991, there were in existence four distinct tariff schedules pertaining to CARICOM trade with extra-regional countries: (a) the Montserrat tariff; (b) the Belize tariff; (c) the CET applied by MDCs; and (d) the OECS tariff (excluding Montserrat).
5. Some authors have argued that progressive reductions in the level of the CET from the 1993 level is perhaps the single most important policy shift among member states of CARICOM during the last decade.
6. Antigua and Barbuda and St Kitts and Nevis have yet to implement phase IV.
7. This gives four classifications: competing inputs, non-competing inputs, competing finished goods and non-competing finished goods.
8. CARICOM and Dominican Republic.

References

Balassa, B. 1965. "Trade Liberalization and Revealed Comparative Advantage". *Manchester School* 33: 99–123.

Baumol, W.J. 1967. "Macroeconomics of Unbalanced Growth: The Anatomy of the Urban Crisis". *American Economic Review* 57: 415–26.

Brecher, R., and E.U. Choudhri. 1984. "New Products and the Factor Content of International Trade". *Journal of Political Economy* 92 (5): 965–71.

Bhagwati, J.N. 1958. "Immiserizing Growth: A Geometrical Note". *Review of Economic Studies* 25: 201–5.

———. 1978. *Foreign Trade Regimes and Economic Development: Anatomy and Consequences of Exchange Control Regimes*. New York: National Bureau of Economic Research.

Brülhart, M. 1994. "Marginal Intra-Industry Trade: Measurement and the Relevance for the Pattern of Industrial Adjustment". *Weltwirtschaftliches Archiv* 130: 600–613.

———. 2002. "Marginal Intra-Industry Trade: Towards a Measure of Non-Disruptive Trade Expansion". In *Frontiers of Research on Intra-Industry Trade*, edited by P.J. Lloyd and H.H. Lee. Basingstoke: Palgrave Macmillan.

Buchan, J., and J. Sochalski. 2004. "The Migration of Nurses: Trends and Policies". *WHO Bulletin* 82: 587–93.

Buerhaus, P., D. Staiger and D. Auerbach. 2000. "Implications of an Ageing Registered Nurse Workforce". *JAMA* 283 (22): 2948–54.

Carrington, W.J., and E. Detragiache. 1998. "How Big Is the Brain Drain?" IMF Working Paper 98/102, Washington, DC.

Caves, R.E. 1981. "Intra-Industry Trade and Market Structure in the Industrial Countries". *Oxford Economic Papers* 33: 203–23.

Central Bank of Trinidad and Tobago. Various years. *Balance of Payments Yearbook* http://www.central-bank.org.tt/content/annual-publications.

Clive, T., R. Hosein and J. Yan. 2005. "Assessing the Export of Nursing Services as a Diversification Option for CARICOM Economies". Report prepared for the Caribbean Commission on Health and Development, May 2005. Washington, DC: Caribbean Commission on Health and Development and the Pan American Health Organization.

Coker, K. 1998. "An Historical Review of the Terms of Trade, 1968–1998 for Trinidad and Tobago". The Balance of Payments of Trinidad and Tobago.

Corden, W.M., and I.P. Neary. 1982. "Booming Sector and Deindustrialization in a Small Open Economy". *Economic Journal* 92 (December): 825–48.

de Mello, L.R., and T.M. Sinclair. 1995. "Foreign Direct Investment, Joint Ventures, and Endogenous Growth". Paper, Department of Economics, University of Kent, UK.

De Rosa, D. 2002. "Trade Policies and Prospects of the Eastern Caribbean States in the New Global Economy". Revised Draft, ADR International Ltd., Arlington, VA.

Drabek, Z., and D. Greenaway. 1984. "Economic Integration and Intra-Industry Trade: The EEC and CMEA Compared". *Kyklos* 37: 444–69.

Economic Intelligence Unit (EIU). Various years. *Country Forecast.* http://country.eiu.com/AllCountries.aspx.

Engel, E. 1857. *Die Produktions- und Consumtionsverhäaltnisse des Käonigreichs Sachsen*, reprinted with Engel (1895), Anlage I, 1–54.

Ethier, W. 1974. "Some of the Theorems of International Trade with Many Goods and Factors". *Journal of International Economics* 4 (2): 199–206.

Faini, R. 2001. "Development Trade and Migration". Development, Trade, and Migration, Revue d'Économie et du Développement, Proceedings from the ABCDE Europe Conference, 1–2, 85–116.

Falvey, R.E. 1981. "Commercial Policy and Intra-Industry Trade". *Journal of International Economics* 11: 495–511.

Falvey, R.E., and H. Kierzkowski. 1987. "Product Quality, Intra-industry Trade, and Imperfect Competition". In *Protection and Competition in International Trade, Essays in Honor of W.M. Corden*, edited by H. Kierzkowski. Basil Blackwell.

Ferto, I., and L.J. Hubbard. 2003. "The Dynamics of Agri-Food Trade Patterns: The Hungarian Case". Conference Paper for the 25th International Conference of Agricultural Economists, 16–22 August, Durban, South Africa.

Friedman, T. 2000. *The Lexus and the Olive Tree: Understanding Globalization.* New York: Anchor Books.

Gagnon, J. E., and A.E. Rose. 1995. "Dynamic Persistence of Industry Trade Balances: How Pervasive Is the Product Cycle?" *Oxford Economic Papers* 47 (2): 229–48.

Gandal, N., G.H. Hanson and M.J. Slaughter. 2000. "Technology, Trade, and Adjustment to Immigration in Israel". Working Paper 7962, National Bureau of Economic Research, Cambridge, MA.

Gonzales, A.P. 1998. "The Vulnerability of Small Island Developing States and the Future of ACP-EU Cooperation: The Search for New Instruments". Paper presented to the Small Island Developing States (SIDS) Conference in Brussels, 1–2 September.

Gray, H.P. 1973. "Two Way International Trade in Manufactures: A Theoretical Underpinning". *Weltwirtschafliches Archiv* 109 (1): 19–39.

Greenaway, D. 1984. "A Cross Section Analysis of Intra-Industry Trade in the UK". *European Economic Review* 25: 39–57.

Greenaway, D., and C. Milner. 1986. *The Economics of Intra-Industry-Trade.* Oxford: Blackwell.

———. 1994. "Determinants of the Inter-Industry Structure of Protection in the UK". *Oxford Bulletin of Economics and Statistics* 56 (4): 399–419.

———. 1995. "Employment Consequences of the Uruguay Round and WTO". *International Labor Review* 134.

Greenaway, D., R.C. Hine, C. Milner and R. Elliott. 1994. "Adjustment and the Measurement of Marginal Intra-Industry Trade". *Weltwirtschaftliches Archiv* 130: 418–27.

Grubel, H.G., and P.J. Lloyd. 1975. *Intra-Industry Trade: The Theory and Measurement of International Trade in Differentiated Products.* London: Macmillan.

Haltmaier, J.T., S. Ahmed, B. Coulibaly, R. Knippenberg, S. Leduc, M. Marazzi and B.A. Wilson. 2007. "China's Role as Engine and Conduit of Growth". Global Implications of China's Trade, Investment and Growth Conference Research Department. Paper presented at Global Implications of

China's Trade, Investment and Growth Conference, 6 April 2007. http://www.imf.org/external/np/seminars/eng/2007/china/pdf/hacklmw.pdf.

Hamilton, C., and P. Kniest. 1991. "Trade Liberalization, Structural Adjustment and Intra-Industry Trade: A Note". *Weltwirtschaftliches Archiv* 127: 356–67.

Heckscher, E.F. 1949. "The Effect of Foreign Trade on the Distribution of Income". In *Readings in the Theory of International Trade*, edited by H.S. Ellis and L.A. Metzler. Homewood, IL: Irwin, 272–300. First published in Swedish in 1919, the original and remarkably sophisticated presentation of the Heckscher-Ohlin theory of trade.

Henegedara, Mahinda. 2011. "Heckscher-Ohlin's Factor Endowment Theory (H-O Theory)". *International Trade* (blog). 26 October. http://real-international-trade.blogspot.com/2011/10/heckscher-ohlins-factor-endowment.html.

Hillman, A.L. 1980. "Observations on the Relations between 'Revealed Comparative Advantage' and Comparative Advantage as Indicated by Pre-Trade Relative Prices". *Welwirtschaftliches Archiv* 116 (2): 315–21.

Hinloopen, J., and C. van Marrewijk. 2006. "On the Empirical Distribution of the Balassa Index". *Weltwirtschaftliches Archiv* 137: 1–35.

Hirsch, S. 1967. *Location of Industry and International Competitiveness*. Oxford: Oxford University Press.

Hufbauer, G. 1966. *Synthetic Materials and the Theory of International Trade*. London: Buckworth.

International Monetary Fund. Various years. *Balance of Payments Statistics Yearbook*. IMF Statistics Department. http://www.imfbookstore.org/ProdDetails.asp?ID=BYIET0011995&PG=1&Type=BL.

International Organization for Migration. 2003. "World Migration Report: Managing Migration – Challenges and Responses for People on the Move". Geneva, Switzerland.

Itam, S., S. Cueva, E. Lundback, J. Stotsky and S. Tokarick. 2000. "Developments and Challenges in the Caribbean Region". *IMF.org*. 31 December. http://www.imf.org/external/pubs/nft/op/201/index.htm.

Jalilian H. 1996. "Foreign Investment Location in Less Developed Countries: Theoretical Framework". *Journal of Economic Studies* 23 (4): 18–30.

Jasso, G., M.R. Rosenzweig and J.P. Smith. 1998. "The Changing Skill of New Immigrants to the United States: Recent Trends and Their Determinants". Working Paper 6764, National Bureau of Economic Research, Cambridge, MA.

Johns, R.A. 1985. *International Trade Theories and the Evolving International Economy*. New York: St. Martin's Press.

Jones, R.W. 1965. "The Structure of Simple General Equilibrium Models". *Journal of Political Economy* 73 (6): 557–72.

Jorgenson, D., and K. Vu. 2005. "Information Technology and the World Economy". *Scandinavian Journal of Economics* 107 (4): 631–50.

Kingma, M. 2001. "Nurse Migration: Global Treasure Hunt or Disaster in the Making?" *Nursing Inquiry* 8 (4): 205–12.

Kojima, K. 1964. "The Pattern of International Trade among Advanced Countries". *Hitotsubashi Journal of Economics* 5 (1): 17–36.

Lenin, V. 1916. "Imperialism, the Highest Stage of Capitalism". in Lenin, Selected Works, 167–257. Moscow: Progress Publishers (fourth printing, 1977).

Lerner, A.P. 1936. "The Symmetry between Import and Export Taxes". *Economica* 3 (11): 306–13.

Lewis, W.A. 1954. "Economic Development with Unlimited Supplies of Labor". *The Manchester School of Economic and Social Studies* 22: 139–91.

Liesner, H.H. 1958. "The European Common Market and British Industry". *Economic Journal* 68 (270): 302–16.

Linder, S. 1961. *An Essay on Trade and Transformation*. Uppsala: Almqvist and Wiksells.

Lucas, R.E. 1988. "On the Mechanics of Economic Development". *Journal of Monetary Economics* 22: 3–42.

MacDougall, D. 1951. "British and American Exports: A Study Suggested by the Theory of Comparative Costs. Part I". *Economic Journal* 61: 697–724.

Marchese, S., and F.N. de Simone. 1989. "Monotonicity of Indices of 'Revealed' Comparative Advantage: Empirical Evidence on Hillman's Condition". *Weltwirtschaftliches Archiv* 125 (1): 158–67.

Martin, P. 1990. "Labor Migration and Economic Development". Report of the Commission for the Study of International Migration and Cooperative Economic Development. Washington, DC: Government Printing Office.

Ministry of Finance of Trinidad and Tobago. Various years. *National Income Accounts.*

———. Various years. *Review of the Economy.*

Mun, T. 1664. *England's Treasure by Forraign Trade.* London: Macmillan.

Nurse, K. 2004. "Diaspora, Migration and Development in the Americas". http://library.fes.de/pdf-files/id/ipg/200402nurse.pdf.

Ohlin, B. 1933. *Inter-regional and International Trade.* Cambridge, MA: Harvard University Press.

Pan American Health Organization. 2002. "Health in the Americas". Technical and Scientific Publication No. 587. Washington, DC: PAHO.

Porter, M. 1990. *The Competitive Advantage of Nations.* London: Macmillan.

Posner M.V. 1961. "International Trade and Technological Change". *Oxford Economic Paper* 13: 323–41.

Prebisch, R. 1959. "Commercial Policy in the Underdeveloped Countries". *American Economic Review* 4 (2): 251–73.

Ricardo, D. 1951. "On Foreign Trade". In *The Works and Correspondence of David Ricardo,* vol. 1, edited by P. Sraffa and M.H. Dobb. Cambridge, UK: Cambridge University Press.

Romer. P. 1994. "The Origins of Endogenous Growth". *Journal of Economic Perspectives* 8 (1): 3–22.

Rowthorn, R.E., and R. Ramaswamy. 1998. "Growth, Trade, and Deindustrialization". WP/98/60. IMF Working Paper.

Rowthorn, R.E., and J.R. Wells. 1987. *De-industrialization and Foreign Trade.* Cambridge: Cambridge University Press.

Rubenstein, H. 1982. "The Impact of Remittances in the Rural English Speaking Caribbean: Notes on the Literature". In *Return Migration and Remittances Developing a Caribbean Perspective,* edited by W.F. Stinner, Klaus De Alburqurque and R.S. Bryce-Laporte. Washington, DC: The Smithsonian Institute.

Russell, S.S. 1986. "Remittances from International Migration: A Review in Perspective". *World Development* 14 (6): 677–96.

Salmon, M., J. Yan, H. Hewitt and V. Guisinger. 2007. "Managed Migration: The Caribbean Approach to Addressing Nursing Services Capacity". *Health Services Research* 42 (3): 1354–72.

Singer, H. 1950. "The Distribution of Gains between Investing and Borrowing Countries". *American Economic Review, Papers and Proceedings* 40: 473–85.

Slaughter, M., and D. Blanchflower. 1998. "The Causes and Consequences of Changing Income Inequality: Whither the Debate?" Centre for Economic Performance Institute of Economics Papers, no. 27. http://ideas.repec.org/s/fth/cepies.html.

Thom, R., and M. McDowell. 1999. "Measuring Marginal Intra-Industry Trade". *Weltwirtschaftliches Archiv* 135: 48–61.

Torrens, R. 1844. *The Budget: On Commercial and Colonial Policy.* London: Smith, Elder, and Co.

Trinidad and Tobago. Ministry of Energy and Natural Resources. 1984. *Accounting for the Petrodollar 1973–1983.* Port of Spain: Government Printery.

———. Ministry of Trade and Industry. 2008. *The CARIFORUM/EU EconomicPartnership Agreement:*

An Executive Summary. http://www.tradeind.gov.tt/Portals/0/Documents/EPA/EPA2/EPA%20 Summary.pdf.

———. Ministry of Trade, Industry and Investment. N.d. http://www.tradeind.gov.tt/Agreements/ TradeAgreements/EconomicPartnershipAgreementEPA/EconomicPartnershipAgreementEPA Overview.asp.

UNECLAC/Caribbean Development and Cooperation Committee. 2003. *Emigration of Nurses from the Caribbean: Causes and Consequences for the Socio-Economic Welfare of the Country: Trinidad and Tobago – A Case Study*. Port of Spain: UNECLAC.

United Nations. Various years. *International Trade Statistics Yearbook*. Geneva: United Nations.

United Nations Conference on Trade and Development. Various years. *Statistical Handbook*. Geneva: United Nations.

———. Various years. *World Investment Report*. Geneva: United Nations. http://www.unctad.org.

United Nations Development Programme. Various years. *Human Development Report*. Geneva: United Nations.

United Nations Economic Commission for Latin America and the Caribbean (UNECLAC). 1991. "Remesas y Economia Familiar En El Salvador, Guatemala, and Nicaragua". Prepared for El Proyecto CEPAL/Gobierno de los Paises Bajos.

———. 2001. "Trade, Environment and Development: Implications for the Caribbean". (LC/ CAR/G.669), Port of Spain. ECLAC Subregional Headquarters for the Caribbean, November.

Venables, A.J. 1987. "Trade and Trade Policy with Differentiated Products: A Chamberlinian-Ricardian Model". *Economic Journal* 97 (387): 700–717.

Verdoorn, P.J. 1960. "The Intra-Block Trade of the Benelux". In *Economic Consequences of the Size of Nations*, edited by E.A.G. Robinson. London: Macmillan.

Vernon, R. 1966. "International Investment and International Trade in the Product Cycle". *Quarterly Journal of Economics* 80 (May): 190–207.

Vollrath, T. 1991. "A Theoretical Evaluation of Alternative Trade Intensity Measures of Revealed Comparative Advantage". *Weltwirtschaftliches Archiv* 127: 265–80.

World Bank. 2000. "Small States: Meeting Challenges in the Global Economy". Report of the Commonwealth Secretariat/World Bank Joint Task Force on Small States, Washington, DC.

———. 2007. *World Bank Development Report*. Washington, DC: World Bank.

———. Various years. *World Bank Development Indicators*. Washington, DC: World Bank. http:// www.worldbank.org.

World Economic Forum. Various years. *Global Competitiveness Report*. Geneva: Palgrave Macmillan.

World Trade Organization. 2005. "Exploring the Links between Trade Standards and the WTO". World Trade Report, Geneva.

———. 2005. "Trade Policies and Practices by Measure". http://www.wto.org/english/tratop_e/tpr_e/ tp251_e.htm.

Websites and Databases

Caribbean Community Regional Statistics. http://www.caricomstats.org.

International Monetary Fund. http://elibrary-data.imf.org.

Trade Statistics For International Business Development. http://www.trademap.org.

United Nations Commodity Trade Database. http://comtrade.un.org/db.

United Nations Conference on Trade and Development. http://unctadstat.unctad.org/ReportFolders/ reportFolders.aspx?sCS_referer=&sCS_ChosenLang=en.

United Nations Economic Commission for Latin America and the Caribbean database. http://www .eclac.cl/estadisticas/default.asp?idioma=IN.

United States International Trade Commission. http://www.usitc.gov.

Answer Key

Chapter 1		Chapter 2		Chapter 3		Chapter 4	
1	e	1	a	1	c	1	d
2	d	2	a	2	c	2	c
3	c	3	c	3	c	3	a
4	d	4	c	4	d	4	b
5	a	5	c	5	b	5	d
Chapter 5		**Chapter 6**		**Chapter 7**		**Chapter 8**	
1	c	1	a	1	a	1	a
2	b	2	c	2	b	2	b
3	a	3	a	3	d	3	a
4	c	4	d	4	c	4	d
5	a	5	b	5	a	5	d
Chapter 9		**Chapter 10**		**Chapter 11**		**Chapter 12**	
1	a	1	d	1	b	1	b
2	d	2	d	2	a	2	c
3	c	3	a	3	c	3	b
4	d	4	d			4	d
5	c	5	c			5	b

.

Index

Note: The letters *f* and *t* indicate that the entry refers to a figure or a table, respectively.

www.ingramcontent.com/pod-product-compliance
Lightning Source LLC
Chambersburg PA
CBHW082352270326
41935CB00013B/1595